THE LIFELONG SEASON

About the author

Keith Duggan is a sportswriter for *The Irish Times*, for whom he writes features, and also a weekly column on a wide variety of subjects. He is from Ballyshannon in County Donegal and lives in Galway.

THE LIFELONG SEASON

At the Heart of Gaelic Games

KEITH DUGGAN

TOWN
HOUSE
DUBLIN

First published in 2004 by

TownHouse, Dublin
THCH Ltd
Trinity House
Charleston Road
Ranelagh
Dublin 6
Ireland

www.townhouse.ie

© Keith Duggan, 2004

1 2 3 4 5 6 7 8 9 10

A CIP catalogue record for this book is available from
the British Library.

ISBN: 1-86059-219-8

Printed by Cox & Wyman Ltd, Reading, Berks.

Contents

Introduction

My first hero in Gaelic games was a lad by the name of Tommy McDermott. During my early school years, he used to eat dinner at the same table as myself in a brilliant and happy house on West Rock, Ballyshannon. He was in his late teens then, preoccupied with football, exams, girlfriends and the usual. To those of us in primary school, McDermott represented an excellence that even then we knew we would probably never match. His grandfather and father both played football for Donegal and by his late teens, it was apparent that McDermott was destined for similar fulfilment. He was sunny and outgoing and because magnified in our mind's eye, he could be a little scary whenever he directed a few words down our grubby-sleeved way.

He was a defender, tough and polished and the opposite of the typically solemn and frowning Ulster defender in that he had this movie-star smile that he used a lot. He hit as hard as any of them though. McDermott played corner-back on the Donegal team of 1983 that lost an All-Ireland semi-final to Galway in circumstances too depressing to recount. No subsequent sporting experience ever really touched the disappointment I felt that evening. That was about as hurtful as it got. Within a few years, life took McDermott to London, where he is still deeply involved in Gaelic football. It was just as well: Donegal football went through a lean spell for the remainder of the 1980s. By the time the county won its only All-Ireland title in 1992, Tommy's day in the sun had passed but when he comes home on holidays old acquaintances note – with some envy – that he looks the very same as when he roamed the back line for Donegal. The relative shortness of his career meant that Tommy was never going to become a particularly famous name nationally – although at his best he could have marked many of the most celebrated names of any period into oblivion. For some of us though, at that age when sport and its heroes were a deathly serious business, Tommy McDermott stood alone. And it was all the better that he also stood in the crowd outside John Monday's shop on the way back to school.

Although I have only met him about twice in the last twenty years, I think about McDermott whenever that 1983 game comes up in conversation with friends. In the grand scheme of things, he is just another in the great hall of men who have represented their county in Gaelic games. Yet it remains a hell of a thing, to have come within a kick of a ball of being in an All-Ireland football final, an experience only a select number of players have attained. He was too smart and impatient to sup in his local on tales of what might have been: he walked, started a career and a family. And he was always easy about the football scene anyway, wearing it on his sleeve.

Still, two decades on, a generation of guys I know can summon a clear and shimmering memory of McDermott in his pomp – that he was the only Donegal player ever to sport a virtual Afro is a help. He would – and will – be mortified at the notion but it is the truth.

The idea of this book was to try see what happens behind those transcendent bursts of illumination that the very best leave behind as their gift to those of us who watch from the shadows. The people who feature in the following pages are mainly those whom I have come to admire since my involvement in Gaelic games deepened through working with *The Irish Times*. Some are among the very revered names in the history of our native games. Others are not so well known but equally important. What they share is a commitment and love of Gaelic games that is not uncommon – because hundreds of other men and women share it – but it is truly rare. It would be easy to brand what they have as an obsession with the game they love but that is not quite it. It is more that the games have provided the truest reflection of their value system and beliefs. They all fell into Gaelic games for different reasons – some because they loved the games, others because they simply could not help being brilliant at them.

I knew none of the people I met for the purpose of this book very well and the majority I knew not at all. Because of that, their generosity of time and spirit has been humbling. They are all remarkable and exceptional people; I just hope the following pages do some justice to that fact.

And the thing is, they might have been any one of the hundreds of men and women whose association with Gaelic games remains constant through the rain and shine of many decades. God knows what drives them. But we best hope it survives in tomorrow's generation as well, this spark that is found in only a few souls, for it alone lights the great summer furnace and the games we don't forget.

Keith Duggan
October 2004

1

There is a Light that Never Goes Out

Brian McEniff has been in his car for about ten seconds when he encounters the first problem of the evening. He has not yet had time to ease the silver Volvo out of first gear or to flick on the Radio One news, and the thermal heating system that cosies the seats has not even reached tepid, but ahead is a sight to send his own temperature soaring.

The McEniff home is tucked behind the original family hotel, the Holyrood, in the heart of the main street in Bundoran. As he leaves the hotel car park for a training session with the Donegal team in Castlefin, a red car – one of those unnameable jazzed-up rally numbers with stickers and trinkets – pulls sharply into the entrance lane of the car park. The car gives the appearance of actually trembling from the bass level of an aggressive stereo. The driver door opens and a young man hops out and skips through the entrance of a nearby pub. He has not even bothered closing the car door and McEniff gazes after him, trying to confirm to himself that he has just seen this youngster abandoning his car as if it was a bike on a footpath.

The silhouette of passengers behind the darkened windshield becomes apparent as McEniff rolls down his own electric window.

'Hey,' he calls to the occupants, peering at the shaded interior of the other car.

'Hey, you can't park there. This is a through road to a car park. You are blocking people.'

He has to shout this and as he finishes, another smooth-faced young lad pokes his head out.

'I'm nat parkin' anywhere. Sure I'm nat even drivin.'

The boy stares in comfortable defiance at this sallow-coloured man in a silver car who is dressed in an immaculate suit.

'Right,' snaps McEniff, taking out a mobile phone and making to press buttons. 'I'll have the guards up here in two minutes to see about who is driving.'

The teenager shrugs and fades back into the sound. McEniff breathes deeply. Over the years, he has had a million of these minor civic debates with the juvenile quarter of Bundoran's pleasure-seeking constituency. And he knows that part of the thrill that kids of a certain age get is spinning around in spit-polished low-engine racers looking for authority figures to rouse. But he has never quite learned how to prevent them from getting under his skin. He looks for a long, fathomless moment at the kid who returns his stare blithely, convinced that the issue of his friend's ditching of the car has nothing to do with him. He takes another deep breath and, for an instant, it looks as if he is about to leave his own car to deliver a more memorable lesson in driving etiquette. Certainly, that would have been the solution in previous decades. A life in the hotel business and half a century of football dressing rooms makes for easy meat of truculent street kids.

But the electric clock already shows five-thirty in the evening and he is racked by a cold and he has people to collect and so he turns the wheel away from the offending car, the automatic window of his own car purring calmly and drawing a tinted veil on the confrontation.

'Ah, I'll only annoy myself now if I hang around trying to sort it out,' he sighs and indicates right.

He departs. The saloon car moves up the town past the amusement arcades and bars and ice-cream parlours and the stern 1940s townhouses of the east end, and by the time it sweeps around O'Gorman's corner and past the Kentucky Fried Chicken drive-through, McEniff's mood of high humour has returned. He has a sheet of typed names with corresponding phone numbers pinned against the steering wheel. Roper, Devenney, Cassidy, Diver, Hegarty: names that starred in last summer's slightly hallucinatory, left-field championship adventure that was as unexpected as a flare in the middle of the ocean. McEniff and Donegal have long been regarded as a classic combination but, much like Bogart and Bacall, they represented a certain epoch: nobody expected the pair to be back except in late-night re-runs on the television. Yet late last August, McEniff, the grandfather, confounded all expectations when he led a Donegal team to its first All-Ireland semi-final since 1992, the year the radar went haywire in the county. This time, his team lost narrowly and unluckily to Armagh, but the end did not diminish what was arguably McEniff's most shining achievement, as contrary as it was unexpected. In truth, the early season was so singularly grim that qualifying for the All-Ireland final would have troubled the borders of credulity of even the most fevered of Donegal fans and McEniff was the epitome of gallantry as he shook the hand of Big Joe Kernan at the final whistle. That moment was to be the very last encore. McEniff was only back because the county could find no other manager and he publicly promised himself that this would be his final season. And what a perfect setting: Croke Park ablaze after a fervid, rugged all-Ulster confrontation made beautiful by a goal that was as good as any scored by a McEniff team. There was a touching honesty and grandeur about the manner in which the young team lost. The sense that afternoon was of a noble conclusion to an improbable season and all that was left to do for McEniff was to round the team up in the dressing room and deliver his valedictory.

'I stayed with them that evening,' he remembers. 'We rang ahead to a hotel in Virginia and got a few bottles for them from an off-licence and they sang a few songs on the bus down. We had arranged to go to Donegal Town for a meal that evening so we went ahead with that. I was anxious to get them back to the county as quickly as possible because I thought we would have been preparing for the All-Ireland final.'

But there was to be no final and as the season ended on a note of Tyrone glory, no replacement manager was announced in Donegal, as McEniff, also acting as county chairman, went searching for his own successor. He had key men in mind: the smart lads from 1992 – Donal Reid, Martin McHugh, Anthony Molloy – but for various reasons they had to decline. Meanwhile, letters from around the county fell onto the hallway carpet asking him to stay and, more tellingly, the current boys were leaving messages on the mobile. Come back. One more season. All the way. Sometimes his phone would beep in the small hours and when he replayed the message McEniff would hear the sound of nightlife in the background as a player, struck by one of those dance-club epiphanies, felt compelled to leave his words of support there and then. Some were pricelessly funny and he stored them all away with the intention of playing them back at a team party somewhere down the line. You could speculate that even as he saved those words, he knew. He would not be walking away. He did not want to stay but could not leave unless he was satisfied they were going the right way. Or perhaps he sort of did want to stay. Or perhaps wild horses couldn't have dragged him away. This was his team again: his boys. And gathering speed past Finner Camp, he is doing what he likes to do best. He calls them. McEniff is a compulsive user of phones. Next to the Steinway and the hand-pass, the mobile phone is the invention he refers to most often. The knowledge that the boys are always reachable is soothing when you have a restless nature.

He dials a series of numbers and talks on speakerphone.

'Yes, Cass.'

'Ah, yes, how's the form, Brian?'

'Where are ya?'

'I'm already down at the pitch, Brian. I want ta get a bit a kickin' in.'

'Good boy. Good enough.'

He punches in the next number and then the next and finally he rings his brother Liam, a doctor, to try to get something medicinal for the cold he feels settling in his bones. At Clery's garage in Ballyshannon, he stops for Charlie Gillespie, the team physiotherapist and Brendan Boyle, a quiet and likeable young Ardara lad studying in Sligo. The talk is of the recent Sigerson Cup final, which wreaked a catastrophic series of injuries on the Donegal members of the Sligo IT side, but once they hit the open road to Donegal there is a lull for the main evening news.

'How's things anyway, Boyler?' McEniff asks eventually.

'Aye, grand. Busy enough, hey. Trying to get this oul paper out of the way.'

'Paper? What's the paper on?'

Boyler says something like: 'The effects of phosphorous on water.'

'Oh, fuck,' responds McEniff.

'Kind of a conversation killer,' says Charlie, and Boyler laughs.

'Science always wrecked me,' McEniff says then. 'Irish and English and Latin I loved and I could do my sums, as they say.

But science had me ruined. I don't know how you do it, Boyler. How's that leg? Will you be all right for Sunday?'

'Sunday' is a league game against Clare. If Donegal win, they will gain promotion to division one. Last year, in his first time back in charge since 1994, McEniff watched his team flounder in the league and drop to the second division, a new and somewhat chastening experience for him. Although those early games were forgotten by the public during the July and August awakening, he has remembered and he dearly wants to get promotion again, just to balance the books.

It is already darkening when the manager's car arrives at the ground and the players are in the changing room or on the field. The evening is clear and bright and icily cold but there are three men in the shed watching training, among them Dessie Kelly, a local man and a well-known Donegal supporter. He had been in Croke Park the day before, St Patrick's Day, for the All-Ireland club finals and was still delighting in the spectacle the Meehan boys from Caltra had put on. Yards from where we stand, the Donegal players run a swift, concentrated series of ball drills – three-man weaves, spot-to-spot passes and give-and-go drills – all carried out at an urgent pace. Joe McBrearty, the trainer from Killybegs, is the lone voice through the sound of athletes running and breathing. Even here, against the backdrop of blackened fields, in heavy winter gear and hats, under floodlights, Donegal players transferring a football at speed are a joy to watch.

McEniff observes. He stands on the fringes with PJ McGowan and Michael Oliver McIntyre, like breeders watching stallions in the ring. The days of the manager barking orders at training are a thing of the past, and tonight, McEniff would not have the throat for shouting anyway. When he speaks, it is in low, private consultation with a player. There have been times when he has been demonstrative at training. McEniff endured the worst week of his football life with this generation of Donegal footballers early last summer when they lost the first round of the championship 0-11 to 0-6 to Fermanagh. After a disheartening league, the manner of this defeat was too much and as he departed Enniskillen on a drizzly Sunday evening, he felt broken.

'I still do not understand it. I can't. There is something in the Donegal psyche that just allows these things to happen every so often with no real reason. I do remember, though, that on that terrible day, we stopped off in Pettigo on the way to Enniskillen for a bite to eat. And we got a tremendous reception, as one always will in Pettigo. But as we were walking in for our meal, "From Bundoran to the Rosses", the old Margo song from 1992 was playing. It was a well-meant gesture but it gave me a funny feeling. I just thought, "no, this is not they what they need." 1992 has no relevance to these boys. And we never mention it. In fact, from the beginning, I made a point of saying to them that they were all that mattered in Donegal football.'

But it was to the old ghosts he turned late that night. McEniff is an insomniac at the best of times and at home he felt agitated and drained of all verve. He felt out of touch and at a loss and so he went to the voices he knew: the Wee Man, Martin McHugh; Pauric McShea, his friend and Donegal team-mate from the 1970s; Anthony Molloy, the man who lifted the Sam Maguire in 1992; Arthur McRory, his cousin and the great Tyrone football man. The hotel was busy that bank holiday Monday and he went through the motions of working and, on the Tuesday night, feeling all of his fifty-eight years of age, he went back to training. The pitch at Ballybofey was shrouded in a wet, Irish summer mist and the players were spiritless. The manager, wearing an old pair of multi-studs that had lain in the boot of his car for months, walked onto the field at the beginning of the session and kicked a ball over the bar from fourteen metres. Then he got another ball and kicked it over the bar from the same spot. He had their attention now. He took the ball a third time and kicked it over the bar. Then he moved deliberately out to the twenty-one-yard line and belted another accurately over the bar. Twice, he repeated the kick, never looking at the players, as if he was perfectly alone on the practice field.

Although he was twice an All-Star for Donegal and played football until the age of fifty-one, most of the players would never have seen McEniff truly kick a football. To them, he is the smiling man in the green peaked hat, the eternal manager. Many had been primary school boys in September 1992, when football fever was like pollen in the air and McEniff and the Sam Maguire and the team were barnstorming the county. They remembered him when he was king and, as they developed as footballers, they probably learned about how Donegal football wasn't just a game to him. About how he was sacked three times but kept coming back for more. Or about how he would try to solve the life problems that confronted his players every now and then by arranging for jobs to fall their way or a few quid here or there. That even though he was a pioneer, he could appear drunk on life when a moment enraptured him. They probably heard stories about how psyched he could get in dressing rooms, truly furious and frothing. Or the tale about the half-time speech when he walked in, looked at each player in silent contempt, spat on the stone floor and walked out again – a game that was won. Older boys probably told them that no matter how deeply they believed they cared for Donegal football, with McEniff that compulsion was not a phase in life, it was life. Five decades have not been enough to calm his unrest. That was why he was here, a man whose team-mates from the 1960s were dealing with issues like retirement and mortality and the Internet while he was stuck on the old training ground of their youth, hammering a football in the rain as if his life depended on it. A bunch of twenty-something-year-old men watching him from a respectful distance and learning that kicking points was nothing mysterious: that if McEniff, the great survivor of county football could nail it, so could they. Finally, the manager moved out to the thirty-yard line.

'I kicked two of the three over the bar from there,' he remembers quietly, bowing to the small glimmer of competitive pride that stays with all sportsmen long after the gloves have been hung.

To know Brian McEniff, you have to know Bundoran. It is not an ordinary town. It is not even an ordinary seaside town. The prevailing attitude towards the place depends on the perspective from which it is viewed. If you get stuck in all-day traffic along the neon main street on a rainy weekend day around the twelfth of July, it can seem loud and claustrophobic. Ulster kids prowl the streets and caravan parks waiting for Bacchanalia to visit. When the beach is damp and useless, families have to retreat to the bars and amusement arcades and restaurants and so there is no relief from people, from the swings at the east end to the turn-off for Rougey cliffs at the far end of town. But if you walk the path along those cliffs during the calmer weeks of June or August, it is different. Catch Bundoran around tea-time after a hot day when the sky is incandescent and the great, bashed coastline somehow complements the electric soul of the town below and all of it framed by the still mass of Ben Bulben, there is an imposing self-assurance and beauty about the place.

The town has shaped McEniff as much as his family has shaped the town. At present, the McEniff Hotel Group is one of the largest private hotel businesses in Ireland, with eleven premises scattered around the country. Over the years, the profiles of McEniff that have appeared in the sports pages have made cheery references to 'the hotelier'. Business reports generally allude to his long association with Donegal football. They create the impression that he is in control of two neat and parallel existences but the opposite is true. Football and work always went hand in hand. Some summer Sundays seemed to involve nipping out from the Holyrood kitchen to play a championship game in Clones but still managing to be back in front of the grill in time to turn the steaks.

That the family settled in Bundoran was something of an accident. John McEniff had decided to quit Newbliss in Monaghan for a life in Minneapolis and visited the Donegal resort on impulse to say goodbye to a relative.

During his stay, he met Elizabeth Begley from Carraigmor, a nurse who was working in a café located where Joe O'Neill's pub is today. That put paid to his voyage. They married and rented a small shop. When the family arrived, all boys, they lived upstairs. Brian was a middle child and probably the most attuned to helping his mother run the café and later the small bed and breakfast service they operated from the two spare rooms when the older boys went to college. He spent entire summers washing dishes that his older brother Pat would dry. Elizabeth McEniff had a ferocious work ethic and an unwavering belief that there was a right way and a wrong way to do things. She was devoted to the former. Her husband had a milder nature: Brian McEniff struggles to remember his father ever scolding him. His mother still does to this day. But together, they made a formidable couple and just took to grabbing each ascending rung on the ladder through the 1940s and 1950s. Every penny was accounted for and most of it was channelled into sending their boys on to third-level education. As a consequence, luxuries in the house were few.

'None,' remembers Brian. 'We had absolutely no wealth. But at the same time my mother would have always taken very good care of us. She had a very high standard of hygiene from the nursing background. She would scrub you – and I mean scrub you. She would darn your socks. But whatever she had, she spent on her kids. If you sat down at the table, you never got up from it. You washed your hands, you sat down, the plate was put down and if you wanted anything, she got up and she served. We said a Rosary every night – she was and still is an extremely Catholic woman. My father was a good-living man but not to the same extent. He was not a cross man. I only ever got a slap from him once. Funny, my brother Pat was also mild-mannered but he was the one who always contrived to get himself into trouble. It was never me – I suppose I was a good home boy and would have enjoyed working for my mother. When we started keeping guests, I would have been the one going under the beds with the duster and cleaning them and stuff like that there. I was happy in the house – which was why going boarding to St McCartan's was a huge jolt. I never took to it. I just enjoyed the home environment. It would be wrong to say we were poor as such, but it was a very small existence. They worked hard – my father would have done a bit of travelling as well as running the shop. My mother, though, was a savage worker in terms of effort and the hours, the lot. And it was all for the family because she never spent anything on herself or went away or things like that. She worked and prayed. Like, she used to bake these huge brown loaves about the size of a coffee table, until about seven years ago. It got to the stage where she could no longer lift them. We try to talk to her but I mean, you don't tell her anything and that is it. She is a real Carrickmore woman.'

It was in Mrs McEniff that the entrepreneurial streak burned strongest. In the late 1940s, she negotiated the rent of a small guesthouse called Lourdesville from the McNulty family and then bought it outright after a couple of seasons. In 1951, the Holyrood, a twelve-bedroom hotel beside Lourdesville, came up for sale.

'For whatever reason, they took a mad notion to buy it,' says Brian. It was a decision that affected the direction of his life. When Sean, his eldest brother, came home from boarding school and got married, he was sold the original family interest, the shop across the road, in which to set up a business and home. It meant that the Holyrood became home for the younger members of the family. Because Pat was already half way through an expensive college course in dentistry, Brian was the obvious candidate to go into the hotel business, something that held no appeal for him.

'I had imagined myself going on to study – maybe law or languages or something. We had a great professor in McCartan's who taught the Classics and Latin and he could have taught you anything; I had great respect for him. Funnily, my brother Pat would have had a strong interest in the family business but my father could not see him giving up three years of dentistry. On top of that, there would have been a personality clash – the three could never function. So I was dispatched to hotel school. I really did not want to go. When I did the interview for Cathal Brugha Street, I was embarrassed because when I did the entrance exam, I felt I could have sat it before I did the Intermediate. I remember going back to McCartan's and I was nearly ashamed to tell the boys what I had been going for. But I have nothing but good memories of Cathal Brugha Street now.'

Those college years – when he was kicking football and working part time as a waiter – were probably the only carefree years of his life but it was all preparation for a return to Bundoran. McEniff has a complex relationship with his home town: he loves the place but admits that if he was to start over again, he is not sure he would rear a family there. He has never become used to the extremities of the seasons: the heat and crowds and long nights of summer were always music to him but the winters unnerved him. As a boy, he did the normal things – learned piano from Mrs Mulhearn in the east end, kicked football and went with his father to watch Donegal and Sligo Rovers. He followed Ipswich Town and Celtic. But he was still quite young when he realised how reductive a force winter was on his town. Not only did the tourists leave, so did many of those he knew.

'Many years, Bundoran would qualify for the final of this competition or that and by the time the game was played in Autumn, half our team would be gone. Emigration had a fierce effect here. You had July and August full of tourists and then September was when the farmers took holidays. And then suddenly the place closed down and was empty. I look over Bundoran teams from the last forty years and ask where did Nixie Johnson or where did David Keane go. They went off, never to return, a lot of them. And I find that sad. A nun from the convent once said to me that Bundoran was lacking in community spirit and it struck me because I had never been conscious of that. And that spirit was always something I got such a strong sense of in places like Kilcar and Killybegs. Even Ballyshannon would be a better town than Bundoran in that way. So the off-season in the town could be tough. But then the summer would roll around again and there would be so much life about the place that you would forget all about it.'

He might have left himself. He set off for Canada after qualifying in Cathal Brugha Street, working as a chef and selling insurance in Toronto and playing a guest role on football teams across the States. One of his favourite lines in trivia is that he is the only Donegal man to possess a league medal, won with New York in 1964 against Dublin. He bought a house in Toronto and considered going to Australia. He kept in touch by telephone: Bundoran 22 was the number. His father would reproach him for wasting all that money and persisted in replying to his son through long, elegant letters. His son had no time for writing, though. He was always on the move but knew deep down that all the energy could only lead back to one destination. It was while in Canada that he developed a fondness for warbling Irish ballads and he used to stalk the Irish halls to hear them. It was a way of bridging distance. He also got *The Democrat* posted out to him regularly, learning to his astonishment that Bundoran GAA club had amalgamated with its detested neighbours, Aodh Ruadh of Ballyshannon, to form a new club, St Joseph's. In fanciful moments, he told himself that he was done with home but he knew that if and when the call came, he would obey it. When he returned from Canada, his parents had bought the house between the Holyrood and the Lourdesville guesthouse and borrowed heavily to amalgamate all three buildings into one large hotel.

'When I came back into the hotel in 1965 it was strange, especially living there as I had my own house across in Canada. My father was taking a good drink then and I could see he was having difficulty. Then he took the stroke – they told him he had three years. And he lived two years and nine months but he made a total recovery from the stroke. It was a heart attack eventually. Whatever damage was done was done.'

Gradually, he assumed a fuller responsibility for the hotel, his early diligence and responsibility spurring him on. It is within this context that his emergence as a footballer of note has to be viewed. Even those who did not like McEniff in Donegal conceded that he had class and craft on the field. He was eighteen when he made his senior county debut in 1961 before disappearing across the Atlantic. His return to Ireland coincided with Donegal's second ever appearance in an Ulster final in 1966. It was against Down and took place the day after England had won the World Cup.

'We lost by two points to a bad, bad Down team. It was the first time an Ulster final was televised. The boys went up to stay in Belfast the night before but we had a big wedding in Bundoran so I travelled up in the morning. I was only in the substitutes anyway – I wasn't long back from Canada. But God, I was disappointed. I saw Cecil King shortly after the final whistle and asked him if he was heading home. He was leaving immediately so I just grabbed my bag. Cecil had a big Mercedes and I think I was back in the hotel two hours after the final whistle.'

He made straight for the kitchen, banishing all thoughts of the game and serving up order after order. When the kitchen closed and was mopped and wiped down, he put on a fresh shirt and jacket and sat down at the piano in the lobby. Sing-songs in those days were more informal but McEniff regularly accompanied local musicians like Phonsie Bogle and Cormac McCready.

'My mother was astonished I was back so soon. She never once questioned me about the football no matter how busy we were in the hotel. But it was just the way I saw things. I remember we had our biggest ever bar sales that Easter Sunday. And this was a busy August bank holiday so I worked my arse off to attain a certain figure just to beat that. I must have played the piano for four hours straight. I'll always remember that my fingers were raw the next day because there was no amplification and you had to really hit the keys.'

It was around this period that McEniff's force of personality began to resonate in Donegal football circles. His great friend Pauric McShea often tells the story that when McEniff returned from his Canadian hiatus, he could not wait to be officially invited back onto Gerry Griffin's county panel. McShea jumped into Bernard Brady's car in Ballyshannon one evening and there was McEniff, sitting in shorts and socks, as if he had never been away. It was not the act of a prima donna – he was content to reclaim his senior status by impressing on the junior side for a time. Rather, it just never occurred to McEniff not to be there. Although he was absent for the formation of St Joseph's he played wingback for the team that won its first county championship in 1965. Forty years on, sitting in his living room in front of a coal fire and flicking between a rugby international featuring England and Wales and Juventus against Udinese in the Serie A, McEniff still sounds genuinely enthralled when he talks of the brand of football St Joseph's patented.

'God, they played great football. Had we really committed, we would have won two or three club All-Irelands. They were nearly too pure a team. You couldn't but like the kind of football they played. They might put away four or five goals in any one game. And these were quality goals, now. And this was without ever really training.

'But the players who were around then... God. In goals, you had Sean McHugh or Alan Keane – both Donegal players. In the back line, there was Brady, McShea of Donegal and Ulster and Ray Sheerin of Donegal and Roscommon. Fr Ray McDaid played for Donegal. Sean Meade had three All-Irelands won with Galway at this stage.

'Then you had younger lads like Josie Boyle and Michael Pat Daly of Bundoran. We had Kieran Dolan and Brendan Dowling of the ESB, exceptionally talented lads. Meself. Declan O'Carroll and the late Brendan McHugh, a big strong man who played minor and senior for Donegal and Sligo. Up front you had Mickey McLoone, an outstanding player, a great eye – a prototype for Martin McHugh. And Peter Quinn, "The Fat Man", my oldest friend and a very fine footballer. You had Seamie Granaghan and Thomas Quinn. Dan McHugh, a Cliffoney man living in this area at the time. And Martin Carney – I don't have to say it but Jesus, he was a brilliant, brilliant player. I'm forgetting lads now, I know I am. But God they were a dream.'

St Joseph's won county championships in 1965, 1966, 1968, 1970, 1973, 1974, 1975 and 1976. They won Ulster club championships in 1966 and 1968 and also won the first unofficial club All-Ireland that autumn against the Donnellan-inspired Dunmore McHales. That final was played in Bundoran and McEniff was captain.

'See that, ' he says, pointing to a big, handsome cup that sits on a mahogany table beside a piano, the only piece of sporting ware on display in the room. 'That is the origin of everything good that happened in Donegal football afterwards.'

The St Joseph's experiment kind of petered out after the final county championship success in 1976. It had probably run its natural lifespan and there was a local consensus that it was high time that Ballyshannon and Bundoran teams returned to their rightful state of mutual hatred. By then, the trajectory of Donegal football had altered beyond recognition, as had McEniff's influence in the game. After managing the county minor team in 1969 because nobody else was interested, he found himself in charge of the senior team in 1971. It had been McEniff's idea to try to persuade an 'outsider' to take charge, but despite the bright aura that St Joseph's had created, the senior county side was something of a shambles that winter. When Mick Higgins of Cavan declined an offer of management but did promise to come on board as an assistant, St Joseph's proposed McEniff for player-manager. Austin Coughlan, the only other viable candidate, withdrew and, at twenty-eight, McEniff was in charge of the county, with Coughlan, Higgins and Columba McDyer as his backroom team. The rest is history that has been recounted often. A year later, he led Donegal to its first ever Ulster championship. He received Donegal's first ever All-Star award at the end of the season. The county took Ulster again in 1974. He was sacked in 1975 but stayed involved as a player under his successor, John Hannigan. When the post fell vacant after Hannigan stepped down, McEniff again filled the void but was replaced shortly after by Sean O'Donnell. He came back in 1980 to lead the county to its third Ulster championship in 1983 and was sacked again in 1985. He came back for more after the 1989 season and took Donegal to Ulster finals in 1990, 1991 and again in 1992 when they won the All-Ireland. After that, he was granted the privilege of calling time on himself. That moment arrived after a forlorn and demoralising Ulster semi-final loss against Tyrone in 1994 when the last vestiges of the 1992 team fell apart. By then, he was ready to take his leave and retained a strong interest in the team when PJ McGowan and later Declan Bonner assumed control. Gradually, the boys of 1992 fell away. McEniff paid a courtesy call to the Donegal dressing room after the 1998 Ulster final loss and found himself shedding a tear beside big Brian Murray from Ballyshannon, a gruff, heart-of-gold midfielder who was disconsolate that his Donegal career was ending to the worst chorus imaginable: Derry cheers. By 2002, when Mickey Moran took the team to the All-Ireland quarter-finals, McEniff was county chairman and its happiest supporter. It was the most relaxed football season of his life. He knew the players vaguely: if he bumped into many of them in a bank queue, he would have been hard-pressed to place them. That was certainly the case when he addressed them in a dressing room in January of 2003. He was as astonished as everybody else that he was taking on a county team that had made a bonfire of its own reputation by going publicly and recklessly on the beer for forty-eight lost hours between the drawn All-Ireland quarter-final against Dublin and the inglorious replay. McEniff, as chairman, led a protracted and almost embarrassing search for a successor to Moran before it became clear that Donegal were considered untouchable. The position was gravely affecting the collective confidence of the players, a generally modest and likeable bunch. So McEniff, the embodiment of a bright and irrevocable past for most Donegal people, risked his own assured place in the county by taking control again. People shook their heads and said he was mad. In retrospect, though, it was the most logical solution in the world. When, in McEniff's adult life, had Donegal ever whistled but he came running?

Those are the bones of his Donegal football life, now well into its fifth decade, but they should be reviewed in tandem with his working life. When Pat Britton, the family solicitor, took McEniff aside early in 1967 and advised him to quit the county scene to concentrate on home, he did so instantly. He was gone at twenty-five, kicking football with St Joseph's and playing a bit of soccer. The sense of duty and the work ethic he inherited from his mother never left.

'The night my father died I was down refereeing an indoor football tournament in St Patrick's Hall. We had won the first semi-final and so I refereed the second match. A call was put through to the hall and at half-time I was told my father was not well. The local priest, Fr Finnegan, was there in the hall so I told him to come up right away. We walked up to the hotel and I remember I switched off this sign – we had bought a big electric sign for the side of the hotel. And then I went up to the room and sat down close to him and asked him how he was. And he said, 'It's all over.'

Those three words stayed with the son, of course, but it was not until early this year, when he went through a heart operation in Blackrock himself, that he felt their full weight. Early in the procedure, he was told he would feel tightness in his chest that was symptomatic of a heart attack.

'So I understood then what it must have been like for my father, although the sensation would have been multiplied for him. But he knew. And he died within five minutes of me getting there that night. He was sixty-four. It was hard because I never really got the time to know him. And the sad thing was, I played my best football after he died. I remember though, funnily, St Joseph's played a club semi-final against my mother's home place in Carrickmore just weeks before he died. She travelled down to the game with me but even though I was captain, she was making no bones about cheering for them. But he was also a mad Carrickmore man. So we won the game by a point and maybe we got a few favours from Joe O'Loughlin, a Fermanagh referee. I landed back in the house and my father said congratulations. But he was very fair-minded and he did say, "Let's be honest, it might have been different if not for the referee." It stayed with me. Afterwards, I tried to get to know him from what people would tell me about him. But I never got the time with him as distinct from with my mother. I spent a lifetime with her.'

He was enticed back to the county panel in the spring of 1967 and juggled the art of just keeping one hotel afloat with playing and then managing Donegal. There remained a sizeable debt to be paid on the extension to the hotel. Then the bombs began exploding across Ulster and the Northern crowds stopped coming to Bundoran. In fact, everybody stopped coming anywhere near the border. McEniff had already committed to buying another hotel on the block near the Holyrood, the Hamilton's place, in order to get a shed that could be converted to a dance hall. He borrowed heavily at a time when interest was 8½ per cent and when business was lamentable. The first half of the 1970s was just about survival.

'The football was flying but the hotel wasn't doing so well. But I had a great staff and life was good at the same time. Funny, the sacking in 1975 came at the right time. We were beaten by Cavan in Ballybofey in early May and got three conferences in the hotel in the same period and we did quite well from those. I had been toying with the idea of building a ballroom and went ahead with that. Suddenly the banks went on strike in 1976 and it gave everybody a break from the interest rates. So I thrashed away and built it. Bands were fierce popular then and we used to get some big acts in Bundoran. The ballroom did well for me; 1976 was a wee lift.'

In 1982, the Great Northern Hotel, a sprawling building owned by CIÉ and located on a promontory overlooking the Atlantic, came up for sale and McEniff decided to bid for it along with his brothers.

'It was Sean, my brother, that got involved originally and

then Pat and myself came in. I had it sold to him, but no more than myself, he had no money and he sold it back to me about an hour later. It's a true story. I walked in to Cautie and told her we had just bought the Northern. And she nearly cried, she didn't want to know. I persuaded her that we should just run it for a few years and see how it went.'

Not that he was above the pressure. That summer, 1982, McEniff was playing for Bundoran – against Ballyshannon – when he felt constantly breathless. He had been in such good shape that there was talk of his returning as a player-manager some six years after his final game for the county, but suddenly, he could not run. For a while, he fought it and finished training sessions wheezing, like a heavy smoker. Asthma was diagnosed and he was told it was stress-related.

'I can pinpoint it to the very weeks I bought the Northern. I couldn't believe it. But I am a stressful person, Jesus I am. What can I do?'

That diagnosis led to cursory tests in the Blackrock clinic every year and it was there, just before Christmas of 2003, that his touch of heart trouble was discovered. He persuaded four different doctors that there was no need for an angiogram: he was just tired, he would run it off. It was the family general practitioner who advised him to submit himself to testing and, early last January, he was told that he would need an operation to alleviate 30 per cent blockage in the arteries.

'It was a shock, like the asthma. I thought this body of mine was indestructible.'

But everything began to make sense. At training, the breathlessness was growing more severe. And just after the All-Ireland semi-final defeat to Armagh, Austin O'Kennedy, the team doctor, looked at McEniff and told him he needed a rest, that he looked 'ashen'.

'That's all you need to hear when you have just lost an All-

Ireland semi-final,' he laughs. 'But I just put it down to the stress of the game.'

As it transpired, it was genetic. It did not matter that McEniff had attended literally thousands of training sessions or that he never bothered with alcohol or tobacco. It was in the genes. Brian's diagnosis disturbed his brothers who understandably deduced that if Brian, with his abstemious ways, had to go under the knife, God only knew what was in store for them.

'Pat was the boy that was most worried because he, now, tore through life. I got a call on the mobile that morning when he was finished the check-up in Dublin. He got the complete all clear. "Fuck you," he says to me. "I'm away for a double Bush."'

When the league resumed this spring, McEniff was still in rehabilitation and under strict instructions to stay away from anywhere that even resembled a football field. Those first games were torture and he spent the Sunday in his house plaguing family members who were at the games with phone calls and texts looking for the latest scores. He was permitted to attend the Leitrim game on condition he refrained from actually managing. He started out by sitting up in the press box in Boyle but felt agitated and cooped up. By the second half, he was down at the wire that separated the crowd from the players and the field, 'following them up and down like a madman.'

County players have the act of appearing for and leaving a training session down to an art form. In high summer, with a defining game on the horizon, there is probably a temptation to linger on the field after the session ends, but on a cold spring night, they train and depart with military economy. Almost all of the players would have travelled straight to Castlefin from work and, although the ground is centrally located, some of the boys, like the Sweeneys from Dungloe, have at least another hour in the car before they will see home. The training session finishes up with fifteen minutes of shooting.

After the players leave, the management gathers up the footballs. When it is discovered that one is missing, PJ McGowan disappears among the fir trees behind the goalposts to search, his orange bib darting through the black branches. This is a man who has managed Donegal to the All-Ireland under-twenty-one championship of 1987 – its second ever and most recent success at that grade, yet – who thinks nothing of scrambling around woodland in the dark until he finds a lost football.

In a small kitchen across from the dressing rooms a lady is serving out an evening dinner of chicken in cream sauce with mashed potatoes and vegetables. A bowl of fruit and a basket of sandwiches sit on the counter. When the players have showered and changed they begin to drift into the small kitchen and sit on plastic chairs to eat their meals, the plates sitting on their knees. There is not much conversation; already their minds are focusing on the road home or on tomorrow's work or on the daily chores that await them. It is hard to reconcile this group of young men, dressed now in track suits or denim jackets or shirts and ties, with the team that starred in front of 80,000 people on a hot Sunday afternoon last August. The atmosphere around Castlefin is so nocturnal and still that the championship adventure seems terribly remote. McEniff eats with the players, swallowing his meal impatiently so he can call the team meeting. Now, he belongs with them just as much as he belonged with the Donegal team of the 1960s, the 1970s, the 1980s and the 1990s. More than with any other bunch of men he has worked with, it seems true to say that, with this present group, he has achieved something heart-warming and unexpected. Many hours after Donegal beat Galway in the All-Ireland quarter-final on a balmy evening in Castlebar last

August, McEniff got a call from John Cunningham, a tough campaigner from the 1990s.

'That was the best day of my life,' he told his former manager. McEniff found this staggering because Cunningham, although not on the field for the final, was an All-Ireland medal holder in 1992. He reminded the Killybegs man about that.

'No, that there was as good.'

That call was like a vindication of his decision to come back. In 1983, when Donegal had suffered a cruel loss to Galway through a late goal in that year's semi-final, McEniff had famously sat on a park bench in Belgrave Park in Rathmines all through the night, sober and silent and absolutely overwrought with sadness and confusion. When the end came this year against Armagh, he was better able to cope with the disappointment and put it into context.

'It happens with age. Anyway, I asked the boys to go out and play with flamboyance, to express themselves as a true Donegal team and they did that. I was proud. Wee things went against us. We had a man sent off for two nothing fouls really in comparison to other challenges in the game. But I thought then it was my last match. I really was drained and did not see any point in saying anything to the referee; I just felt I should get out of there as quickly as I could and get into the boys. It is hard to say [if we could have won the All-Ireland] with Tyrone so strong but I must say that given the way Tyrone played in the final, then it was possible because we were getting better day by day.'

It all meant that by September of last year, the McEniff legend had taken on another dimension.

Years ago, when Bundoran used to play down in Ballybofey, a local woman used to take a position above the tunnel where the teams ran onto the field so that she could try to bash McEniff on the head with her umbrella. He never did anything specifically to provoke her ire and only got to know her name in later years, but in those years, the young McEniff was the most potent symbol of power and politics in the fearfully localised arena of Donegal football. So it was his head she aimed for. The parochial subtleties in Donegal are infinite, so universal acclaim was never going to come cheaply. The point about McEniff is that he was never the ordained king of his county and did not always have things his own way. There have been several times when McEniff has been treated casually by the delegates of the county board and yet he always had the humility to show up a few years later and plead his case for another shot at management. In 1975, he was axed for having played a meaningless summer game for the New York exiles against Donegal. His mistake was to give a distinguished performance, and that led to discontent at home.

'I suppose if I look back, a few people got together that decided they wanted rid of McEniff. In 1986, I remember saying to Pauric McShea coming out of Breffni Park having been beaten by Cavan, "That's it. I'm gone." But it was right in this respect: Tom Conaghan was entitled to his period in charge then. It's true though that certain people just don't like you – they won't like you as a person or as a Bundoran man or whatever. But I think over the years people with reservations learned to see me not as a businessman or a Bundoran man but just as a football man, a wild Donegal man.'

When he was dropped in 1975, he took up an invitation to train the Sligo football team across the border and on impulse, he took it. Almost inevitably, he guided them to that year's Connacht title, a feat that has eluded the county since. That was his lone adventure beyond the borders of Donegal and he argues that it does not really count because his own county had already been knocked out of the championship. And that short term away was enough to convince him that managing any county other than Donegal felt wrong; he never repeated it, despite many offers.

There are very few men in the history of the GAA who have put in as many years with their own county as McEniff has given to Donegal, and none of them are still involved in the game. He is the last of a rare breed and when you ask him why he is still bound to the whole mad carousel, he smiles as if confronted with a riddle and simply says: 'Because I love it.'

He claims to care little for immortality within Donegal and is certainly indifferent to how he is perceived beyond the borders. If he has any regrets, it is that there were years when he was so obsessed with the football seasons that he failed to notice his children growing up. He and Cautie have ten, three sons and seven daughters.

'Some of the kids got great pieces of me and others didn't. It all depends on what stage the football was at. There was a photo in all the national newspapers after the Armagh game of this Donegal kid with tears in his eyes and nobody knew the significance of it. That was Diarmuid Long, my daughter Fiona's boy. I get a great buzz out of all the grandchildren now and I think they enjoy seeing their grandfather involved with the team.'

Most of his children are now involved in the hotel business that is now sometimes referred to in newspapers as an 'empire.' Whatever it is, McEniff insists it developed accidentally. He is singularly uninterested in the affectations of wealth but does allow that the years have moulded him into a natural hotelier. He has the glide and the quick smile of a man used to sweeping through lobbies at galas and receptions and speaks in a low tone of confidentiality, as if all the things he tells you are a secret. And although he is uncommonly approachable and decent with his time, there is always the sense with McEniff that only a very select and chosen group of people in this world are permitted to truly know him.

He has a thespian's gift for accentuating a good yarn and many of the best invariably revolve around the September orb of 1992. On the day of that All-Ireland final, Cautie stood before him as he made his way out through the front door of the hotel and asked him not to be disappointed if Donegal lost the game.

'Woman,' he replied, 'move aside from the door. There is no way we are going to lose this game.'

The reason he can get away with delivering a line that sounds like something from a John Ford western is that McEniff is so obviously influenced by a strong matriarchal family. His wife did not get to witness the finest hour first-hand. She never grew accustomed to seeing her husband so stressed and animated during games and so, while the rest of Donegal obsessed on every passing second of the 1992 final, she drove through the midlands with their youngest girl, turning on and off Mícheál Ó Muircheartaigh's commentary. The last ten minutes were spent in a church and when she ascertained that Donegal had won, she raced into a Mullingar pub to see the speech and the celebrations. She told the staff who she was but they hardly believed her.

About an hour after the game ended, McEniff went wandering high above the seats in Croke Park in search of a press phone. He had just received an ovation from all the clans in Donegal that in sentiment remains deathless. Still, he phoned the Holyrood and asked for his mother.

'Brian, she said, 'listen to this.'

Elizabeth McEniff held the receiver close to a window on Main Street. All her son could hear were car horns beeping and people cheering and he stood there with the phone against his ear for the longest time. It could never be said Bundoran lacked spirit at that moment.

It could be contended that deep down Brian McEniff yearns to hear that rapture anew and that is why he remains so potent a force in Donegal. After all, he gave the impossible a damn good rattle last year. But the truth is that there is no simple reason why you can find him on Donegal training fields a decade after he has achieved everything and several decades after he stopped owing anything.

To those of us who accept there are limits to everything, McEniff's ongoing defiance of the principle is both mad and beautiful. It is just an inherent want and passion, a consequence of a distinguished football career and the hours and discipline instilled by hotel life and the pianist's romantic desire to always play them one more tune. After the team travelled to London for a league game this year, McEniff sat down at a grand piano in the heart of Cricklewood and tinkled some Percy French. By then, none of his players were surprised.

When the cars shoot away from Castlefin, McEniff is truly tired. He asks Charlie to drive the car home and he sits in the front seat and although he would probably prefer to rest, he is conscious that he has company. Ever the host, ever the entertainer. He remembers a story from the 1960s. He has this boyhood friend from Bundoran, Liam Travers, a professional musician. One night shortly after his father had passed away, Travers called to the door and asked him to help out at a variety concert that had been organised in Ballintra. McEniff was reluctant but he was persuaded just to help load the equipment. In Ballintra, the hall was full but there was no piano. McEniff and Bernard Brady were dispatched to locate one. Several flights of stairs and a tractor-trailer later, they were in business. The piano nearly ended both their football careers. Moving it became a grim and wordless struggle but they persisted because there were customers waiting. It was some sight, two county men on a tractor-trailer holding onto a piano – in the rain. McEniff was soaked by the time they pushed the instrument up through the main hall. The performance was already delayed. Most of the crowd was beginning to wonder if this was part of the act, some kind of ill-advised comedic turn. When they moved the piano onto the stage. Travers managed to twist McEniff's arm into playing it, to accompany the lad on guitar.

'There's just one problem,' his friend whispered as he nudged the young Bundoran footballer on to the stage before a Ballintra audience on its last few grains of patience. 'That boy only started learning guitar last week.'

The Donegal manager laughs in delight as he delivers that line and his car moves on through the moonlit hollow of Barnesmore Gap, the unyielding physical presence down all the years of driving to and from football.

That Sunday, Donegal would beat Clare in Ballyshannon. Brian McEniff had succeeded in returning his beloved county to the first division but his cold was no better.

2

Cathedral

On the hallowed Sundays in September, when thousands of people move through the city streets in a mood of blazing optimism, Croke Park does not surprise. It is a city now, bold and bright and firmly modern, a masterpiece of imagination and perseverance. And when Irish people gather on the dedicated Sundays of All-Ireland finals, flowing like lava along the red-bricked tenements of old, they expect to see nothing less than the great, sweeping curve of cold grey as surely as the risen saints expect to see Heaven's Gate. The warmth and colour of epic crowds balance the sheer vastness of the new theatre and when two counties gather to play contests that will define a season and for some, a lifetime, Croke Park becomes localised again.

It is impossible, when approaching the new stadium, though, not to recall what it arose from, a dark and windblown place. There was something of the mausoleum about the old Croke Park in the way you had to leave the sunshine in your wake as you approached its stiles. Once inside, crowds drifted through a kind of dim wattage twilight, along the broad walkways and narrow stairwells and it felt less like being inside a sporting stadium than like being in the cavernous heart of some geological structure: damp and echoing and ancient. It was as if the hooded stands crouched over the players and the green field to fend off the outside world. It was a singularly unlovable place, grimy and haughty with a superior history. And yet it was loved.

There will be a day when there will be none of us left to remember that stark monument to 1950s Ireland. For the time being, we are all caught in the middle ground of expecting the splendour of the new arena while preserving the mindset in which we approached the old place. Before, Croke Park was an expedition to come prepared for. Then, a well-leafed copy of the *Sunday Press* became a seat cushion. The old Croke Park left its patrons feeling tired, sticky and enchanted. It was a leathery and sharp-boned old maiden, possessed by its own ghosts – suitors like Ring and Purcell – and dependent on its crowds for sentiment. It had enigma. There was, people have acknowledged as it was torn down, 'something about it'.

It is against the memory of that dark atmosphere that today's palace, carpeted and marble-touched and silver shone, is conceived.

The first day of the championship season in Croke Park this year was hot, with temperatures expected to reach the mid-twenties. When the stewards gathered on the side of the field at ten in the morning, the heat was already noticeable and increased the mood of good humour. Although there was a cleaned-out cavity where Hill 16 used to stand, the stadium looked polished and fantastic and the thought of a good afternoon of football and of all the stories that would be played out over the summer created a happy house.

Séamus Ó Midheach, the event controller of Croke Park, covers miles walking through its catacombs every Sunday of the summer season. He has been a stadium staff member for so long that he cheerfully declares himself part of the furniture.

On the first morning of the season, he walked swiftly through the various levels, greeting the security boys and kitchen staff and stewards by first name. He has distilled the art of conversing along with murmuring instructions into a multi-channel walkie-talkie and because he knew all the short cuts, we moved from the sophistication of the corporate level to the oil and rags of the boiler room in seconds flat. The best way to get a feel for Croke Park is to walk in Séamus's shadow for a couple of hours.

Nowadays, departments are so streamlined that everything runs like clockwork but it is still Séamus Ó Midheach's responsibility to eliminate the tiniest percentage chance of things going wrong. In Croke Park, there is a show behind the show: a backstage production that is more or less completely disconnected from what happens on the field in the mid-afternoon. These are the people whom Séamus is concerned with. But as he explained the fine balance of scale and timing and preparation that goes into any Sunday at Croke Park, he frequently referred back to 'the old way' to illustrate a point.

In principle, the working life of Croke Park has not changed. The first staff members arrive at dawn. Stewards are predominantly from the bordering counties of Wicklow, Meath and Kildare and they give their time on a voluntary basis, the chief perk being that they normally get to watch the second half of the main game. Gardaí and a medical team are dedicated to the stadium for the afternoon: the teams are escorted through to the rear entrance of the dressing room and, as always, the movement of the crowd towards the stadium is tightly monitored. The principle of conducting a large crowd through a residential area for the purpose of watching a match is no different from how it was fifty years ago but of course the reality flies in the face of the old ways.

'It is hard to fathom the way we used to do things here,' Ó Midheach said.

'The whole experience has changed, from our point of view and from the customers'. It is apparent from the moment you approach the turnstiles at the ground. When we were dealing with cash, it was a nightmare. It was slow and inefficient and messy. But there was no alternative at that time. Now, everything is designed towards making the day as enjoyable and comfortable for the public as possible.'

Because of that, the majority of the 2,000 Croke Park staff members who sign on for match day are involved in catering. Food is a serious business in Croke Park. In the main kitchens, located on the lower floor of the Cusack stand, Derek McLaughlin, the head chef, was busy inspecting a tiered dessert trolley when we walked in. Although the team dressing rooms are only twenty metres down the hallway, this might have been the kitchen of any *haute cuisine* restaurant and McLaughlin expects his food to be judged on those standards.

'Our clients in the corporate boxes pay fairly handsomely for the privilege of being there so we do try and treat them well,' he said.

In July 1996, corporate boxes for the Cusack stand were leased for ten years at £250,000 for a double suite and £150,000 for a single. By May of 1999, £1 million of premium seat tickets – sold at £5,500 for a ten-year period – were taken up within three days of going on the market. The plushest and largest of the executive suites sold at £320,000 while the smaller suites sold at £160,000. The innovation of the corporate boxes, adopted from the American philosophy of sports stadiums, meant that when the GAA was considering financing for the new Cusack stand, the first phase of development, they could rely on the corporate fraternity to cover the cost without dominating the available seats. The devoted premium seats and corporate suites, located at mezzanine level, number only 3,000 of the 24,000 seats in the stand.

Having marketed what was in the mid-1990s an unproven

strategy with great effect, the association felt that the interior and detail of the corporate sections should reflect the appreciation that it felt towards its benefactors from the business world. Having invested in the stadium, the corporate community was treated royally from the beginning. There is something of old-world extravagance about the elite section of the stadium and this sense of privilege and exclusivity is symbolised by the cuisine.

Before each season, McLaughlin devises four distinct silver menus which are presented each week and then reviewed on a cyclical basis. The dishes that have proven popular are retained, some are eliminated and others are added.

The menu for the opening day of the season included such delicacies as terrine of hickory smoked chicken with an apricot chutney; baked fillet of sea bass in spring-roll pastry in a lime and sherbet butter sauce, and dark chocolate and orange tart with a compote and citrus *anglais*.

There are about twenty chefs under McLaughlin. They arrive at about eight in the morning on match days and appoint the starters and desserts to polished white plates before delivering them to the cold storage at suite level. Generally, all seventy-eight corporate boxes are in operation on All-Ireland final days, with anywhere from between fifteen to thirty-five people in each box. The time when orders come in varies. Some companies like to spend some time in the stadium bars before going into the corporate suite. Most prefer to eat between games. Generally, by half-time of the main match of the day, the food has been served.

'Thursday is the critical day. It we get our information right and plan ahead, the actual day of the game can be fairly smooth and, if I am not looking, some of the chefs might try and sneak out to see the end of the game. But it is a bit like the approach of the hurling and football teams here. If we are organised and understand the demands that lie ahead, we don't encounter any problems.'

Regional habits have not gone unnoticed. Northern customers tend to eat heartily. Visitors from Kerry and Cork consume what is put on their plate. People residing closer to the city eat more sparingly. Vegetarianism is rare. Everything is logged and recorded and stored for when the same counties return for another game. It is all business. There are days when the crowd above sounds like a distant thunderclap as McLaughlin shouts orders through the clatter of the kitchens. And it only occurs to him much later on, when Croke Park is silent and moonlit and he is exhausted, that he has not the faintest idea of who won the game.

The garda meeting takes place at eleven o'clock in the auditorium that is part of the GAA museum. For a day of this nature – a Leinster football championship double bill and expected to draw a crowd of around 35,000 – about 40 gardaí have been assigned posts in the ground.

The list of issues outlined by the chief superintendent ranges from the trivial – children hurling water balloons from the upper decks of the stand – to the worst possible scenario – bomb threats and evacuations.

Before the 1994 ceasefire in Northern Ireland, Croke Park regularly received bomb warnings, often through the Samaritans and with a recognised code word.

'It was quite stressful,' remembered Séamus Ó Midheach.

'Generally, the calls came through early in the morning and we were always able to search the stands with dog units so we knew by the time people came in that the ground was perfectly safe. Thankfully we haven't received a coded warning now for many years.'

Evacuating a full house at Croke Park has been timed at eight minutes flat. The internal communications system allows the gardaí and the stewards to work in tandem.

Although the stadium started last summer working with an eight-camera surveillance system, it has been updated to a state-of-the-art successor. It features 100 individual cameras that provide a complete picture of the interior and exterior of Croke Park, with lenses powerful enough to read the small print on the newspapers that blow abandoned around the stadium after every big match day.

The other potential nightmare for Séamus Ó Midheach and the staff is of a crowd crush.

'Dubs arriving late,' was his response when asked what he feared most about a match day. Two years ago, the Dublin vs Donegal All-Ireland quarter-final replay, scheduled for five o'clock on an August Saturday, was delayed by fifteen minutes at Ó Midheach's directive.

'Because there was no early game on, there was no incentive to arrive in the ground early. And we knew it irritated people who had arrived in time that we seemed to accommodate those people who showed up at the last minute. But fifteen minutes before that game was due to start, there was less than half of the expected crowd in the ground. It came down to an issue of people's safety. We could see from the cameras the crowd that was gathering along the Clonliffe Road and heading towards Hill 16. Those extra fifteen minutes cleared that pressure with no danger to anyone. Once you have the crowd inside, your worry eases. There is never the same concentrated time period about leaving the ground. Individual habits come back. The supporters of losing teams generally leave smartly but some hang around to gather themselves. Winning fans drift out in their own time. Counties that win an All-Ireland for the first time stay in the ground as long as possible, savouring the day. Then you have the counties that are habitual winners and they just about hang on for the presentation.'

Because Armagh and Tyrone were the maiden winners of the past two All-Ireland football championships, the requests for supporters to remain in their seats after the final whistles went gloriously unheeded. Most GAA followers regard the swamping of the pitch on September Sundays as a venerable tradition but such occurrences are becoming much less frequent. The ironic thing is that the field has never been more accessible. A cordon of stewards forms a human barrier at the end of the All-Ireland finals, a line of resistance that is ultimately dependent on co-operation. In the old Croke Park, with tall mesh gates separating the crowd from the field, there was a look of circus trainers releasing their charges when the gates were opened on All-Ireland final days. As it was, negotiating entrance to the field was tricky, particularly from the Canal end, with its low terracing.

'It was a headache, with people rushing out onto the field while others found it difficult to step up through the gate. And in the excitement of the moment, people invariably fell on the field and went home to discover a bruise or a twist.'

The pandemonium of the field was a no man's land. It was a pickpocket's heaven. It was also a fertile land when it came to insurance claims. After many All-Irelands, Séamus Ó Midheach found himself driving the length of Ireland with Ciarán O'Neill to hear cases of claimants of injuries received during the All-Ireland-day celebrations.

'When we used to let people onto the field, Ciarán O'Neill, who was in charge of stadium insurance, and I travelled up and down the country to court cases where people had come onto the field and had fallen in the excitement and went home and discovered this knock or that bruise. Coming in off the old Canal end when the gates were open was a particularly common problem. But that is almost a thing of the past.'

In the medical control centre, Seamus Grant spends his day in front of a laptop screen monitoring the calls that come in before and after the match. Crowds of between 30,000 and 90,000 people mean a standard list of complaints: headaches, sprains, sunburn, sickness, vertigo, Rarely has a Sunday passed without a ticket-holder finding themselves gasping for air on their first visit to the upper slopes of the Hogan or Cusack stands. The gradient is very gentle, but because of the fine view of the city and because the players look so very faraway on the field below, sitting close to the front edge can make you feel vulnerable. Croke Park manages to accommodate confirmed vertigo sufferers elsewhere but some require a visit to the medical centre before turning back to the sport.

Every season brings its cardiac arrests, sometimes fatal. As recently as twenty years ago, stadiums were dependent on 'runners' to alert medical staff to a person in distress. Now, even as Seamus Grant receives the data, one of the medical teams in the ground is dispatched to the precise location. This summer, the stewards were trained in giving emergency medical attention to customers. During the training course, two stewards were sitting in the museum café at lunchtime when a member of the public collapsed with a cardiac complaint. They administered medical attention and three weeks later their patient had recovered sufficiently to call and thank them.

In the control room in the Hogan stand, two gardaí studied the television monitors of the crowds that had begun to thicken on the approach roads. The critical time is about half an hour before throw-in but because this was a double bill of modest scale, the avenues were not expected to come under serious pressure.

By one o'clock in the afternoon, though, the premium levels were doing brisk business. There is something about the polished floors and bright brass beer taps and white linen cloths and the sheer linear majesty of the premium levels that is redolent of luxury cruise liners. Turn your back to the glass panels that run the length of the premium levels and you could be in the foyer of any opulent hotel, with waiting staff carrying silver trays and customers standing at counters sipping drinks.

In the suites, the atmosphere is even more sedate. Clients need never even leave the rooms, which are fitted with personalised bars and television screens and dedicated waiting staff. And when the dining is complete, they are just steps away from the glass-panelled doors and the private box seating, designed to maximise seclusion without compromising the noise and atmosphere all around.

There are lone arguments that the corporate slant of the new Croke Park is a lamentable development which dilutes the purity of the Jones's Road experience that many people grew up with. The tiered structure undeniably reinforces the class system and there is something of the old Coliseum about the notion of the aristocrats engaging in fine dining while beneath them the sport rages on. But it is ultimately a reactionary grievance because the design of the stadium improves the quality of the experience for all spectators in the house.

In 1941, the artist Warner was commissioned to produce a sketch visualising Croke Park fifty years on. The image was published in an annual celebrating the opening of the new Hogan stand last year. Warner imagined a vast, open, dome-like creation, with a circular pitch. The emblem was of two hurleys that stretch 150 feet into the air, with a giant *sliotar* resting at the base. There is a lot of shrubbery and what appears to be a sleek railway line running under the pitch and there are glass chutes in which elevators ferry people to the upper echelons of the stands. People are dining at tables located near the base of one of the chutes and the stands appear to be adorned with private boxes, like the enclosures reserved for the royal family at London theatres.

In reality, Warner's vision looks a bit unworkable and concedes to occasional flights of fantasy – not least in the appearance of an extremely menacing and huge double-finned aircraft circling the stadium. But in spirit, with its dramatic, cupped shape and the emphasis on space and sky and cleanliness and most of all in the total boldness of the creation, the artist was spookily close.

Deep beneath the clinking of glasses in the corporate boxes is the serious stuff. The tunnels underneath the stands allow the team buses to deliver the players to the door of their dressing room.

When the teams arrive some time after midday, Joe Rock is there to greet them as he has always been. Joe is a Croke Park institution.

'The Rocks,' he explained one morning when we sat in 'the Dublin' dressing room under the Cusack stand, 'are the foundation of Croke Park.'

Joe was seventy-eight this year and he began working in the stadium on match days with his father. William Rock was the Custodian of the Ball in the stadium for many decades.

'It was he who, with due dignity, brought in with measured stride the football or the *sliotar* to the referee before the game began,' wrote Padraig Puirseal in the *Irish Press* in a 1977 article, 'and Croke Park experts knew exactly what he expected from the match to come. If he wore his best bowler hat, he anticipated a game worthy of the occasion. If he wore a cloth cap, one assumed he was just hoping for the best.'

On All-Ireland days, he always embellished his suit with the hard hat and walked around the field dispensing the footballs or *sliotar*s to the teams and collecting them afterwards. The Rocks predate Croke Park: they used to live on Love Lane, which is still at the rear of the stadium, but later moved to nearby Russell Avenue, where Joe still walks today.

Even when he was six, Joe Rock was aware of the immense pride and seriousness that his father invested in this Sunday tradition and it was something he inherited. When he was first brought along to the game, he was told to collect the orange peels that the players used to discard at half-time. Teams never returned to the dressing rooms then, so he dodged in and out among the strange, urgent accents collecting the scattered peels in his bucket, too young to know or care which teams were playing. It was enough to be following in his father's footsteps.

'Some days, he would let me carry one of the football bags onto the field. And I used to feel like the proudest fella in the place.'

Joe was probably in Croke Park for the Thunder and Lightning final of 1939 and on the September day in 1956 when Ring was chaired around the field by Wexford, but he does not recall them. Although he loves the games, he remembers them through the prism of the dressing rooms. His was – and remains – a role that demanded sensitivity and subtlety and he takes it seriously. There is a gallows element about dressing rooms, particularly on All-Ireland final day. Once a team enters a dressing room, they do so in the knowledge that when they eventually leave, their lives will have changed in a minor but significant way. They will have won or lost. For some men, Joe Rock moving unobtrusively among them was a comfort because he lived these hours every single September and that bestowed upon him some sort of indirect power.

In a way, he was like the man preparing the last meal for the condemned on the eve of execution: the last kindly face they might meet before they departed for the hereafter.

Some teams found him a lucky charm. Some guys liked to engage him in talk. Others were too wrapped up in the moment to notice his existence.

'Nothing really has changed except that now, it is all business. Years ago, fellas were more lackadaisical about the games and about life. I just do what I always did. The bus pulls up outside the rear doors. Normally there are a few lads from RTÉ there now. We make sure the dressing rooms are perfect for them and then show the teams through. I make the managers a cup of tea if they so desire and see if they need anything else. Then I just keep out of sight but I'd be close at hand if they need anything. I just let them chat. I never interfere.'

Nobody has seen the epic games like Joe Rock. Loitering in the shadows of the old Hogan and Cusack stands, drifting out to where the tunnel met the field to catch glimpses, he has caught just fleeting sequences of so many great matches. But he was at the heart of the unforgettable consequences, the chaotic minutes where the separating line between victory and loss was still asserting itself, leaving the bleak, steamed-up corridors of the old arena in bedlam.

Things stand out. Sometimes he walks into an empty dressing room and remembers a scene from the vintage days of Heffernan's Dublin – Paddy Cullen sitting in his usual corner or Joe's nephew Barney, pale and elegant and restrained in the corner.

Joe Rock loved the 1970s era when Croke Park felt like it truly belonged to that raucous and charismatic city bunch, boys who he came to know by name and enjoyed fussing over as the sounds from the Hill rumbled through the very bones of the stadium. The involvement of his nephew Barney heightened his pride in that era and, in those times, he found himself drawn to the edge of the field more and more, lurking in the mouth of the tunnel, engrossed in the game. He can talk clearly and fondly about some of Barney Rock's splendid moments in the stadium that his father and grandfather and uncles roamed for decades. And he remembers vividly the attrition that existed between his nephew and the feared Meath defender, Liam Harnan.

'Big strong men. When you had the reputation of being a good player the way Barney has, then you had to expect the consequences.'

Joe was in the tunnel on the mean and notorious day in September 1983 when the players of Galway and Dublin got involved in a fight at half-time, one of the more dismal episodes of violence in GAA history. Joe Rock witnessed that – or at least some of what occurred – but he did not want to implicate anyone.

'A few days after the final, Kevin Heffernan called up to Russell Avenue to ask me what I knew about what went on but I told him I didn't see anything. And I was close by for the thing with Talty [Brian Talty of Galway] but ah, none of it was my business. Like, I saw many things before and after that day that nobody ever heard about.'

Joe saw himself as being outside the immediate politics of the game, however incendiary they became. His role was to cater for the teams when they entered his dominion. It cost him. One year, when a large crowd managed to gain access to the dressing-room area through the tunnel, he was doing his best to keep the door closed when it shot open and caught him flush in the face. He lost the sight in one eye permanently. That was nearly fifty years ago, but the incident never made him bitter or turned him off a position that was largely ceremonial, something he did out of a sense of honour to his familial role in the stadium.

'It was a hard thing to have happen you and I didn't see so well after that. But that was it, you got on with it.'

Some individuals made his summer. He remembers Jack Lynch of Cork as an absolute prince of a man, at once regal and unassuming regardless of how events transpired on the field. He does not believe Jack Lynch ever left the dressing rooms without seeking him out to say thank you and goodbye. He still has a good relationship with Seán Boylan. Meath fascinates him. He believes that no team prepares so perfectly as Meath. One summer at the beginning of the championship, Joe complained to Boylan about kidney-stone problems. Three weeks later, when Meath were back in the capital, Boylan handed him a jar containing a liquid that had the appearance of tea and the taste of nothing he experienced before or since. The herbalist instructed him to drink it twice a day. He was cured before he welcomed Meath again.

During one of the years when the footballers of Kerry were kings of Croke Park, Joe was shuffling around the dressing room, tidying up bags, when he heard the familiar voice of Pat Spillane. This was in the old Cusack-stand dressing room, with a white bathtub that was never filled sitting as the centrepiece of the design. The walls were adorned with wrought-iron coat hooks for the players to hang their shirts and trousers, and the wooden beams on the floor had become so worn and chafed from the years of studs and soaking towels that splinters of wood stood upright. When teams and substitutes and trainers were all in there and bags scattered across the floor, it felt claustrophobic. Spillane, the celebrated and talkative Kerry forward, was making his way across the room in his socks when he trod on a splinter.

'Joe. Jesus. Joe. This floor will have me finished. Come on until we get a hammer and knock these spikes back into the floor.'

And years later, sitting in a bright and salubrious new dressing room, Joe Rock triumphantly recalled his reply: 'So I looked at this Spillane fella and I said, "You must think you're in your granny's now. I don't go knocking spikes into the ground on a Sunday morning."

The spikes stayed. Kerry won anyhow.

The more you listen to Joe Rock talk about his years watching the metamorphosis of teams into champions, the more it reminds you of speaking with a veteran schoolteacher who has excellent recall of the names and faces of those who passed through his classroom but is a bit blurred about the years. Years do not matter so much to Joe Rock. He remembers the great Galway three-in-a-row-team of the 1960s, through the harrowing silence and then the weeping he heard when word was passed on to John Donnellan that his father had passed away in the stands during the match.

The iron-willed, stubble-faced Meath team of the 1980s summon to his mind not the raw tussles in which they engaged Cork, but for a debate he had with Colm O'Rourke over showers. The boiler system in Croke Park then was much the same as any private dwelling: when the tank was empty, you took a cold shower.

O'Rourke, possibly engaged in press duties, was one of the last players to enter the showers after this All-Ireland and when he did, he found the water icy. This, after an hour in the company of Cork's ferocious defence, was too much, so he called for Joe.

'I says to him, "Of course it is cold. While the other boys were in there washing, you were out talking. The fact is that the tank is empty." I said I was sorry but there was nothing I could do. Colm got a bit upset that day but Seán [Boylan] straightened it all out for me.'

William Rock died in November of 1972. Although Joe has vague memories of the original three stands in Croke Park, he associates that era with his father. William Rock was working in the stadium on 20 November, 1920, the day that Michael Hogan of Tipperary was shot dead along with thirteen spectators when the Auxiliaries and the RIC opened fire at random from the centre of the field. The Rocks lived beside an IRA man who was heavily involved in the War of Independence and William Rock told stories of how the Black and Tans would jump up on a milk cart to peer in through the houses in search of this neighbour, who successfully hid himself up chimneys. Joe Rock heard his father talk about Bloody Sunday so often – the abrupt, silencing rat-a-tat of bullets, the screams and the crowds fleeing the ground – that it became real to him.

And the legacy of that day is so potent that although it is rarely explicitly referred to, it remains at the core of the ongoing debate as to whether or not sports like soccer and rugby should be played in the stadium. The nationalist line is that the mere symbol of flying the Union Jack would tarnish the memory of those murdered in the wartime atrocity. It is an unfashionable perspective to hold and is often pilloried as being unenlightened, mired in the past. The lobbyists for 'opening' Croke Park can point to the financial imperative and to the fact that many contemporary players have declared their wish for other sports people to have the opportunity to play there.

It is a sensitive point because the GAA has always been an overtly nationalist organisation and Bloody Sunday was a defining episode in its evolution. To some members, calls to embrace a more liberal and inclusive tone is tantamount to erasing that history, to admitting that because it belongs in the shady years that led to the formation of the Irish State, it no longer matters. But talking with Joe Rock about his father makes it feel as if Bloody Sunday was not all that long ago.

In March of 1977, Joe's brother John Rock was killed leaving Croke Park. All the Rock boys worked the stadium from their early boyhood. John was responsible for checking all the gates and turnstiles in the stadium after the crowds had left. Often, he took a pet dog with him just for company because, when it was empty, Croke Park was a mournful and cold place. When the central council met in the offices of Croke Park, John stood outside until the delegates left, sometimes after midnight, in bitter weather when it seemed like the entire city was sleeping. Then he would lock up and go home. On this evening – 27 March – he left the stadium to meet his wife and, as they walked across the Ballybough Bridge, they were hit by a car whose driver was drunk. Although the driver was apprehended, the charges were ultimately dropped when legal papers pertaining to his arrest somehow got lost. That night, though,

Joe was still in the ground when he got word and it was he who had to go along to the Richmond Hospital to identify the body.

'It's not the kind of thing you like to talk about,' he said. 'It is not the kind of thing you easily forget.'

In an obituary in the *Irish Press* on 6 April, Padraig Puirseal wrote:

'We would sit in the sunshine in the old sideline seats while John's father would talk of the old days of the Albert College students he had known who had gone on to hurling and football stardom. Then when John had left us to climb up to the scoreboard, the old man would trace back to the days when he himself was a lad, when Croke Park was first Butterly's Field and then the City and Suburban Sports Ground; when it housed pony races and trotting as well as hurling and football games, and when more than one gay party went on 'til morning on the wooden pavilion that stood where the first Hogan stand subsequently followed.

'The Rocks always served Croke Park faithfully. When he retired from Cahill's [Printers], John became a kind of combination caretaker and watchman. He was the man who locked up after late night meetings, whose quiet patience seemed almost inexhaustible. In their middle years, John Rock and his wife had known tragedy, a tragedy hauntingly similar to the terrible one that has swept them away so suddenly from their loved ones and from us all. *In Iotlann Dé go gcastar sin.*'

Few families have developed such profound ties with Croke Park as the Rocks. Joe can sit in the ultra-modern facilities of the new dressing room and still have complete recall of the black passages of the vanished stadium because the old place was hand in glove to him. He might gesture off to the left and straight ahead and refer, say, to the Kerry dressing room in 1982, as if they are still down the corridor, side-burned and youthful and brimming with expectation. He could summon the great teams from any era and place them in their dressing room, on their favourite part of the bench.

The day we met, Joe showed me Mass cards of his father William, strong and pleasant-faced, and of his brothers John and Charlie. He also had some family heirlooms – a snap taken of himself and a friend Christy brandishing a pair of hurls as they stood outside their house on Love Lane sometime in the 1930s. He had a grainy photograph of himself with his arm around his young son, Joseph. They were pictured in a dressing room in Croke Park, the panelled wooden walls and coat hangers behind them. He had a steward's rosette, striped with serrated edges that he received in the 1930s. Wrapped in soft white crepe paper was a simple silver medal he had received from the GAA for his services to Croke Park in the centenary year of the association.

He is not sure why Croke Park came to mean so much to his father and brothers or even why his own son Joseph now works there.

'I suppose it is a matter of honour and pride,' he says.

He believes there is probably less conversation now than in former days. Teams tend to look much the same: tense and gaunt young men and voluble managers. Sometimes the depth and extremity of the pre-match speeches amuse him. He has heard them all and wonders if it makes any difference. Sometimes he retreats to one of the spare dressing rooms and watches some of the match on the television screen. In the evenings, a cleaning team comes in to leave the dressing room shining.

It does not seem all that long ago since Croke Park was home to just three full-time staff – the secretary general, Paddy O'Keeffe; his secretary, Miss Moriarty; and the groundsman, Jimmy Curtain. Three people. It makes him smile. Joe Rock doesn't know how long he will keep it going but he is always hopeful there will be another September. He is happy that he has put in his time.

'I daresay I am the longest here,' he said and it was not a claim he made lightly.

At the front entrance of Croke Park, where the Ard Comhairle and other guests of the association gather on match days, stands George Delaney. He is the longest-serving steward in the building and over the years his has become perhaps its most recognisable face. He stands just outside the main hallway, with its electronic turnstiles and a long foyer of polished beige stone, where bronze sculptures of Cusack, Davitt and Archbishop Croke are prominently placed.

George always looks immaculate in a blazer and tie, his hair brill-creamed back, and he has the host's knack of moving from one group to another with the lightness of Astaire, always smiling, greeting and deadly accurate with names. There was a time when stewarding at Croke Park meant herding the masses towards the black, clinking turnstiles as quickly as possible, a practice that seems unbelievably rough in comparison to the relaxed and genteel environment of the present-day seasons.

'Back then there was no chat,' he said over a cup of tea in the staff canteen.

'Nothing. I started off in 1965 – I came up here to work with a crowd of men from Wicklow and I was sent down to the Hill at the time. And with the Dubs, you know, it was fairly hardy. I was working outside the turnstiles. You could hear the referee's whistle just before throw-in and this crowd of people would still be backing out onto the Clonliffe Road. And it was tight because it was all money then at the turnstiles and fellas would be pushing up and getting impatient, especially if they had the few jars in them. Then other lads would be trying to see if they could make a jump through the stiles. And once the crowd would roar inside, then they would be mad to get through and onto the Hill. It was all about trying to keep them contained, trying to keep it smooth. Thinking back, sure we were all mad but at the time, you didn't realise. There was no other way of getting people through. It was just a blessing that most people were good-humoured. But we went home tired, I remember that.'

The old photographs of the Croke Park crowds that congregated in Croke Park in the 1940s, 1950s and 1960s are endlessly fascinating, not only for the expressions – which are lit with the novelty of having a camera bulb flashed at them – but for the sheer numbers. A cavalier attitude towards personal safety was acceptable then and younger men thought nothing of sitting with one leg on either side of the high and precarious wall behind the Hill or on climbing onto the roof of the Hogan or Nally stands. George Delaney remembers supporters arriving at the grounds with ladders and scaling the walls at the Railway end before disappearing into the Canal-end terrace.

'You would shout at them but by the time you'd have made your way over to them, they were long gone. It was different then. It was sort of accepted that people would try anything to get in for free. And it wasn't that they didn't have the few bob in their pockets, it was just for the sake of it. I suppose there was no real harm in it.'

Crowds were hard to determine then. Officially, 90,566 attended the Down–Offaly football final of 1961 but the likelihood is that there were many more people in the ground. The biggest recorded crowd at an All-Ireland hurling final was at the 1954 game between Cork and Wexford when 84, 856 people attended. It is unlikely that those numbers will ever be exceeded.

George worked the gates of all the stands over the years. He admits that when he heard about plans to build a new, revolutionary stadium that would match the great soccer empires of England and the famous baseball houses of America, he just smiled.

'I just couldn't see it, even after the plans were drafted and the model for the stadium was in the old offices. Then, after

1993 when the foundations for the Cusack side were laid, it just hit me. This was going to happen. And the hardest thing to get used to was how quickly then it began to take shape. It took no time for the new to overtake the old.'

For many seasons, by the time George got back to Wicklow, the *Sunday Game* was already finished so although he had spent the day in Croke Park, he had seen no football or hurling. He still remains at his post during the games, trying to read the game from the symphony of the crowd.

'Or there is always some punter arriving late or called away urgently that would tell you the score. But you miss it sometimes, especially when the game seems exciting.'

He admits that he sometimes pines after the steel and wooden crypt of old as well, with its nooks and crannies and its stark, refrigerated atmosphere. He had good fun there over the years. And he met them all, from Ali to De Valera.

'The funniest time was just after a game began and this big lump of a lad came up to me saying that an American presidential candidate wanted to go to the game. It was your man Gary Harte. So I said I would sort him out. He was a nice fella, friendly. But he was fierce scared I would tell the press that he was in the crowd. He kept repeating that nobody could find out he was there. Sure who was I going to tell?'

In recent years, George reckons he has started to feel the length of the seasons. 'Sunday after Sunday it goes right through until October. My wife has passed away now, sadly, so I suppose I am as happy spending the Sundays here. The great thing about working here is that you always run into friends that you have made over the years. That's what makes it worth it for me anyway. And the All-Ireland days are a pleasure now, they are easier than ever. People just seem to arrive in great form. The day seems to give everyone a lift.'

The old press box was a wooden, green-painted enclosure in the middle of the upper deck of the Hogan stand. It had three tiers of hard wooden seats for ticket-holders and the front row, with black-padded swivel chairs and a small bench for writing notes on, was the dominion of the GAA correspondents. To the right of the press area was a small box where the radiomen made their broadcasts. Sound men and technicians had to stoop down with the announcers in these tiny booths with slanting windows that seemed to jut out beyond the rest of the stand, as if the commentators were working from the cockpit of an aeroplane from the old wars. The crowds, ambling along the stone corridors to their seats or trying to negotiate a path into the maelstrom of the washbasin facilities, could peer through the latch-doors into the broadcast booths where Mícheál O'Muircheartaigh's rapid-fire melodies of Irish and English originated.

There was a small windowless room across the corridor from the press box that on All-Ireland final days was transformed into a hospitality suite. Journalists vaulted – or at least gracelessly rolled over – the edge of the press box and fought their way across the tide of paying customers to the other side of a plain brown door. It is astonishing the tenacity and ruthlessness that the most placid pressman can demonstrate when a ham platter is on the line. Plates and plates of sandwiches and *hors d'oeuvres* on paper doilies, iced buns and fruit cake, wine and beer. The women who used to prepare the tables put great care into the presentation and it must have disturbed them to see the speed and devastation with which the trays on the long white tablecloths were stripped. For 'cub' journalists there was the added kick of passing the sugar to former stars of the field who had taken up work as guest columnists or analysts as some kind of atonement for their sins. There were days when it got so crowded in that little room that pressmen became acquainted with one another in ways they would rather have avoided. It was not a place for those given to panic. The thought crossed many minds that if, as the fourth estate gravitated towards the well-stocked refrigerator at the rear of the room, the Ard Stiúrthóir was to come along and just lock the door from the outside, nobody would be any the wiser. No screams would be heard over the din of the crowd and the Ard Stiúrthóir could leave the stadium that night, fling the key into the canal and sleep peacefully in the knowledge that he had done the association and society in general a great service. But it never happened. Seconds before the final whistle, the room was evacuated as smartly as if a fire drill had been called and the green enclosure was filled again. Press people elbowed each other as they settled in for the second half, a silent, scribbling group huddled together in a darkened cavern of noise and passion, wedged into the best seats in the house.

It is hard to believe that the dear old green box was still seating the perpetually disgruntled as recently as 1998. Today, the Hogan stand press facilities are sumptuous. Located on the seventh floor, in the centre of the upper tier, they include an indoor lounge area with televisions and a (dry) bar and snack counter. The working area is vast and spacious, with television monitors at the print desks and all the power points a soul could wish for. If it has brought any of the spirit of the old place with it, it is that the press area is still incredibly cold. Even on days when the sky is brightly lit and the crowds below are basking in short sleeves, it is as if the wind that drifts in across the city to the press area has been transported directly from Everest.

At the final whistle, the press members are escorted down through the vaults of the stadium to the tunnel where the teams leave the field. On All-Ireland final days, it is an uncomfortable experience waiting for the defeated players to leave the field. It is a funny thing, but beaten players never look as tired as those who win. A defeated player bounds off the field, sometimes muttering an oath or slamming a hurl off the wall, still pent up and frustrated, dying to play again, wanting to stay on the move, wanting anything other than to go back into that dressing room and endure the rituals of loss. Winners, though, saunter home in their own good time, relaxed of mind and of body, feeling as complete and fulfilled as they are ever going to in their athletic lives.

The tradition for many years was that the press got access to the dressing rooms. The room with the champions was often just an open house, with county board officials and past players and family members and the press people swarming in through the door, causing bedlam. In those times, you got to hear and see the rarest of things. Dressing rooms are sacrosanct places and in the immediate aftermath of victory or defeat, players are at their most honest. Over the years, unforgettable speeches were recorded or jotted down in the mayhem of All-Ireland dressing rooms.

In recent times, it has become more regulated. The dressing room doors stay shut after matches. Maybe that is as it should be. For teams, they are sacred places.

It means, though, that when the press finally shuffle in, the dressing rooms have been cleansed of their euphoria or desolation. Balance has been restored and managers and players have composed themselves enough to offer some sanitised observations on what has passed. They have, in short, recovered their game faces.

When the teams are showered and dressed, they take the lift to the corporate level where they present passes that entitle them to some drinks and finger food. It is an awkward situation, the defeated unwilling or unable to converse with anyone and the winners trying to contain their happiness out of respect. The worst moment, though, is when the losing players leave the dressing room and make their way across the concourse to the bright green light of the lift. The bus that will eventually take them back to the hotel is generally purring and the whole way along echoes to the sound of bottle crates being ferried away and vacuum cleaners humming and kitchen staff bidding one another good night. All-Ireland finals are built up into such epic, classical entities that it comes as a surprise to find the evening drawing in to such a common accompaniment. Those are the sounds of a season coming to a close and for those players left catatonic with regret, their souls still out there on the darkening, silent field, such sounds are brutal.

After the press collect their pound's worth of quotable words from the players, leaning into the crestfallen and broken losing players like priests hearing confession, they retreat back upstairs to the working room. It is generally close to ten o'clock in the evening when the last of them leave and by then Croke Park is imperial and alone again.

When the dream-makers of Croke Park talk about the origin of the new stadium, they sometimes refer to the 1983 All-Ireland football final. That afternoon was the last stand of a magical and evocative period for the city game but although Dublin won an All-Ireland that afternoon, it was a fretful and disappointing game that seemed to chase away the last scent of charm that had characterised the Dublin renaissance in the 1970s. That night, when they locked the gates of Croke Park, an uneasy air hung over the place. Stripped of people, it looked its age, worn and ugly, even baleful.

The 1980s were a decade when the architecture of so many stadiums – Heysel, Bradford, Hillsborough – was found out. What started out as an intention to modernise the venerable Hill 16 quickly shed light on what might be possible. The astonishing thing, when you trace the development of the new Croke Park from the first tossed brick to the finished, €200 million structure of today, is how steadfast and calmly low-key the GAA officials at the heart of the project remained throughout. Although a decade passed before the plans were invoked, the speed with which the stadium was transformed and the prophetic vision of those who guided it, represents the closest thing to revolution that will ever come to pass in the association.

Although a series of presidents – Paddy Buggy, Dr Mick Loftus, John Dowling, Peter Quinn, Jack Boothman, Joe McDonagh, Seán McCague, Sean Kelly – worked devotedly on the project, the name of Liam Mulivhill, Ard Stiúrthóir through all those administrations, is most closely associated with the realisation of Croke Park. In true tradition, he has publicly said very little about his role in Croke Park. However, he is widely lauded for having the vision and instinct to realise the importance of preserving the association's link with Jones's Road and for promoting the idea of a stadium that was beyond the contemporary imagination.

'We knew then that our reconstruction could not stop at the northern end of the ground,' he wrote in the Croke Park annual, reminiscing about the early studies undertaken of modern sports grounds.

'The realisation came quickly and the practicalities were examined. Croke Park was our pride and joy, our jewel. It was a symbol of where CLG [Cumann Lúthcleas Gael] stood in the Ireland of the late twentieth century.'

Liam Mulvihill is due to step down from his post in 2006. It must be with a sense of tremendous fulfilment that he looks out on the scenes of vivid triumphal celebration on the great days of summer. Years ago, when he came to Croke Park to play with Longford, Mulvihill's clothes were guarded by Joe Rock. Back then, when the dressing rooms were as well lit as a coal-mine and the field had a carnal and merciless aura about it, neither man could have dreamed of the great crossing that Croke Park would make.

Having newly shed its old skin, Croke Park is passing through an ether phase. Because the physical manifestation of the ground graced by men like Ring, like Mackey, like Michael

Hogan, no longer exists, so their deeds seem further removed from the contemporary generation. There are still women and men who can sit in the shiny new seats and look out on the field and summon the glorious details of long-finished matches as though they are happening before their eyes for the first time. But those lines of communication grow more tenuous with each passing year.

For now, though, there remains a spirit of the past about Croke Park, a sense that it is still the field of men and women who would not necessarily approve of the pomp of today's theatre. There is still the sense that the field remains a portal to those whose feats are captured in black-and-white stills and who played when the Irish State was younger and more optimistic, simpler and more mannerly. It is that shivery feeling of walking in the footsteps of the gods of a previous age that makes the place something deeper than a monument to design and money. It is in the way that Joe Rock will gesture down the hallway when he talks of Jack Lynch, as if the tall fellow might appear at any moment, polite and angular and wearing the plain red shirt of Cork.

And perhaps it is so: that long after the final whistles sound, after the cameras are wheeled away, after the crowds melt into the city twilight and the gates are bolted, after nightfall, the ghosts of all those Croke Park games have the freedom of the field.

3

After the Ball is Over

It was sometime in the Autumn of 1967 when the Morris Minor made its approach to Thurles. Of all the vehicles in Ireland at that time, this particular Morris was best acquainted with the provincial back roads that led to GAA grounds all over the country. There were some Sunday-night journeys back to Dublin city when it was as if the small car had the bone-rattling Irish road network to itself, chugging across the moonlit bog lands of Offaly and the gaping plains of Kildare without ever encountering any other traffic. On those occasions, if its occupant motored alone, the radio dial would be tweaked until it happened upon an operatic frequency, turned to full volume and a passenger window opened to allow some cigar smoke to escape. After the tumult and splendour of another Sunday game, after many painstaking hours with a pen and paper, this was peace. More often than not though, the Morris Minor was crammed with regular guests.

On this particular afternoon, one of those mackerel-coloured Irish days late in the year that never bothers brightening, there were just two men in the car and they were nervous. The driver was Paddy Downey, Gaelic games correspondent with *The Irish*

Times, a tall, angular and impressive man, always immaculately turned out and Yeatsian in his deportment. When he spoke, with a gravely musical tone that still held clear echoes from his childhood days in West Cork, people felt compelled to listen. Beside him was John D Hickey, GAA correspondent for the *Irish Independent*, small and compact and bristling with energy and humour and attitude. They had little in common as people, other than a fierce love of, and pride in this curious and privileged job that they shared, writing reports on Gaelic matches that were phoned back to Dublin, printed onto the news sheets and transported on trains and trucks around the country. That was enough to draw a tight bond between them. Years later, the two men, along with Padraig Puirseal of the *Irish Press*, would be regarded as the key figures in popularising and broadening the newspaper coverage of Gaelic games.

At this time though, they were merely the leaders of a cavalier group of eccentrics, a colourful troop that would arrive in a flurry of raincoats and pencils. During the period they became instantly recognisable to the GAA's cognoscenti and its players. They were the press boys. They numbered only five or six – Downey and Sean Kilfeather in *The Irish Times*, John D Hickey and Donal Carroll of the Independent Group, Peadar O'Brien and Mick Dunne of the *Press* and also RTÉ, Val Dorgan and later Jim O'Sullivan of the *Examiner*. And if you wanted to know the story of a match that took place hundreds of miles from your home, this group was the only source.

John D was especially jumpy on this journey. They were travelling to make peace with the Tipperary county board following an entire summer of a stony feud between the press and that august body. The trouble began on a Monday morning in May when the national reports appeared after that year's league final between Kilkenny and Tipperary.

'It was a massive and unrelenting intense rivalry during that period,' remembers Downey. 'As fierce as anything that ever went on between Cork and Tipperary.'

'It was responsible really for Kilkenny changing their style subsequently and adapting a more physical game. The match really got very heated. Eddie Keher, a notably clean hurler, was blamed for starting something and the thing degenerated into a real dogfight.'

Skirmishes broke out all over the field, most seriously between Kilkenny goalkeeper Ollie Walsh and John Flanagan, Tipperary's big-boned full forward. In this period, press boxes were a rarity. More often that not, the reporters sat on the sideline near the teams, sometimes spoke to the managers afterwards and then made haste to a local tavern to compose both themselves and their words. These events left them all especially breathless, but when they privately considered the incidents, it transpired that they were unanimous in their agreement that Tipperary had been the aggressors and they began asserting as much in print. This left John D, Thurles-reared and Tipperary through and through, in an uncomfortable position, but, loyal to his character, his report was the most lacerating of all.

All of Tipperary was incensed with what was perceived as the nakedly jaundiced perspective offered in most of the morning newspapers. After a meeting, the county board simply blackballed the national media. They were not allowed into Thurles. So began a long-hot summer of discontent during which the Tipperary hurlers thrived. Coverage of their All-Ireland championship feats, however, practically disappeared with the reporters making a pact not even to mention the county by name.

'I remember in the weeks before the All-Ireland final getting into trouble for referring to Tipperary as "you-know-who",' remembers Donal Carroll.

'We were wrong,' Downey insists now. 'We felt we were doing the right thing at the time but no.'

Tipperary inevitably advanced to the All-Ireland final and a press night was arranged to which none of the 'national' boys were permitted. At that point, though, the impossibility of the situation was beginning to dawn on all camps and Jim Ryan from Moneygall went to untold efforts to broker a settlement. That year's final was covered satisfactorily if not as wholeheartedly as would have pleased the reporters and, shortly after that, peace was declared. The press boys were formally invited down to the Anner Hotel for a meal and a meeting to close the affair. It was time to bury differences.

'John D, however, felt it would be too much to accept a meal after all that happened and I agreed with him,' says Downey. 'We all did. We decided we would go and meet the officials and settle the matter amicably and briefly and leave.'

Peadar O'Brien was covering the meeting for the *Irish Press* and *Evening Herald*. O'Brien is full of brim and brass and is as funny as they come. Nothing has ever intimidated him and although he would usually travel with the gang, probably bare cheek and nerve convinced him that he would go alone on this day. So it was that Downey and John D had each other for company and though neither man liked to admit it, they were a touch apprehensive. They joked to each other that the whole thing was a trap and that they were about to be burnt at the stake. A couple of miles after they passed Two-Mile-Borris, they saw a lone figure walking at some distance on the road ahead. As the Morris Minor charged gamely along, its passengers presently saw that the man, who offered them a reassuring smile as they passed, was carrying a shotgun under his arm.

'Christ,' said John D. 'They are out looking for us.'

Some minutes later, they entered Thurles town. It had begun to rain heavily and as they were a few minutes early for the meeting, they decided to pass the Anner and drive up towards the famous square and Hayes' Hotel. When they rounded the corner at the bridge, they saw that the town was heaving with people. This was not a match Sunday so it should have been deserted. Through the rain and manic wipers, the gathering could have been a lynch mob.

'It's not looking good, boy,' whispered John D.

Then they passed the cathedral and just as they looked, instinctively blessing themselves, there appeared four men at the shadowed, arched door carrying a brand new coffin on their shoulders.

'Ah, we're done for,' cried John D. 'Look. They've already fucking got O'Brien.'

The two men roared with laughter and by that evening, they were trading yarns with the Tipperary boys.

Stories. It is what Paddy Downey's generation does best. It is as if life was lived primarily so that experiences could be translated into tales to be passed on at the various hotel pubs and country pubs that they used to descend upon late on Sunday evenings after winter and summer games. Although they regarded the task of writing match critiques and previews as a craft, they also approached it with a light heart. Irish society moved at a leisurely pace then and once the deadlines were met, the press boys were never in a rush – it was a given that they would meet in some place or another regardless of the hour. Then the stories and rows would begin, about players, about games, about score lines and about each other. When you turned shillings by travelling the length and breadth of Ireland through the 1960s and 1970s, things happened. Writing on Gaelic games felt like a privilege to them. It felt like they had each, for reasons they could never fully articulate, been handed a get-out clause from the structured and heavily governed environments their friends and family worked in. And because their number was so select and they came to prominence during a period when newspapers mattered deeply in this country, it was as if Edmund Burke's (attributed) phrase about the press being the fourth estate was apt. Their words and opinions carried true weight.

'John D was a legend,' says Donal Carroll, 'and a beautiful writer. But I was always consciously different when I followed him in the *Independent*. Because I remember travelling on a bus up to Cavan to cover a championship game in the 1960s for the *Independent*. I fell into conversation with a young lady, and she kept repeating about how her whole family would gather around the kitchen on the Monday after a big match involving Cavan to see what Paddy Puirseal said in the *Press*. And she kept repeating the *Press* and that annoyed me after a while. And I said to her eventually, "Would ye not read the *Independent* the odd time?" And she replied, "Ah, John D is too high-falutin' for me. I can't understand him." And that stuck with me and for that reason I always kept it simple.'

John D was a classicist as was Paddy Downey, who wrote on matches in prose that even today shines with a sort of rain-washed glaze of elegy. Downey was, by his own admission, tortuously slow; for decades he was the last to finish a report, the last to go through the often-complex procedure of phoning his copy through and the last to join the others at the bar for an amber short. 'A tincture,' as he famously says himself.

Peadar O'Brien frequently tells a story about an evening in the Killeshin Hotel in Portlaoise. After a match in Nenagh or Roscrea, himself and Paddy and John D Hickey regularly stopped off to write their reports and ring them through. Peter Byrne of *The Irish Times* happened to be covering an athletics meeting in the area and the GAA boys were just finishing their writing when he walked in, followed by Tom O'Riordan of the *Independent*. When the others gathered around the bar for a late drink, Paddy Downey was crouched in the phone booth down the hallway calling out his match report. On passing from the toilets one of the party overheard a line or two.

'Jesus, lads, Downey is after saying that Cork played like a spavined drayhorse.'

'A spavined effin' drayhorse?'

'What in God's name is that?'

'Haven't a notion.'

None of them knew. Sometimes, Paddy just left everyone for dead. A plan was hatched. Downey eventually returned, relieved that another report was whistling down the darkness of the telephone wires for the purring presses on D'Olier Street. He sighed in satisfaction, elaborately lit a cigar and settled back for an evening of conversation. An hour or so later, just as the group was considering resuming the journey back, Byrne said, 'By the way, Peadar, I meant to ask you how Cork played today.'

'Jesus, Peter, they were terrible. Really now. To be honest with you, they played like a spavined drayhorse.'

Paddy's mouth dropped open.

'You,' he boomed. 'You little so and so. Did you use that phrase? Where did you get it?'

'Course I did,' snapped O'Brien. 'Sure I thought of it so I used it.'

'My God,' deliberated Paddy. 'This is a disaster. You bloody nuisance. I have used the same thing.'

The others fell back as if in horror.

'Jesus, Paddy, you'd better change it.'

'Sure Peadar sent in his report first.'

'It must be his by right.'

'I will change nothing.'

'There's nothing for it, Paddy. Fair is fair.'

'Get on the phone before it's too late.'

Paddy has a terrific and colourful temper that rises and vanishes like a Mediterranean summer storm. In minutes, they had him banging his cane like Lear and hurling insults at

O'Brien, who was by now purple with repressed mirth. Eventually, the truth came out and they headed off up towards Dublin, tear-faced with the laughter. The phrase 'spavined drayhorse' was retired in honour of that moment.

Another time, John D and Peadar found themselves on a train to Leitrim for reasons that have long ceased to be of consequence. At the station in Mohill, they were pleased, if not quite astonished, to find an official welcoming party waiting. Most of the county board was huddled on the platform in the cold night and a few local dignitaries shook their hands. They were assured that it was a great honour to have two esteemed members of the press in the locality and they were escorted to a local bar where a sumptuous feast and drinks were laid on. Feeling highly agreeable with this state of affairs, the guests of the nation sat back and duly gave their considered opinion on Gaelic games, on Ireland, on life in general. Their audience listened in rapt attention and, eventually, a youngster was plucked from the crowd. Peadar shudders still when he thinks of his cherub's face. The lad was sat before them on a high stool.

'Ask this buck anything you like about the GAA,' was the instruction.

'Anything.'

John D looked at O'Brien and O'Brien could hear both their hearts crashing like stones in a well. They fired football questions at the child. They quizzed him on long-finished hurling teams, on dates, on historical facts. They began asking questions the answers to which they themselves did not know. The boy was a wizard and he reeled off answers in the deadpan way a child rhymes out his five-times tables.

'Now. Maybe young Tommy here will get his chance to ask the experts a question or two.'

And so started the longest night of their lives. Some time long after midnight they traipsed towards their Bed and

Breakfast with the broken walk of lads heading home with wretched exam results. By the next Sunday night, they were at the other end of country, reliving the humiliation.

'If I saw that little fecker today,' vows O'Brien, 'I'd still run a mile.'

Paddy Downey is a story in his own right. It is very difficult to imagine what Paddy's life would have been without the GAA, although one can presume it would not have been boring. And it is completely impossible to imagine the GAA without Downey.

For five decades, he has been a quiet, constant and dignified voice whose involvement with the association distinguished it. Although he would reject the assertion, he was one of the key figures in the evolution of the GAA in a way that was always subtle and minor but that has become magnified now that so many of the voices of Ireland from 1950 on have fallen eternally quiet.

It is arguable that Downey first became a chronicler of Gaelic games on a Monday evening in September of 1944. The hurlers of Cork had completed their four in a row and, as was tradition at the time, they disembarked from the train at Blackrock so that the team could climb onto an open-back lorry and manoeuvre through the winding streets of Cork city greeting the crowd.

That year was one that changed the direction of Paddy Downey's life.

Early that summer, he had been living a carefree existence in a pastoral area near Schull in west Cork. He was thirteen years old but unnaturally tall for his age at over 6ft 1in. He was involved in athletics and swam a lot. In early August, he took cousins visiting from Dublin down to the local strand. He alone went in for a swim and even as he tramped out of the waves, he felt a deadening cramp in his right leg. Late that night, he developed a severe headache that lasted all of the next day. His leg became immovable and several doctors were consulted before he was transferred to the North Fever Hospital in Cork City, where all cases of infectious diseases were treated. The diagnosis was polio. Paddy had never heard of it. The name sounded like an insult. When they pressed electric currents against the stricken limb, he felt the exiled life return, but once the stimulation stopped, the leg was a dead weight again. After three months of isolation and treatment, he was transferred to the Mercy Hospital. Schull was seventy-three miles from Cork City, and so his parents were rarely able to go and visit him. If a neighbour had to travel into the city for some reason, they always called up, but most days he was alone. The Mercy stood on a height above Murphy's Brewery. On this night, a Dr Hennessy came in and told him the parade would be passing underneath. He helped the young patient across the spare hospital bedroom to the window, sat him in a chair and covered him with blankets. Eventually came the triumphant notes of the brass band and, high above the celebrations, the doctor and his young patient saw Sean Condon waving the cup at the hundreds who had gathered. From their lofty perspective, it was a fantastic sight: noisy and chaotic and spontaneous, lit by the oil-burning street lamps below the general city twilight. Watching that scene, Downey felt a sense of separation, of being slightly outside of the moment, a feeling that would return to him on many afternoons when he sat perched high above the jubilant episodes breaking beneath him on the field at Croke Park, Thurles or Páirc Uí Chaoimh.

He spent a year and three months in hospital and, when he walked again, it was with the aid of crutches and later a cane. These instruments became in later life a mere extension of himself, paraphernalia that he used with a flourish, like his pen or his pipe. Few public houses did not feel the swish of

Downey's cane renting the air on at least one occasion. But at the age of fourteen, his affliction was a tough sentence to bear.

'It was and yet looking back at it, I suppose after the initial shock I just wanted to live. When I went home, I never got despondent or emotionally involved. I tried to keep playing – anything. We actually had two hurleys which was rare for a house in west Cork then. My older brothers had set up the branches of a tree as crossbars and I would stand under one and we would just strike the ball back and forth. I could do that fairly easily. The other children never changed towards me and really, I think my attitude was to make the best of it.'

His initial dream of joining the Army was shot, though. Patrick Downey senior had been in the RIC and Paddy, because of his height and strength, fobbed his way into the local LDF at the age of thirteen. In fact, he was given the command of a unit shortly afterwards and remembers one day during a training exercise marching into a bar and ordering men of thirty and forty years to leave the place immediately.

'The madness of it. But they had to obey because of the rank.'

School fell by the wayside but the solitary months in hospital had guided him towards books and he read anything that fell into his possession. It might have been Tolstoy or the novels based on Buffalo Bill that were in plentiful supply at the time. He read and began to think about writing cowboy stories or something of that nature.

His interest in sport developed simultaneously. His mother Johanna came from Inistiogue in County Kilkenny but even this, perversely, was not enough to introduce him to hurling. His early memories of summer visits to the maternal home place are dominated by games of cricket, which was big in the area.

'Her name was Walsh. We used to hear talk of her brother playing hurling and cricket around Mount Juliet. And it was along the lines of the English thing where the squire would have his tea and watch the play. So before I ever saw Gaelic games, I knew more about cricket. She explained the basic rules, that there were stumps that one threw a ball at, trying to beat the batsmen. We thought it sounded marvellous. Two friends – sons of a carpenter – produced these stumps from broom handles. But we never had bails. ·

'I remember being very upset one day when a favourite cat of ours died. I must only have been about four. My brothers were six and eight years older. The family had a little pet cemetery at the back garden and this cat was to be officially buried. We had flowers laid, the hole dug and the ceremony was just beginning when I heard these whoops and the two friends – they were twins, I can still see them charging across the garden in identical red jumpers – had arrived with the stumps for the first cricket match. Both my brothers just took off, abandoning the burial, and I was so annoyed and sad. That was the first day I saw in operation the lure of sport.'

His exposure to Gaelic games was confined to newspapers. The *Cork Examiner* was the daily newspaper in the household, although when Patrick Downey used to cycle into Schull to visit John Donovan, a former British Navy officer, he would arrive back armed with stacks of old copies of the *Irish Press* and *The Irish Times*. Three copies of *The Irish Times* were ordered in Schull during that period – one for Donovan, one for the bank and one for the Protestant clergyman. Downey used to study the small space allocated for Pat O's [PD Mehigan's] coverage of Gaelic games and imagine what the particular match was like or what Croke Park was like. He began submitting articles to a publication called *GAA Digest* which was edited by a gentleman called Eugene Powell. Downey would offer his opinion on players and teams of the day.

'Teams that I had never seen nor even heard on the radio. All I knew was what I read in newspapers.'

Around the same time, he applied to Dick Wicks for the post of Gaelic games correspondent for the new *Sunday Press*, having noticed an advertisement amongst the hoard of old sheets his father had acquired on his visits to Schull.

'The temerity of it. I never met the man afterwards, curiously enough, although I received a very polite and kind letter saying that while they would love to consider me, living in Cork would make it impossible. It was a nice way of fobbing me off.'

Dublin, however, beckoned. In 1950, Downey, then almost twenty years of age, accompanied his mother to a cousin's wedding in the city. Although he had no intention of staying, he ventured down one free afternoon to the Polio Fellowship near Herbert Park and was put in contact with a Captain Talbot, one of the benefactors of the association. Within days, it was arranged that he would start a job correcting crosswords at Independent House. It paid sixteen shillings an evening. Shifts began at 6 pm. While he was secluded from the editorial side of the house, he found that the curious smell of the print works made him feel excited and nervous, like the warm smell of machinery at summer funfairs. It was as if the building revved and pitched and keened towards the hour of printing. Paddy Downey would work methodically and meticulously, poring over his allocations of crosswords, but at the back of his mind was the notion that maybe he could get into journalism. Although he pulled the plug on his own lengthy deliberations for *GAA Digest* when payment was not forthcoming, he was on the lookout for other avenues.

One June afternoon, crossing O'Connell Street, he saw his entire future illuminated in the grubby hands of a vendor, a child brandishing a magazine. Standing outside Clery's shop, the boy was selling copies of a magazine called *The Gaelic Sportsman*. Within minutes, Downey had discovered its address and was on his way to Eccles Street. Shyness was not a problem for the young Cork man. Just weeks after arriving in Dublin, he had landed unannounced on the doorstep of Pat O to engage him in a general chat about Gaelic games. PD Mehigan was then over seventy and was undoubtedly astonished but had the grace to ask this stranger, who would ultimately succeed him, into his house for tea, and they spoke at length.

'Can you imagine,' Downey asks fifty years later in mock shame, 'the bloody temerity of it? The cheek to just turn up at this poor man's door. Isn't that terrible? We ended up in O'Brien's of Leeson Street. I asked him who the best hurler he ever saw was. Ring, he told me. Mackey was close but Ring. And maybe that was because Pat was a Cork man but I believe he was an honest judge.'

Just as boldly, he showed up at the office door of Hughie McLoughlin, the famous publisher from Donegal who owned *The Gaelic Sportsman*. Padraig Puirseal was the nominal editor, but as he was immersed in his work at the *Irish Press*, there was an opening for someone young and raw – and inexpensive – like Downey. His first article was about Paddy 'Hands' O'Brien, the great Meath fullback who at the time worked in a shop near Downey's digs in Waterloo Lane. Puirseal accepted the story and so it began.

One night in the mid-1950s, Downey was drinking in Searson's of Baggot Street with his brother Jim and another friend. Dublin in that period has been romanticised over the subsequent decades as an unconsciously bohemian and very local city, a glorified village filled with hard-drinking men of letters as typified by the McDaid's set of Kavanagh, Anthony Cronin and Flann O'Brien.[1] Although Downey insists the era was largely unremarkable, it was definitely a highly enjoyable time to be young and living in Dublin. People sauntered

---

1. Downey saw Flann O'Brien many times leaving his column into *The Irish Times* and drinking in The Pearl Bar but never worked up the courage to go and speak to him.

through weeks. It was a time when you could leave your car unlocked on Parliament Street across from Dublin Castle and stroll back to collect it a few hours later. Although Downey considered the traffic around the city centre horrendous, he regularly caught a bus from Eccles Street to go to Baggot Street for a lunchtime sandwich. Weir's of Grafton Street would polish their most precious stones and leave them on overnight display against a black backdrop. Hidden lights were directed on the jewellery and, in a time of relative paucity, the effect was blinding and intimidating in its loveliness. The display stopped couples in their tracks. And there was nothing between those diamonds and the outside world other than a pane of glass. It is a detail from those years that always stayed with Downey. It may be with the benefit of soft reminiscence, but the city of that time seemed unaccountably safe to him. And contrary to the tidy view of Irish society in the 1950s as one where nothing happened, to him Dublin felt different. Interviewed a few years ago by his old friend Sean Ó Mordha for the TV documentary series, *Seven Ages*, Downey asserted that life went on for those who did not emigrate.

'As I said, I was a free man. I did not feel as if we were all stooped under the burden of Dev or John Charles McQuaid. There was gaiety in Dublin then, genuinely.'

Downey took to pub life slowly but enjoyed the sensation of meeting people. There were journalists' pubs all over the city – The Pearl and The Palace were *The Irish Times'* strongholds, The Oval was the main watering hole for those at Independent House and the *Irish Press* staff drank in The White Horse and Mulligan's.

Downey used to float around them all, meeting people, drifting into an evening of conversation. Although his use of a cane was permanent, walking distances did not trouble him. And there was always the off chance of encountering the city's outrageous characters whose reputations would balloon in later years. On this night in Searson's, he was in a state of excitement. Sitting at the bar alone was Patrick Kavanagh, whose poetry Downey had begun to read and read until the words ran off his tongue. Feeling red-blooded by a couple of half-Guinnesses and a small sherry, he decided to venture a word or two when it was his turn to go up to the counter for drinks. Searson's was a no-frills establishment then. It was poorly lit, had sawdust on the floor and on this occasion, a musty smell emanated from the toilets. There were few clients.

'Excuse me, Mr Kavanagh. I was hoping you might be able to tell me where I might locate a copy of *Ploughman and Other Poems*? I greatly enjoyed *A Soul for Sale* but have had no luck in getting my hands on *Ploughman*.'

Kavanagh half turned but did not look at the questioner.

'Arraagh, don't bother yer arse about it.'

Downey mulled for hours over whether the poet meant that the original collection was not worth reading or that someone like him was not worthy of reading it.

'Maybe if I had offered him a drink things might have gone better. But I didn't think or hadn't enough money – although I would gladly have forsaken my own drink if I had thought. Anyway, I'll never know.'

On his free afternoons, Downey spent many afternoons in Parson's Bookshop which was then co-owned by a lady he knew only as Mrs O'Flaherty from Macroom. She used to allow Kavanagh to come in and read the newspapers and racing pages for free. A little stool was stored underneath the counter for his personal use. Once, she lifted up its underside and showed Downey where she had written 'Patrick's Stool' on the underside. It was through her that he obtained a signed first edition of *Tarry Flynn*. After lengthy enquiries she finally secured a copy and apologised for the cost of fifteen shillings, hefty money in 1956. To sweeten it, she offered to hold it until Kavanagh came in to sign it.

'When I returned a few weeks later, it had been signed, just his name, nothing else. Mrs O'Flaherty told me that she had informed Kavanagh what had been paid for the book. And he had replied, "The man is a bloody fool. He would have picked it up for one and six any day in any book barrow in London."'

'The man is a fool,' Downey repeated joyfully as he told the story over a glass of wine and a cigar on a bright and biting day in Rathgar in January 2004.

But it was through Gaelic games that he finally had a meeting with Kavanagh that did not conclude with an insult. Hughie McLoughlin had decided to launch, with a splash, a new publication, *Gaelic Weekly*, on St Patrick's Day of 1956, commissioning articles on the first decades of the State. As editor, Downey pressed for an approach to Kavanagh to contribute an article on Irish writing since the inception of the Republic.

'So I got a bus from Baggot Street to Pembroke Road at around half past six. I am fairly certain the date was February 8th. I felt it was a time that he was likely to be home and by sheer good luck, just as I was walking up towards his dwelling, he came out of the gate. There is a line in "If Ever You Go To Dublin Town" and, anytime I read it afterwards, it reminded me of seeing him on this evening. So I approached him and introduced myself – although not as the fool who had paid fifteen shillings for his book. And he was perfectly friendly and agreed to do the article and delivered it on time.'

Securing Kavanagh for the inaugural edition of *Gaelic Weekly* would prove a minor footnote in the early part of his career. The magazine business had been enjoyable and unorthodox. In the beginning, Hughie McLoughlin simply instructed his novice reporter to go out to the great beyond and return with material. His first real exposure to the stars came in the weeks before the 1950 All-Ireland final between Tipperary and Kilkenny.

When Downey wandered onto the field at Thurles, a tall callow youth with a cane, he was more or less adopted by Mickey 'the Rattler' Byrne who introduced him to all the players. John Doyle was the youngest player on the team at nineteen and detested being reminded of this. Byrne coaxed Downey into asking Doyle how he liked being the baby of the bunch. Doyle responded by breaking his hurl during training and afterwards presenting it to Downey.

'I carried it with me everywhere. I even took it on the bus when I went across to Kilkenny to cover their training camp.'

McLoughlin had given Downey five pounds to cover his expenses. When he returned to Eccles Street after a five-day jaunt, he still had almost three pounds left.

He held the money out in his palm for his boss to take.

'Keep it,' advised McLoughlin with the briefest glance. 'That will pay you for the next four articles.'

After that, he learned never to return with change from advances. It was a busy time. To polish his budding journalistic career, he went to Potter's College in Blackrock to take shorthand and typing. Tommy Potter had been stricken with polio also. He secured Downey a job with an auctioneer's firm and, for a few months, he sold houses and wrote on Gaelic games. To be more exact, he sold one house. The games were sucking him in. Then, as suddenly and inexplicably as polio had visited his body, he contracted TB. He was ripped as forcibly and completely from his young working life as he had been from his adolescence. A year and five months were spent recuperating in the Richmond Hospital, from 1952 to early 1954. Now his parents had to cope with trips of 240 miles. That entire time is like a void to Downey, reduced to a few images, the most surreal being on the night of his initial operation. In the early days of his illness, he had been listening to a cricket game on the radio. When he awoke, some hours after being wheeled out of theatre following an operation, he was heavily sedated on morphine. All through the night, he lay on his side and watched two of Australia's great fast bowlers, Miller and Waugh, come bowling at him from the end of the bed.

'And I was the batsman. I must have had several centuries. It was a vivid experience and it lasted for hours but not in the least bit frightening.'

He was desperately gaunt and pale when he returned, blinking, to the city again.

His guardians had not forgotten him. Padraig Puirseal had bought *The Sportsman* in the interim and offered him a job straight away. He was also in demand with Michael O'Farrell's *Gaelic Weekly*.

Although he slotted back into the underground world of GAA periodicals, collecting advertisement rates on Saturday afternoons, attending games at Croke Park or down the country on Sunday and enjoying the independence of the city, he wanted to deepen his involvement. One evening he met Ken Gray through an acquaintance. The deputy editor of *The Irish Times* suggested he should apply for a post in a new paper they were launching, *The Sunday Review*. Gray's tip was almost like an imprimatur and Downey penned a letter to Austin Walsh, believing that it was tantamount to a letter of acceptance. A few days later, he discovered he hadn't got the job. It had been offered to Mick Dunne, who was second to Puirseal in the *Irish Press*.

'Years later, Paddy Puirseal told me that the *Press* were so anxious to hold on to Mick that they made Paddy features editor and gave Mick the job of GAA correspondent. When that happened, Austin Walsh gave me a call. I remember going down to the office in a daze, knowing I would probably be offered something and half wishing I had the nerve to turn it down having been overlooked in the first place.'

He didn't. He worked for four years with *The Sunday Review*, subbing and editing. One Monday morning, he arrived into work and fell into conversation with the journalist Paddy McGowan. Kilkenny and Tipperary had played a hurling league semi-final in Nenagh the day before and *The Irish Times* had neglected to carry a word on it, not even the score line. Pat O was over eighty years of age at this stage and it was impossible for him to travel the breadth of the country and hustle to find a phone line and file copy through. The sports editor then was Paul McWeeney, a man who wrote with great knowledge and skill on golf and rugby but who held a minimal interest in Gaelic games. Even so, the absence of even a cursory recording of the league semi-final was an embarrassment and further dented the newspaper's reputation of having a negligent attitude towards Gaelic games. For years, Pat O had fought a lone fight but he no longer had the energy for the post. Liam McGowan went off to see Douglas Gageby, then managing director of *The Irish Times* and, later that afternoon, Downey got a call from McWeeney to meet him in The Pearl for a chat. He was groomed to gradually assume responsibility for covering GAA matters along with Pat O. The changing of the guard was to be low key and understated. It was the summer when Paddy Downey covered his first big game for *The Irish Times*, that year's Munster hurling final between Cork and Tipperary. Typically, he arrived on the scene with immaculate timing. It was on that fiery afternoon that the venerable Christy Ring was accused of striking Tipperary's Tom Moloughney, an incident that is still bitterly contested across the province.

He did not get a by-line, only 'By A Special Correspondent', but there was no mistaking the style. He had arrived.

The pleasures of the game were unceasing. Downey spent over thirty years as the voice of *The Irish Times* on Gaelic games. It was a lifelong season involving God knows how many drives to Casement in Belfast, to Castlebar or Clones or Cork or the ritual of Thurles, the scene of countless gladiatorial summers. Those three decades vanished, he says now, in the blink of an eye. He always loved the job. In fact, he never regarded what he did as a job. The dreamlike Galway football team of the 1960s flowered and went, the Kerry phenomenon lit the 1970s, the holy trinity of hurling – Cork, Kilkenny and Tipperary – rumbled through the years remorselessly.

Late one evening in The Pearl Bar, Downey and other drinkers heard a ferocious blast emanating from O'Connell Street. They abandoned their glasses and hurried across the bridge where they encountered the rubble of Nelson's Pillar. GAA presidents came and went. Paddy Puirseal died suddenly, news of his passing causing Downey to pale and grip the steering wheel of his car tightly on his way down to Kerry for a match. He pulled in to the side of the road to compose himself and offer a silent blessing. The Pearl became Bowes. Mick Dunne switched over to RTÉ television, which in the 1970s broadened the appeal of the games for the public. Among his specialities were post All-Ireland dressing-room interviews, claustrophobic affairs shot in close up and often dominated by a heavily furred microphone Mick used to carry. They were brilliant and rich and spontaneous minutes. The GAA went technicolour. Downey and John D and the others got together and devised the first All-Stars scheme in 1972.

That decade more so than any other marked frequent transatlantic passages for the promotion of the home games in the Irish boroughs of the great American cities. Donal Carroll recalls making three trips in one season before the games lapsed into hollow challenge games of little consequence. Downey remembers a hellish evening in Balboa stadium in San Francisco in 1973. It was an hour or so after the All-Star exhibition game and he sat with John D and Jim O'Sullivan in the press box, modern and comfortable by the standards they were accustomed to. Jim had arranged for somebody from ITT, the international telex-company, to come by and collect his typed report. The other two men were phoning theirs back. One of the delights of the American trip was that you picked up a phone and were speaking to someone in Abbey Street or D'Olier Street with less fuss than it often took to get connected from Mayo or Wexford.

Downey tried first on this evening. It was already mid-afternoon in San Francisco, the game over and nobody in the stadium except a janitor ambling through the seats with a brush. He picked up the receiver and gave the number of *The Irish Times*.

'Sorry, sir, there is currently a four-hour delay on all calls to Eye-re-land.'

Downey almost choked. He couldn't understand. There must be some mistake, dear lady. Your communications system is without parallel. We always get put through without even a second of delay. Please try again. This may be a matter of life and death. And there is an appointment with several players in a San Francisco tavern to be honoured. Please.

'I know sir, but it is Mother's Day.'

Of course it was. Every emigrant from Boston to San Diego was clogging up the line. Between them, John D and Downey cursed every Irish mammy they could think of and cursed their tears of gratitude. Couldn't they write? They had about three-quarters of an hour before the first print run and were unable to get in touch with their office to explain the dilemma. Neither man had ever missed a deadline and to fail from the other side of the world would be unforgivable. More grievously, it would almost certainly jeopardise future trips. Both journalists shared a cold sweat when the ITT man came bounding up the stairs. Jim O'Sullivan explained the situation and the messenger, a breezy West Coast boy, offered to take the other two reports as well. John D fetched his report, clearly typed out on white paper, tailor-made for telex machines. Downey held up his own production, a ream of notes scrawled in his own half-invented shorthand. It was writing, though not immediately recognisable as English.

'Gee pal, ' said the ITT man. 'I think you're fucked.'

O'Sullivan and John D offered to wait with their colleague who now felt like those death-row prisoners they read about in the American press whose last-minute appeals were rejected by the governor. He slumped over the desk, hands on his head.

'Go. Go.'

The pair disappeared into suburbia. Downey was king of Balboa stadium, alone in his grief. He tried the phone line. Obligingly, it was engaged. He tried it again, and then every two minutes. Always the same reply. He laughed bitterly at his fate and wondered how the house-selling market back home was going. Finally, just to sweeten the agony, he tried one last time, ten minutes before his deadline elapsed.

'Certainly sir, putting you through.'

To his astonishment, his copy taker, the familiar voice with whom he had shivered through so many half-hour conversations from frozen phone boxes in Urlingford and hotel offices in Limerick or Belfast was there, formal and reliable as ever. Grateful and delighted, Downey began calling out his introduction. That evening was spent at the bar, celebrating his own skin. The next afternoon he bumped into John D and Jim in the hotel lobby, both looking particularly glum. ITT had messed up and neither of their reports had got through.

'Suppose the bloody phone let you down as well,' said John D but when he looked up, he saw that his friend was doing his best to suppress an urge to dance a jig.

'I felt sorry for them, I really did,' pleads Downey. 'But at the same time, I was delighted for myself. That was as close as I came to missing the boat.'[2]

2. Harold Lloyd-type adventures seemed to have been the speciality of *Irish Times* sports correspondents of that period. Paddy Downey has a great friend, Michael O'Farrell, who was racing correspondent with the newspaper for many years. O'Farrell is similarly lean and

It is impossible to record adequately all or even a small number of the episodes that occurred around Paddy Downey's working life. At the heart of all those Sundays sit the match reports and colour pieces, stored in microfilm in *The Irish Times* offices and in the National Library. Those are the immutable legacy, each the result of several hours of serene concentration. But behind those reports, as tight and cemented as brick walls, are stories about people. Choose any game in any year and, inevitably, some anecdote would come galloping out of the mists on a white horse, some unlikely twist or line that became associated with a certain game. An Ulster final of the late 1960s is remembered not for its own merit but the journey back down to Dublin from Belfast. John D had arranged a lift from a freelance photographer who had spent years in Australia. Downey travelled with them and, in the dressing room after the match, Joe Lennon of Down asked if they had room to spare in the car as he didn't fancy getting the train back. Lennon taught in Dublin at this time. John D told him that was fine and they arranged a meeting spot. The four men talked about northern politics, about music and about the game. Eventually the photographer turned companionably to Lennon, who had excelled in front of 30,000 people hours earlier, and asked, 'Do you play a bit yourself?' They were almost at Dundalk when Joe, teeth clenched with indignation, broke the silence.

---

dapper and wonderfully spoken. One night he was travelling on a Dublin-bound train that was due to arrive in Heuston at seven o'clock. His plan was to get home and ring in whatever report he was doing then. However, the train stopped dead on the tracks in the middle of the black countryside. A half-hour passed and then an hour and he realised he was in danger of missing his deadline. He consulted the ticket master and, after interminable negotiations, was instructed to follow an official down the dark track. Some hundreds of metres away was a pole with an emergency telephone box attached.

'As far as I know,' said Farrell telling the story, ' I am the only journalist to have dispatched a report while dangling from a telephone pole above a railway line.'

Of all the pieces Paddy Downey phoned in to *The Irish Times*, however, one stands out for pure ornery perseverance. The year is 1981 now. Already, the scene has begun to change; press boxes are getting fuller and the younger players seemed slightly more hurried than used to be the case. There is a legend that Mick O'Dwyer once held up training to wait for Downey and O'Brien, who were expected to attend, but O'Brien swears it's just a myth. What was true, however, was that either of them could just wander up to Mick, ask him if Páidí or Mikey or Tim could speak and O'Dwyer would call that player over immediately. That casual informality, based on mutual trust, was beginning to disappear as the press boxes started to expand.

By 1981, a torrid summer during which the sporting year was overshadowed by the hunger strikes, things felt different. John D was gone, taken after a long illness, on 16 June 1977.[3] And while there was less elbowroom in press boxes in the subsequent years, they always felt somehow emptier to the likes of Downey and O'Brien.

'A tough, funny bastard. A legend,' is O'Brien's tribute.

Travelling down for the Munster championship hurling semi-final between Cork and Clare, Downey was feeling miserable and all too mortal. A few weeks earlier, he had been sitting in Doyle's pub with his great friend Donal Foley when they had both noticed a shake in the GAA writer's hand.

'It's time you gave up the bloody drink, Downey,' Foley said a bit irritably before going to the counter to fetch them both another round.

---

3. It was just a year after John D's retirement. It surprised his family that after he left the *Irish Independent* at Christmas of 1975 he never seemed to go through withdrawal symptoms. He told one of his daughters-in-law, 'I'm in a state of euphoria.' He attended the 1976 All-Ireland final as a spectator and enjoyed the carefree feeling of just watching. Illness came upon him when he was driving up O'Connell Street one afternoon. He was a heavy smoker, a Churchman's sixty-a-day man. His son Paddy never remembers a time when he did not cough, especially towards the end.

On this day, he was not at all himself, feeling a little breathless and jaded. They stopped in Offaly to see if a couple of brandies would revive him but it was not to be. By the time he was ensconced in the press box in Thurles, he was feeling completely wretched. Making his way down the narrow steps towards the tea-room reserved for press and guests of the local association, Downey happened upon the team doctor of the Tipperary team who was in the crowd. He took one look at the journalist and warned him to wait in the press box after the match. When the crowds cleared, the doctor came up and examined him and informed him he was sending him to hospital. Downey protested that he had a report to write. The doctor had the final word: he feared that Downey had had, was in the midst of, or was shortly about to have a heart attack. Minutes later, he was in the back seat of a car driven by a local priest.

'Much later it was discovered that I had a condition known as hyperthyroidism. It accounted for the shakes and losing weight and everything – although Foley had a point too. The drink probably shook me. But they ran a series of tests and gave me a number of injections. And whatever was in them, I began to feel remarkably better. But of course at this stage they still suspected it was the heart so I was under tight observation.'

At this stage in his life, however, he was something of an expert on hospital etiquette. He knew the typical layout and knew how to charm the staff. He lay there and got to thinking about his match report. It had been a phenomenal afternoon of hurling. Clare, the romantics' choice, the eternally put-upon county of southern hurling, had banished Cork from the championship on a score line of 2-15 to 2-13. It was the story of the summer.

Word had been dispatched to *The Irish Times* to the effect that a local correspondent would file notes on the match as Downey was going downhill fast. Still, it was only eight o'clock in the evening. He realised he had plenty of time. He gathered what notes he had, cleared his throat and summoned a passing nurse.

Ten minutes later, he was sitting in his hospital bed at the reception desk in the corridor. White coats hovered all around him. He had his notes in one hand and the phone in the other. Triumphantly, he announced himself to the copy taker: fine thanks. Just one of those things. No, no, no, reports of his demise greatly exaggerated. Now. First Paragraph.

'Well, there ye are; dee-di-dee-dum; it's a strange world and no mistake. You will forgive us dear readers for that sort of waffle; it's just we are trying to talk ourselves out of jam having written here on Saturday that Cork was the only team playing yesterday with a real chance of appearing in an All-Ireland final next September. And that meant of course that they were confidently expected to beat Clare in the semi-final of the Munster Hurling championship at Semple Stadium, Thurles.

'Seldom in the history of this championship has the prediction of a result been so decisively and brilliantly shattered by the so-called "outsiders". We retreated from Thurles in some confusion but with gladness in our hearts that Clare are again stepping out strongly on the road to somewhere.'

Not bad for a man who had just had a heart attack. It is safe to say he was remembered in Thurles hospital for some time afterwards.

'It was extremely kind of them to wheel the bed out for me. I presume they thought I was mad,' he said.

There was a bittersweet edge to the adventure. Although he considered himself cured, Downey was still seriously ill and was transferred to the Mater. One of his first visitors was Donal Foley. Having hurled for Waterford, Foley understood Gaelic games much more than most editorial people in *The Irish Times* and also wrote on the subject with great knowledge and feeling. Downey and he became fast friends and lost many hours arguing over players and games in The Pearl or The Fleet and on the road together on Sundays. They made a dangerous and almost chemical combination. One time in the 1970s, they travelled for a mundane league game to Thurles along with Con Howard who worked in foreign affairs. On a whim, they decided to stay over the Sunday evening in the Anner Hotel. It was late on Wednesday afternoon when they finally checked out, all feeling the worse for wear. Downey had an engagement to be at the Australian Embassy that evening for a reception for an Australian under-age team that was visiting for the fledgling experiment that would become the International Rules. Downey sped up the road (now in a Renault 1.8) feeling shook. His companions insisted they would accompany him to the reception. It was a sedate affair in some leafy mansion, with trays of polite food and, more pertinently, polite drinks.

'It was a disaster. Howard pulled the ambassador, a lady, up to dance even though there was no bloody dance on. Foley was looking for some class of drink they didn't have. I banged out five or six paragraphs and gave up the ghost.'

Those epic jaunts were rare and tended to happen only when they got together. So it was no surprise when Foley showed and visited Downey in hospital again the next day. On a Friday afternoon, however, Sean Kilfeather and Gerry Noone from the office came in, but Foley was absent. Downey thought this strange but said nothing. He wasn't obliged to visit, after all. On Saturday, Sean Ó Mordha called in and in the course of their conversation said: 'Donal is feeling better anyway.' Again, Downey said nothing but began to suspect all was not as it might be. On Monday, he received a phone call from Donal's daughter Deirdre to say her father had died. Against medical advice, Downey attended the service in Kilmacud. It was there, during the graveyard murmuring after a crowded funeral service that he heard from a mutual friend that just days after their last meeting in the hospital, Donal had warned the friend, 'You better get up to the hospital and see Downey quickly. I think he is fucked.'

Twenty years on, that sentence still gives him the shivers.

'It was one of the saddest things I ever heard. Poor Donal.'

That Waterford might return as a hurling force was Foley's abiding wish. Naturally, after decades of black results, they made it to a Munster final in 1982, a year after his passing. Downey wrote a poem in memory of his friend that appeared in *The Irish Times* on the eve of the match.[4]

He covered the final, a lopsided, dispiriting afternoon that imploded upon Waterford, with a heavy heart.[5] Back in Dublin, he met Jack Fagan, an *Irish Times* colleague who had played minor football with Meath. Fagan told him a story that cheered him up.

---

4. The poem, entitled 'In Memory of Donal Foley', appeared in June 1982. It reads: 'Why did you die, friend/Before the joy stored/Up. This shining summer/of delight, dawned/For Waterford./You were not the only one/Watching for the dawn/The dark hour, endless/ Fretted with defeat,/Broke neither pride nor/Hope. Fiercely you clung/To hope brittle as wafer ice/Counting lost chances, goals/That might have been/Slip-by like milestones/Slipping by the window/Of a train.

At this time of year, height/Of the hurling season,/We held conclaves, planned/Journeys. Of Sundays facing South to Munster Towns/The road shortened with your/Talk. It was Waterford,/ Always Waterford, and tales/Old but green as hurling/Fields echoing the fame/Of the Wares and Keane.

Now with the time at hand/To celebrate/Waterford's summer comes/For you too late.'

5. This final is also distinguished in that it was almost certainly the only GAA match covered by *Playboy*. Jim McGuinness of Bord Fáilte rang Downey looking for a ticket for a writer with the magazine who was coming to do a piece on hurling. He duly obtained one and on the day found himself sitting beside a burly, bearded stranger who greeted him in heavily accented English. Downey guessed it was either the representative from the banned magazine or else the *Waterford Star* had gone radical. The visitor, a German, was utterly fascinated by the match and arranged to meet

Some hours after the game, Fagan had been in The Pearl when somebody asked how Waterford had got on in the match.

'They were annihilated,' replied somebody, 'Destroyed. It was 5-31 to 3-06.'

'Oh,' said another person. 'Isn't it as well Foley is dead? 'Twould have killed him.'

He believes it is a story his friend would have enjoyed.

Paddy Downey retired as Gaelic games correspondent of *The Irish Times* in 1994.[6]

He was succeeded by Seán Moran, only the third specialist GAA writer in the history of the newspaper; Pat O, who played in the All-Ireland final for Cork in the first years of the century was the first. When Downey bowed out, the media coverage of the games and his newspaper's attitude towards them had altered beyond recognition. For many years, Downey had endured the light taunting from the others in the press box about *The Irish Times'* traditionally Protestant readership.

'I'll tell ya, Paddy,' O'Brien would say during some sleepy October league game, 'Major Algernon Smyth-Carmichael will be furious about this over the porridge tomorrow morning. He'll never recover from the number of Offaly wides.'

One night on a train, John D and O'Brien were laying it on thick for their own amusement when a deep, resonant voice across the carriage silenced them with, 'My own father is a Kerryman and a GAA man and he always read *The Irish Times*.'

It was a young Moss Keane, whom all three recognised.

Downey in Dublin for lunch on Monday where they spoke about the likes of John Doyle and Hugh Hefner. Downey has two regrets. One is that he never got the man to send him the 'black' of his article so he could read his impressions of the game. The other is that he never got to tell the story to Foley. Needless to say, he never saw the magazine and presumes that Jimmy Barry Murphy was not the cover star.

6. He always insisted on that title as opposed to GAA correspondent, arguing that those who covered soccer were not FAI correspondents.

Before Downey had time to bask in the relief of this defence, Keane continued, 'It always cheered him up because he found on days he read *The Irish Times* not half as many people had died as on days he read the *Independent*.'

John D banged the ceramic table in salute of an irrevocable victory.

Downey remained long enough in the game to experience the dubious advantages of technological enlightenment. It all happened quite suddenly. As recently as 1986, *The Irish Times* was the only newspaper in the country that possessed a fax machine. So the advent of laptops was a transition of space-age proportions. Downey remembers the ignominy of calling through a report one afternoon on one of the first mobile phones he had ever seen. The instrument was marginally lighter than a sack of coal and made a discouraging reptilian hissing sound as he tried to call his report through.[7] Worst of all, he had to endure a crowd of kids hurling insults like 'Yuppie' at him as he stood under the Mackey stand in Limerick. His final congress took place in the Slieve Russell Hotel in Cavan that spring. Several times he sent test reports through his shining new laptop, all of which obligingly arrived in the system in Dublin seconds later. But cometh the hour, the machinery betrayed him. He had five pieces lined up to go – five easy pieces – but try as he might they failed to breach the mysteries of the microchip.

'So what did I have to do? Phone every blasted one in.'

---

7. Instances of misheard lines leading to embarrassing mistakes in print are a hazard of the trade. Over the years, Paddy Downey endured many. His favourite involves his time covering a hurling match between Kilkenny and New York at Nowlan Park. It was a brutally tough game and the general feeling among the press and those in the crowd was that it would degenerate into a brawl when the teams returned after half-time. 'In the second half, we were sitting on a powder keg,' he wrote.

At least that's what he thought he wrote. What appeared was, 'In the second half, we were sitting on a powdered cake.'

When his working life suddenly stopped, he missed it. The absence of the game hit him hard. The strangeness of a newspaper appearing uncaring of his erased by-line got him down. He missed the camaraderie, missed those sudden bursts of reaction that fled through the stands when something splendid occurred and he missed not so much the writing of the reports but his completion of them – the fleeting satisfaction of another Sunday down. After a few years, though, he became reconciled to the joy of just being a spectator at a game.

One story they all tell about Paddy has acquired cult status. The gang might have been coming back from Cork. Or Belfast. John D was definitely there, in the front. Peadar was somewhere in the back, and Dave Guiney was among them, and Mick Dunne. They had stopped off to work and have a sandwich and a drink and it was a pitch-black Irish night in winter. It felt as if the only waking life in the country was contained in this car. Paddy, with a magician's flourish, produced a flask, and asked John D if he would care for a drop. From the back came a polite cough. It was Donal Carroll, who did not drink. For mischief, he enquired if it was advisable to be offering a flask while driving. Downey was perfectly fine to drive but still, there was a chance of getting him going.

'Are you insinuating my driving is below par?'

'I'm insinuating you should keep this side of the white line.'

John D nodded in grave agreement and said that he supported Donal. So did somebody else. Paddy abruptly halted the car.

'Out.' 'Every one of you out.'

This was not expected and the others tried to plead with Downey but to no avail. He demanded they leave the car. Through all this, Mick Dunne had been fast asleep in the corner, oblivious to the commotion. Finally he stirred and blearily enquired what all the fuss was about. He opened his eyes to be greeted by Paddy glaring at him and shouting, 'and you can bloody walk home as well, Dunne.'

Needless to say, he didn't. Some of that gang have passed on now. O'Brien, though, still works the circuit, covering games for *The Irish Sun* and he remains as sharp as a whistle. On sunny days in Croke Park, the remaining statesmen frequently show up, dressed in shirt and tie and jacket as was their practice on match day. There must be over a hundred press people in Croke Park on banner days now but it is still easy to distinguish that generation from the rest of us. It is something in their bearing. It was their fortune – and that of the association – that they covered Gaelic games in the period that they did. The country was smaller, the association was smaller and perhaps because of that, the games of that period seemed magnified in importance.

There is a passage in Peter Kavanagh's book *Sacred Keeper*, a book detailing the letters exchanged between him and his poet brother, which has always delighted Paddy Downey. It is the second paragraph from a letter by Patrick, dated 1956.

'Last night the editor of a GAA [newspaper] offered me five guineas for an article. That is the kind of thing that keeps a man solvent.'

Over a pipe in the late afternoon when the radio was getting loud and the office crowds were coming in flushed from the raw January chill, Downey smiled as he considered that sentence.

'That is the kind of thing that keeps a man solvent.' Lovely. Well, my name was not in it so I won't be in posterity for offering Kavanagh an article.'

Instead, he will make it through his own ink.

4

Jarlath's for the Cup

The Christmas opera is traditionally the giddiest time of the year at St Jarlath's College. Football does not really heat up until February and the show breaks up the forlorn winter months; it carries the students and staff through the ever-darkening afternoons that announce the autumn term and seem to linger until the New Year. St Jarlath's is situated smack in the middle of Tuam town, tucked away under the shadow of the cathedral and located, in a touch of delicious cruelty, within a stone's throw of the girl's Mercy Convent. A high and heartless wall separates both scholarly universes and, in the decades past, the boys used to gaze across it longingly, like East Berliners. The grounds of the college, with its elm trees and football pitches, its scuffed basketball court and trimmed grass, its stained glass and the simple, potent plaque above the arched wooden door all communicate an ancient feeling that in Jarlath's the outside does not matter. It ticks to its own calendar time. During autumn term, the sky over east Galway is chilled and black when the president, Conal Eustace, Jarlath's class of '62, unlocks the arched entrance of the 'new college' at seven-thirty every morning, and it has turned sullen silver by the end of senior football practice in the evening.

The opera, a sixty-year tradition, is the school's colourful and boisterous response to the dimness of the Irish winter. It means painting and singing and an opportunity for a bit of organised chaos, a chance to filch a smoke or carry props around the college. And it also means weeks of evening practice with the Mercy girls, with whom the show has been performed since 1969 – Irish Catholicism's belated nod to the summer of love. Back in Conal's day – *Brigadoon* was his first opera – the senior boys, often the school football stars, played the main roles while the youngsters with unbroken vocal cords were prevailed upon to don the rouge and heels and mimic the damsels.

'You would end up in make-up, dancing with boys that you regarded as heroes,' he laughs. 'It really doesn't bear thinking about any more.'

Conal is sprightly and energetic and always in fine, warm humour. Although he is school president, he is also taking the Senior A football team for the year. The first evening we met, he had just completed a Tuesday football session and strode across the yard to his house to get rid of the heavy coat and Wellingtons he wears on the pitch. It will be Conal's fate or privilege to preside over the end of boarding at St Jarlath's – the closing of a way of life that had a permanent impact on the thousands of boys whose teenage years were shaped by the whims and rules and glories of the place. Some boys hated it and cursed their boarding years, others return as rotund, brandy-drinking grey-haired men, misty eyed after the reminiscences of another reunion. Most just got through and moved on until the school receded into an unremarkable memory of bells and mushy food and the snoring of the lad across the room whose young lad, when last they heard, was a decent county minor. St Jarlath's is primarily an educational stronghold, a beacon for families across Connacht with a particularly strong affinity with Mayo. For that reason, among others, it was never fully embraced in Tuam as the town school; that distinction went to the Christian Brothers' school, St Patrick's. Jarlath's has a more complicated relationship with local people for, although regarded as a separate entity, it has heaped honour on Tuam. For Jarlath's is, of course, nationally famous as a Gaelic football academy – the school is the untouchable master of the Hogan Cup with twelve victories to date. That legacy is palpable not only on the football fields where true giants like Sean Purcell took their first steps but also in the school building. The past decorates the bright corridor where the framed black-and-white photographs of the twelve champion seasons are hung. It is evoked in the worn wooden stairs that lead to the dormitories where the ghosts of cane-waving deans still roam, in the dining room with its bursts of epic commotion and in the main hall, the scene of all the football homecomings.

Details of virtually every Hogan Cup season just pour from Conal. Football is not only an obsession here but also a guiding light that sustained many generations of boarding pupils and staff. At best, football provided the most exciting moments of one's schooldays. At worst, it was something to talk about. It was a way of belonging.

A couple of years ago, the final class of first-year boarding pupils was accepted and in just two years' time, the school will be emptied of night students for the first time in 200 years. Jarlath's is to be amalgamated with St Patrick's and will educate 'day' boys only. No evening meal, no study, no lights out, no deans waiting for muffled laughs or some lone brave trying to sneak out – just the solitary click of the front door locking around 6 pm and silence.

Boarding schools lend themselves to certain associations. For those of us who have never been, they are a half-imagined world of grubby-fisted posh kids in expensive blazers, they have a tuck shop and cloisters, a haunted room or two and packages from home filled with confectionery delights. Headmasters with freaky black gowns sweep along rooms; there is a common room, origin of endless tricks and adventures and wheezes, midnight feasts, maybe even a Mam'zelle and somewhere, a blinking bespectacled fat kid. They are the stuff of Frank Richards and Enid Blyton, in other words, children's fiction that was lapped up in this country in the 1960s and 1970s.

St Jarlath's, of course, is nothing like that. It is prosaic and sensible and traditionally tough. Jarlath's is country. There is no uniform here for a start and it is always a surprise to see photographs of the disastrous teenage fashions of the day as modelled by well-known football men like Pat Holmes or Brian Talty. The college does possess a certain understated hauteur but that is because of a deep and comfortable conviction of its value, of its role and influence on the boys it houses. Once, it was a fearsome place with unstinting rituals that could be brutal to more sensitive boys, but not now. It is a little disconcerting, to be honest, how light the atmosphere is. The timetable is roughly similar to that which prevailed centuries ago but, of course, 'first toll of bell' is no longer six in the morning and students are not honour bound to the code of grim silence that was demanded of pupils until after nine in the morning. If St Jarlath's boys of the mid-1800s, or even the early-twentieth century, could spend but one afternoon in the contemporary school, they would probably be shocked back to the grave at the cheerfulness of it all, the freedom. Yet the principal theory is the same. Boys eat, sleep, learn, fight loneliness and each other; they play football, obsess about Mercy girls, yearn for home, sit exams and, if they are lucky, they laugh a lot under the same roof. And the staff members here become, after a few years, governed by the very lifestyle they supervise – men like Conal and Charlie Kelly, a dean in the boarding school, and Fr Oliver Hughes, the past president and the man associated with all of Jarlath's great modern football teams.

It was in the mid-1980s, when Gay Byrne was telling his constituency daily that the country was banjaxed, that St Jarlath's peaked as a boarding school with over 300 students wintering there. Parents might have ferried their boys to the front gates in beaten-up Cortinas, but they found the fees somewhere. The lowest ever studentship was during the Famine of 1845 when about seventeen pupils, including future college president Ulick Burke, survived on drastically low food rations. The college was founded at the start of the nineteenth century on the pragmatism of Archbishop Oliver Kelly who rented what was Ffrench's Bank, a financial company ruined by the end of the Napoleonic War. Lord Ffrench committed suicide and it was left to his sister to tidy up his affairs. Renting to the Church was a convenient form of income and once the archbishop had established a formal school there, the Ffrench family later invited purchase of the building. That marked the beginning of what would become a handsome estate, with the 'new college' completed in 1859. Land was acquired for a college farm to provide milk and butter, a vacuum cleaner from Electrolux was purchased in 1903 and, oh luxury of luxuries, an indoor swimming pool was added in the 1930s. There are also several town houses, front facing onto Bishop Street and backing into the rear of the college grounds. In these houses the Jarlath's priests now live and, shoving open an unlocked back door, Conal excused himself, pausing to show the wretched state in which his pet cat has left the wallpaper next to the stairs. And the shredded lower portion revealed layer after layer of old wallpaper.

'These are grand houses,' Conal said after he changed from his outdoor wear. 'Plain enough but fine. It does great for me anyway.' And we headed back towards the main college, where on every floor the lights in the big and old-fashioned windows burned steadfast in the night.

The staff room is the epicentre of the world for the Jarlath's teachers. It is there that the house teachers like Fr Fintan Monahan and Fr Seán Cunningham and Fr Brendán Kilcoyne gather for lunch – soup followed by a meat dish and vegetables and perhaps a trifle for dessert. There is always a cup of tea on the go and the room faces onto the football pitch, so when it is particularly bitter, you can keep an eye on training without succumbing to frostbite. At night-time when the lay teachers have gone home the remaining priests often sit and correct copies here and gather for a chat before heading over to their own quarters around nine o'clock. Rotating duties often mean you never know who will be in the staff room at any given hour. Conal often takes charge of the students' dining room at lunchtime. The most impressive aspect of this duty is that he manages to complete it without the aid of earmuffs. The student meals are wonderfully loud and rushed affairs and the acoustics of the big dining hall make it deafening. Jarlath's never had any ambition to gain a Michelin star for its culinary presentations but the infamous reputation it acquired for food is probably undeserved. Nowadays, day students can buy a three-course meal for €2. Conal reckons it costs as much to dispose of the meals, what with the recycling of food, paper and plastic, but at least the kids are eating something relatively healthy. The students wolf their meals at astonishing speed, and silence prevails only during the grace after meals. That ritual has become a bit like the national anthem at big summer games in that the screech of chairs, the roar and mass exodus begin as the last words of the prayer are chanted. In the old days, when Conal was a student here, such loose observation of prayer would not so much have been dreamt of. But that was then.

Because many kids clear home at the weekends and because

they have money in their pockets, food is not the issue it used to be at the college. For many students who passed through the school in the era of an unbending disciplinary regime, food became the abiding memory of the college. As is the case today, students sat eight at a table and there was an appointed monitor to supervise the division of the tray of food. Generally it was accepted that the further away you sat from the monitor, the stingier your portions were. Every pupil had a small round portion of butter, about the size of a penny. In the 1940s, though, these were often rancid. Generally proceedings were relatively civilised but sometimes high spirits or high hunger would lead to a 'grab', a spontaneous free for all at a given table where the more timid or mannerly would be left with next to nothing.

Occasionally, things got desperate. During the white winter of 1947, when the country was ravaged by relentless snowfalls, most of the school fell ill with influenza. Pupils of the period recall the kitchens serving up fried sausages and eggs and bacon three and four days a week in an effort to revive spirits and health – a display of generosity that for Jarlath's bordered on the ostentatious. One hundred years before that, the catering situation was even more grim, with famine-relief supplies regularly pillaged before they made it as far as Tuam from Galway City. Under the presidency of Anthony O'Regan, later the Archbishop of Chicago, the student body grew more wasted and spectral by the week. A confederacy of teachers devised a plan secretly to slay a college sheep that then might be reported to the president and ultimately eaten by those in the house. The bloody deed was carried out at night and the poor sheep duly 'discovered' and reported to Fr O'Regan.

To the teacher's horror, however, O'Regan, ever the accountant, openly wondered how much the carcass might fetch on the open market. They rushed to beg him to deliver the sheep to the school kitchens and, grumbling, he assented.

So it was that during the leanest, most threatened period of its history, Jarlath's came to serve up a prime roast of lamb.

After he finished saying grace at this particular lunchtime, Conal hung the resident microphone back on a little hook attached to a pillar in the middle of the room and moved through the crowd of boys towards the staff room for his own meal. There were still a few of the other staff members around – Charlie Kelly, John McLoughlin, Fintan, and Seán, who was preparing to leave for class. The afternoon bell signalled the boys back to afternoon class and, after what sounded like the evacuation of Normandy, a restful quiet fell.

Soon enough, the conversation in the staff room turned to the opera. This year was St Jarlath's first ever production of *Joseph and his Amazing Technicolour Dreamcoat*. John, a burly dean in his fifties, has an encyclopaedic knowledge of West End musicals and is unquestionably one of the western world's leading authorities on *Blood Brothers*, having delivered Jarlath's boys to its performance at St Martin in the Fields more than fifty times.

'He introduces more kids to musicals or theatre than any man alive,' vouched Conal. 'They all remember their first time in theatre – either to the Abbey or London. Go through your London tour, John. This is well worth hearing.'

The compressed nature of John's London trip is famous and students sign up in the knowledge that what awaits is something between a sightseeing tour and a military training camp.

'OK,' agreed John and launched into his itinerary like a man reciting verse.

'Well, this year. Let's see, we left on a Friday and got the ferry in on Saturday. Very much a sightseeing day because the kids generally stay awake all night on the ferry and you cannot take the chance sitting them down. So Buckingham Palace, Downing Street, the War Rooms and then we finish up by getting evening mass at Westminster. Many years ago we chanced a film on the Saturday night up in the Odeon in Swiss Cottage. It was packed and we had about forty kids spread out all over the cinema, absolutely shattered with tiredness. They were out for the count after ten minutes and next this outraged Londoner stands up to shout, "And why is everybody sleeping?"

'So we learned our lesson there. But Petticoat Lane started the Sunday for us and then on to Speaker's Corner, which always gets a laugh. Then to White Hart Lane for a Spurs game. And that being Sunday night we went to a film. *Intolerable Cruelty*, or something. Monday morning then, up early and to Waterloo and a train to the World of Adventures, a great day out. Back in then to a crowded Waterloo and the gang of us would walk then from Charing Cross and have a bite to eat before going to The Field at Charing Cross Road for *Blood Brothers*. And *Blood Brothers* has never failed – I have been three times each year over fifteen or sixteen years. Tuesday then is traditionally a trip on the river to Greenwich and that's always nice. In the afternoon then we justify our existence by going to the British Museum and the Natural History Museum. And the teachers are a bit tired by that stage so they might sit down. And the last particular Tuesday night we visited, we went to New London Theatre where we had seen *Cats* for so long but this time the show was *Joseph and His Amazing Technicolour Dreamcoat*. And we decided to walk home rather than take the underground because the boys were so high. Wednesday then is the visit to the big shops – Harrods and Lilywhites and what not. The afternoon then, we prepare for home, get the seven o'clock out of Euston to Holyhead and we were back in the college on Thursday morning.'

'And how much?' pressed Conal.

'About €250 all in. We wouldn't be staying at the Ritz, now. Let's just say the sleeping bags come in handy.'

There was tea going and John optimistically inspected a box of Kimberly chocolate creams that lay open on the linen tablecloth and then threw his hands up in mock despair. The others revelled in his bad timing. Irish staff-rooms are not exactly known as sanctuaries when it comes to quality biscuits.

'Was there one left when you last looked?' Conal asked with mock sympathy.

'Sunday's dessert was in there too but it was thrown out yesterday, I think. Anyhow, opera rehearsal is going well but it is not a time to intrude. It's a kind of private grief. And yet you know that come Friday it will go like clockwork. I can never understand that. At least with a football team it is up to themselves but a show is different – people expect a certain level.'

'Yeah, I don't know, I think I would crack up,' Charlie said.

Charlie is another Jarlath's 'lifer' – a former student, a former footballer in the 1966 championship season, and now a dean. Although he has been there for several decades, Charlie has retained a youthful look and, to observe him in the corridors, it is obvious he is a great favourite with the pupils.

Charlie reckons that this is his favourite term in the school year, these few weeks leading up to Christmas when it is dry and cold out and the college seems fresh with possibility. He shares the duty of dean with John, ensuring that the boys settle after lights out at 10.30 pm and, later, after satisfying himself that the school is secure, he turns in himself, the sole figure of authority in the boarding school through the long night.

'Ah, you couldn't blame the college. Deans don't come cheap,' Fr Charlie teased.

'Ferocious expensive,' agreed Conal, 'so we can't afford to have any more than one on in the evening time.'

They began talking about the role of the dean and of the

experience of living in the college as the only adult in a habitat filled with adolescents.

'Working here, you feel there is life in the place all of the time,' Conal said. 'That is the great thing. There are very few hours when these halls are actually quiet. It is nice to come over here early in the morning and hear the din at breakfast time.'

'Priests that leave the school will tell you that the sense of camaraderie is what they miss most,' Charlie explained. 'You go out to a parochial house and suddenly you are on your own every single day and it is not an easy thing to accept.'

'I often say to people that on any given day here I laugh more than in a year out in Clifden which, let me add, is no reflection on Clifden,' Conal adds. 'But the kids energise you. Even the problems they have, it keeps you interested and guessing. The school year flies.'

'And we spend our time talking about them and laughing at the things that get them upset and animate them. It is astonishing how pupils pass through here and their five years are gone before you know it.'

'But the day you haven't it will be an awfully dark day,' Charlie said. 'In three years' time when it just goes away.'

Conal nodded. 'It is almost unthinkable.'

'Sure we are institutionalised at this stage,' Charlie said. 'So I figure we will end up in some sort of home for the bewildered. But just maybe we might be allowed to patrol the corridors a little bit.'

The men laughed, then the shrill bell rang and, from the timber floors overhead and along the polished stone floors of the corridor and from the tarmac outside, came the sound of hundreds and hundreds of footsteps, like thunder clapping.

The opera is performed annually the weekend before Christmas. On the Saturday night of the *Joseph* production, St Jarlath's Hall drew a capacity crowd. This weekend has more or less evolved into an unofficial open evening for the parents of students. They come to see the performance and then take the long, time-honoured stroll from the hall and up the stairs, along the corridor with the photographs of all the celebrated football teams and into the main dining room where they have tea and buns until close to midnight. It gives a sense of what the school is like, and the cleaning staff and kitchen ladies work overtime to make sure the building is at its most high wattage and radiant.

Oliver Hughes, a former student, teacher and president of Jarlath's for thirty-one years, is back on the old sod this evening to see the musical. To him, it is a treat to be anticipated as much as a Hogan Cup match.

'You'll be surprised. It is more like a professional production than a school show,' he promised after we were escorted to seats at the rear of the hall.

And he wasn't far wrong. Some of the leads were terrific and the show tunes were instantly recognisable. But it was unmistakably a typically Irish school production that was set in a classic Irish parish hall. The hall had that dense, perfumed warmth of bingo although outside it was a beautiful, seasonal night of clean frost. There were tickets to raffle and kids paraded their finery, up late and getting to see their older brothers and sisters on stage. Parents who vaguely knew each other said hello and scrambled to find seats before the lights dipped and Fr Seán and Fr Fintan directed the audience towards the vacant spots. And all of a sudden a piano struck up and the curtains parted like the Red Sea, hesitantly at first and then drawn back in a rush and the audience was transported to the land of the Israelites by way of actors from Tuam and Mountbellew and wherever. And the teenagers threw their hearts into it. They stood up and lustily sang the sweet and infectious and dated songs and it was clear that a lot of work had gone into the production, that the performers were proud of it and, because of that, the whole event was touching. The scene could have belonged to any decade in Jarlath's (except that the female parts are played by real girls now) and it flew in the face of endless reports of Ireland's subterranean teenagers on a blind crusade to get wantonly ruined on drink or drugs or over-consumption of anything. Perhaps they traded the greasepaint for mascara and aftershave and got blitzed at a disco in Tuam on the nights after the opera, but still. There was an optimistic and healthy pulse here; these were not young people you would be fearful for.

'Children today are absolutely wonderful,' Oliver maintained later on when asked about this. 'Confident and responsive, a joy. At least that is my belief. It was the early Seventies, I think, when kids were at their worst. I'm not sure why – there was hostility in this country towards authority and maybe for the first time a willingness and climate to challenge it. It is nothing like that today. There is a contentment and confidence there.'

Oliver was as enamoured by this show as any of the previous forty he must have witnessed in his time here as a student and teacher. He applauded each solo vigorously and sometimes audibly inhaled at a little lighting trick or a clever turn of choreography.

One of the kids, Dónal Ó Healaí, played the Pharaoh and the idea was to do a caricature of Elvis Presley. He arrived on stage in a lavish all-white suit and quiff. This was not a role that called for half measures. If it was method acting, then the method involved ditching all semblance of cool. He gave this marvellous pastiche of The King, Brendan Bowyer and a Greek god and he brought the house down.

'I never did anything like this before,' he confessed afterwards. 'Like, I try to sing a bit all right in a band we have back home but God, never the whole make-up and costume thing. I dunno, it's a bit of *craic*. Gives you confidence, like. I

knew I wanted to give the opera a go anyhow whenever I came
to Jarlath's.'

Dónal is from Spiddal and switched to the school after the
junior cert. A chance meeting with his friend Fiachra
Breathnach convinced him that he wanted to leave his mixed
day school at home and go boarding. Fiachra plays football and
last year he played half-forward on the Jarlath's team that lost
the Hogan Cup final to St Patrick's, Maghera.

'And Fiachra just said to me, come here. It's a different
world. And I could see straight away what the place had done
for him. Fiachra and myself would be quite similar and I was
just struck by his attitude to things.'

His parents weren't immediately taken with the radical
notion of switching, but through the summer, Dónal persisted
and reasoned and argued. And one day when the family was
going to a cousin's confirmation in Corofin, he persuaded them
to stop by Jarlath's and they took a walk across the yard at the
front of the school, serene and stately at the height of a fine
summer.

'I just said to Mum then, Jesus, there is something about this
place. And it does have this aura, I think anyway. Like, I was
certain it was for me.'

And they were among the parents in the audience watching
their kid belting out these show numbers and being happy. He
has a lot going for him, Dónal – bright and outgoing and
athletic. By chance, he was the only cast member on the Senior
A football team. Rehearsals forced him to skip several early-
season training sessions and already he was dreading the
thought of catching up during the unforgiving January sessions
of which he had heard many horror stories. On the eve of the
last night, with the incessant encores and the bouquets and the
regrettable anti-climax that comes almost always with the final
bow, he was convinced that this opera was one of the most
wonderful experiences of his life.

'Just to prove to yourself you can do it, you know, I suppose it's a nice thing to have on your CV as well, that you were in a Jarlath's opera but, ah, it's not really that. You make friends out of it, get to meet people. You know. Girls.'

And how the departed men of the collar would blanch if they saw the way girls, the once unseen creatures from the Mercy, roamed around the stage area of the college hall with impunity. Girls in Jarlath's! Once, it would have provoked a riot.

Now though, the cast members took their folks up the big dining hall, which was brightened in Christmas decorations. Dónal was staying with relatives in Corofin for the weekend but was in no rush, happy to talk at the rear of the hall that quickly emptied of people and its stage magic. The producer, Noel Kerrane – 'he quivers with music,' said Fr Oliver – walked by and saluted his Pharaoh, telling him he did a good job.

'Ah, I dunno, sir, I only got four hours sleep last night. I was worried about getting hoarse. I'll have to have honey and lemon this evening.'

'Or pints of porter,' laughed Kerrane.

'Aw now. Sure that would finish us altogether.'

Dónal talked on about Jarlath's and like every boy that ever spent a night under its roof, he communicated the sheer strangeness of those first few evenings when an unseen hand flicked the light switch off and of how unforgettably loud the first morning bell was. The lack of personal space took getting used to. A stolen half-hour on his own just to read or lie down became a luxury he learned to appreciate. Football season, he predicted, will put paid to that. It had been easier, he agreed, strolling into his own home after school and lounging around with the remote control but he spoke of St Jarlath's as being the key event of his young life.

'And the one thing I would say, you know, is that it has completely changed my attitude to priests. They were always people that I just never even considered talking to. I wouldn't have even known how. Like, that's nothing against the priests at home, they all seem like sound men. But here, I mean, you are listened to and you get respect for saying what you have to say. And it's nothing to do with religion or anything like that. That's left up to yourself. There is a morning mass on at half past seven in the morning and you might get a dozen at it. I have gone myself sometimes, and before coming here, I wouldn't have ever seen that hour on the clock. But no, like, some of the people here are the loveliest I have met.'

For Oliver Hughes, attending St Jarlath's was always an assumed thing. His father Tommy passed through there in the 1920s and several of his grand-uncles went on for the priesthood in Maynooth. Oliver spent his boyhood on a 200-acre Galway farm that was reasonably prosperous and family-orientated and happy. The eldest of a large clan, he worked hard and roamed freely and is still stunned by how coldly and completely his entrance to Jarlath's in the autumn of 1957 closed the door on that boyhood. Those first weeks of bells, waking him and shunting him here and instructing him to eat now and pray now and go outside now drove him to the edge. Sleep could not come fast enough and even that brought its miseries, with the heating system employed minimally by the conservative guardians of the school. The FCA boys were the luckiest in that they were provided with heavy topcoats that doubled as blankets during the frigid winter nights when the school felt like one mammoth ice floe.

'I found it an extremely difficult experience,' he remembers almost half a century later from the parish house in Corofin, where he was recently posted after a working life in the college.

'I think it was a school of its time. What I found difficult was the enormity of the place and how impersonal it was. You wondered then if anybody was interested in you. They were difficult and rough times, the late Fifties – times of great scarcity economically and in personal relationships. So I found it an extraordinarily lonely place.'

Atmosphere was everything. When he recalls that decade, it awakes in him a distinct feeling of uneasiness. All that was spontaneous and joyful about life was suppressed both internally and by the dominant forces of the time. This was not just in St Jarlath's, but across the country in general. The austere influence of the Church spread across the land like a shadow and here he was a young teenager in its very cradle. There was a dean in the school in his early years who terrified them all. He would cane the boys in a way that went beyond mere strict censure and into the realms of cruelty and beyond. Boys were boys even then and there was horseplay and devilment in the evening time but nothing was worth being caught by this particular dean, a man whose name appears in several books about Jarlath's. Oliver was caned, not often but enough to recall the clean whoosh and the stinging rebuke. And Oliver was one of the quiet ones. When he remembers that dean now, it is with sympathy because he reckons he was just lost in the stagnancy of that decade, posted on duty often seven days a week, not very well paid, and fighting the loneliness that came with guarding the dreams of hundreds of boisterous youngsters. The students were the only corporeal unit he could exercise his frustrations on. And so he caned.

'The whole way of life was harsh – the culture of the day was of fear and repression. I think the place just destroyed him and shortly after my time there, he did suffer a lapse. There was no feel for the kind of person or the growth of the personality. It was all rules and regulations. The priests and the guards – and that percolated through to school life.'

He says he has no doubt there are many other former students out there on whom the Jarlath's culture had a profoundly dark impact. His time at the school coincided with the last gasp of wanton birch-rod authoritarianism and the first glimpses of a more humane alternative to education. Although the relationship between the staff – all religious men then – and the pupils was deathly strict, there was a subtle softening, a natural impulse towards kindness overshadowed by a compelling duty to adhere to the strict dictum laid down by the Catholic hierarchy. For a thirteen-year-old, those conflicting currents of emotion were confusing and he found solace in the books and on the football field. For long before he returned as a member of staff, Oliver was anointed as one of the chosen ones at St Jarlath's. He played on the Hogan Cup winning team of 1961, the only season that the college retained the title. Football was both a way of creating a presence for oneself and a way of forgetting; it burnt up the long evenings and helped break the repetition of the boarding regime. And the football field was the one place where self-expression was permissible. It was the streak of crimson through the grey. When Oliver arrived, the game was already established as the core expression of pride in St Jarlath's. Gaelic football was nothing new to him. His father Tommy won an All-Ireland medal with Galway in 1934, but stopped playing shortly after that to concentrate on farming.

'I have no idea where any of his medals are except for one county championship medal he got while playing with Tuam Stars. He never placed any value on them and he used to joke that a brother of his pawned the lot of them during a scarce year. But he never talked about football; it was as if it was just a job he was good at and then it passed. I am told he was a very, very good footballer but I never saw him play. Yet he was wildly excited about my own football career at St Jarlath's. I don't think he ever missed a game.'

Fr Brendan Kavanagh was the trainer at St Jarlath's in that era. Whether by accident or design, the college had a series of trainers who were forensic and futuristic in their approach to the game. The first recorded football game at Jarlath's took place in 1906 when a student combination took on Young Irelands from Tuam Town. It was a rough-hewn sport then and players on both sides took the wise precaution of wearing shin guards and ankle shields. Referees were generally from the staff and were notoriously partisan; one Jarlath's referee, Frank Guy, denied a poor Mountbellew team their only score – a point – in one particular friendly game, on the grounds that the kick was too high. Through the 1920s, Jarlath's boys contented themselves with friendly games against schools like St Flannan's and St Nathy's. In 1929, however, Canon Joseph Walsh entered the college in the newly established Connacht Colleges' competition, and the task of training the football team was given to Fr Michael Malone. Thus began the college's first golden era; the Jarlath's housekeeper polished the Connacht Cup from 1932 right through until 1940. Fr Malone's unorthodox techniques have become the stuff of myth. As a coaching manual, he carried around a scrapbook of studies and drills from other sports, inspirational pictures and words of advice. It was nicknamed 'the Koran'. He was devoted to the idea of a two-dimensional player to the extent that he would physically tie down a reluctant player's stronger foot to force him to employ his weaker side. Malone's principal beliefs – innovation, excellence and teamwork – formed the lasting framework for all future Jarlath's football coaches. One of his students, Dr Michael Mooney, played on the 1933 team and through him the torch was passed; it was Mooney, appointed to the staff in 1943, who led St Jarlath's into the Hogan Cup era.

The first ever All-Ireland Colleges was held in 1946 and Jarlath's were the omnipotent champions of Connacht. Although they lost that year's final to St Patrick's of Armagh, beaten 3-11 to 4-7, they became champions of Ireland in 1947, the bitterest winter of the century. There was a sense of manifest destiny, with Sean Purcell, born in the shadow of the college on Bishop Street, displaying the nascent genius that would flare so memorably over Galway's brightest-ever footballing era.

That team, captained by Vincent McHale, took revenge on Armagh in Croke Park on Sunday, 11 May. The final score was 4-10 to 3-8. The match was broadcast live on radio and, back in the school, the Jarlath's boys gathered and lived every moment through the crackling, glamorous broadcast. The following night, a Monday evening, bonfires were fired on the edge of Tuam Town, and the Boys' Band trumpeted the heroes into the square where town commissioners waited in all their pomp and glittering chains. At the gates of the college waited Archbishop Joseph Walsh and the staff and hundreds of Jarlath's boys crowding the yard, standing on heights, awe-struck faces pressed against the upper window panes for a better view. St Jarlath's had its first night of glory and thereafter the chase would be permanent. Although the All-Ireland series was abandoned after 1948 because the Catholic hierarchy feared its powers to seduce students from study, football lost no stature in Jarlath's, and when the national competition was revived a decade later, Fr Brendan Kavanagh was in place as the games master of the college. He was as thorough and ambitious as Malone twenty years earlier and, suddenly, the All-Ireland titles began to roll in: 1960, 1961, 1964 and 1966, with lost finals in both 1962 and 1967. It was in this environment that Oliver Hughes found his way.

'Brendan was someone we all had tremendous time for, he was a very humane man but on the field he could be unforgiving ... he would get lost in it really,' he says now smiling.

'I remember one evening at training – he would regularly take part in the training with us – things got a bit heated and he clipped one of the boys. I somehow got involved and bam, next thing I knew I got a belt in the mouth. But that night, we were both called out of study and he took us into Galway for a big

slap-up meal. And it was just to say sorry. It cut him up. And
we understood that and the whole thing was forgotten about
the next day.'

When Oliver was a player, the All-Ireland Colleges scene
was a tremendous deal. In 1960, 15,000 people showed up in
Athlone to see St Jarlath's victory over St Finian's of Mullingar.
That team featured Enda Colleran, Pat Donnellan, John Morley
and Pat Sheridan. The tradition in the college from the early
days was that the team used to travel with the priests in the
cars. That was partly out of necessity – public transport was
notoriously whimsical then – and also it gave the team a feeling
of importance, as if they were being chauffeured.

'And there was the added thing that the priest would
generally stop and buy us chocolate and drinks and whatever on
the way home from the bigger games. Boarders did not regard
treats like that very lightly.'

Oliver insists that despite making two Hogan Cup teams,
the big games made him nervous. The pressure on St Jarlath's
teams to deliver was implicit but nonetheless deeply apparent.
Football was the instrument through which the college
communicated its substance to the greater world. Academics
were taken as seriously, but examination results were an
individual matter between the student and his teachers.
Football was about a glorious collective identity. Forty years
on, he has clear recall of some of the big games but not many.
He admits that in his senior year being on the first team gave
him a quasi-celebrity status in the college among the younger
kids. But you believe him when he says none of that mattered,
not even the winning. Perhaps he is a chip off the old block in
that way. What Oliver valued most when he finally left St
Jarlath's one gorgeous May morning with aspirations to join the
missionaries was the recollection of the pure and countless
evenings when his hands were red raw with cold and it was
getting too dark to see the ball properly. When they were

playing for the joy of playing. Those were the times that got him by and he remembered that when, out of the blue, chance and the Church returned him to St Jarlath's seven years after he thought he had walked out of its gates for the final time.

Kids: they are the wages of sin. If Francis Stockwell had a pound for every hard bullet of chewing gum he has scraped clear from the underside of a desk, he would be a rich man. Summer has always been his consolation. Summer means the school is as it should be: free of children. At least that is what he tells himself. But when the long quiet days do arrive, he always notes that it is a pity that the youngsters do not get to enjoy the warm airiness that the long summer months bring. St Jarlath's often looks at its most magnificent on those hypnotic July days when there is nobody around to marvel at it. It is typical of the obtuse nature of the place. In those months, Francis Stockwell puts order on the school again. He paints the school rooms and repairs the doors, polishes the dormitories, planes away the graffiti and mends locks, and works his way through the endless inventory created by housing hundreds of west of Ireland boys for a school year. Then, before he knows it, the first golden leaves fall across the famous football field, the evenings gather in and they come galloping back. Kids. Put on this earth to drive him mad. And he loves it.

'The kids are great really,' he remarked one evening when we watched a senior team session. 'It's funny, nothing really changes here. It is the same now as it was when I was here. Although maybe the boys are more confident now, more outgoing about things.'

'Stockie' is what they call him. He holds a mezzanine level of authority in the school; he is of the staff fraternity but separate – someone the boys are impelled to obey but still someone they can have a laugh with and not someone they mind seeing if they are trying to mitch off class. They complain to him about the injustices of the school and he reminds them that he is not a teacher.

But if he thinks the youngsters have a worthwhile grievance then he will pass it on and the teachers listen. Many of them taught Stockwell during the Jarlath's period of the late 1970s. He hasn't changed much, with the impish grin and the quick, bouncing step. Oliver remembers him as one of the most delightful and infuriating pupils that ever sat before him.

'A nightmare. But one you didn't mind, one with not an ounce of badness in it.'

Stockwell is a football name that echoes through the tight streets of Tuam and all across Galway. Frank Stockwell senior formed 'the Terrible Twins' partnership with Sean Purcell. They were born within ten days of each other on Bishop Street. They palled together in the town and then Frank went to the CBS and Sean attended St Jarlath's. Following in his father's footsteps never bothered Francis too much. He inherited his father's flair for the game but, in his early teenage years, size counted against him. Oliver Hughes remembers marching him through every shoe shop in Galway one afternoon trying to find a replacement pair of boots small enough to fit him. The young Stockwell had enormous energy. It was as if his tiny frame could not contain the ferocious abundance of energy that pinged around inside him. His parents decided that boarding school would be the best way to control him and so it was that he used to walk one minute to St Jarlath's gate on a Monday morning of each new term, his suitcase packed.

'From the upstairs toilets, I used to be able to see the gable of our house,' he laughs now. 'So I suppose it was never as lonely or tough for me as it would have been for some of the others. And we had a half-day Wednesday so I could go home and get fed. I always liked it here I have to say. I know some that didn't. It just kind of suited me.'

Stockwell possesses his own piece of St Jarlath's folklore.

The college team travelled to the 1979 Hogan Cup final in Tullamore as reigning champions against Ard Scoil Rís from Dublin. The city school's presence in a Hogan Cup final was a stunning feat as it had been opened by president Éamon de Valera only seven years earlier. Their unlikely ascent through the city and provincial championship made the Griffith Avenue side the sweethearts of that year's competition and their appearance in the final against the Galway powerhouse gave that year's Hogan Cup an added dimension. Pat Flynn from Ard Scoil Rís delivered a free in the dying seconds to level the game at ten points each at full time. Seven thousand people showed up at Tullamore for the replay, a game that is remembered in Tuam as Stockwell's final. He hit two penalties, the first one wide and the second one against the post. Jarlath's lost by two points, 2-9 to 1-10.

'If I clipped both of them over the bar, we would have had a draw,' he smiled with a shrug some twenty-four years later.

It didn't matter that Stockwell was the highest scorer in that final series with five points both days. The missed kicks will always be remembered. Oliver remembers practising penalties with Stockwell during those years. He would stand a 7-Up bottle in the goalmouth and, nine times out of ten, Stockwell would send it flying with the ball.

'We would never have been near a final that season if it hadn't been for Francis Stockwell. He was an absolutely beautiful place kicker of a football. That first penalty was just a bad shot. The second one, in retrospect, he took with concussion but I didn't realise that until afterwards. He had taken a knock and we thought he was all right but he was fairly groggy. It was just bad luck.'

Years later, Stockwell ended up at a disco in Tullamore, his first time back in the town since that traumatic game. A fight broke out under the flashing lights and although the Galway man was completely innocent even as to the identity of the warring factions, he somehow managed to get thrown out with the pack. So it was he found himself out on the street at one o'clock on a wet night in a town that he visited twice and was made miserable by twice.

'To be honest, if the Pope himself asked me to come and visit him in Tullamore, I don't know if I would go.'

Stockwell still made it to the gallery of champions that hangs in the corridor, however. The season before, he had been gifted enough to make it onto the 1978 team as a fifth year. He played corner-forward on a team often regarded as the strongest St Jarlath's team in history and they went through that season without facing a truly tough challenge, beating Greg Blaney's St Colman's of Newry team by 2-11 to 2-04 in the Hogan Cup final.

'They were the untouchables,' reckoned Conal, studying the photograph one afternoon alongside Stockwell.

The team wears the all-white uniform, and the Hogan Cup, a long, narrow urn, rests at the feet of the captain, Martin Joyce. Fr Hughes is standing to the left of his team, slender and with the precise posture he favoured for photographs in his own playing days. His left arm is slightly raised as if in presentation, as if to say: 'This is who we are.' At the opposite end of the back row stands Aengus Murphy, a tall athletic wing back who would lose his life on duty with the Irish Army in Lebanon years later.

'They really played some of the best football I have ever seen.'

Francis threw his eyes to heaven at this remark and sauntered away to his work again. According to him, the college has not changed greatly since his student days. The sense of uncompromising strictness had evaporated some years before he began and there was always scope for fun. He has a particular memory of a spring evening shortly before one of the finals. The weather was muggy and everyone was too restless to study. At first, just one or two but, before long, dozens of students jumped out the windows and headed down towards the wall where the Mercy Convent was.

The Elvis Costello song, 'Oliver's Army', had just been released and the Jarlath's boys hijacked the song as a paean to the football team. There must have been over a hundred boys, Francis recalled, books abandoned, burning off those furnaces of teenage energy, singing the chorus into the night and hearing no reply.

Conal told this story against himself. It was some weeks before the 1982 Hogan Cup semi-final in which St Jarlath's were pitted against their eternal rivals, St Mel's of Longford. Conal was taking charge of the college hurlers that season, a team fated to persevere along a noble if anonymous route while the football team shone. It so happened that the senior football captain, Rory O'Dwyer from Urhan in west Cork, was also one of the best hurlers in the college. In the last minute of a contest that Conal cannot even remember the relevance of, O'Dwyer was sent off.

The referee happened to be a good friend of Conal's and as they were all leaving the field he joked, 'I hope that wasn't one of your footballers I sent off.'

Conal, pale at this stage, informed him that he had just red-carded the Jarlath's senior captain. The man almost choked on his whistle. The dismissal, coming practically on the eve of the All-Ireland semi-final, would rule O'Dwyer out of the St Mel's match and Conal drove home wondering how best to present the bad news in the staff-room.

While the hurling team were on their adventures, however, separate legislative problems had arisen. On St Patrick's Day, Jarlath's had defeated St Colman's of Claremorris in the provincial final on a score of 1-09 to 2-05. It emerged that a St Jarlath's player named Michael Molloy, who had shortly before enrolled as a senior student, had actually played for another school prior to his arrival He was therefore quite possibly ineligible and St Colman's, devastated by the narrowness of their defeat, pressed for a ruling on the incident. The Jarlath's fraternity was in shock and poor Molloy inconsolable. The case went from a tangle of provincial meetings to a late night session at Croke Park.

'It was just crazy,' recalls Conal. 'I remember clearly the night we were all waiting for word to come down from Dublin. And the phone was hopping with newspaper people wondering what was going on. Eventually I think we just left a taped message.'

Ultimately, it was ruled that St Jarlath's had not been guilty of anything and, inevitably, they not only beat St Mel's but won the final against Skibbereen after a replay. Shortly afterwards, Eugene McGee, the talismanic Longford journalist and football authority for whom 1982 would distinguish itself as quite a year, wrote an article that hinted at conspiracy. His theory was that the St Colman's protest was just a ruse to delay the semi-final by a few weeks, thereby ensuring that Rory O'Dwyer, Jarlath's most influential player, would be clear to play.

'And it was a grand theory,' says Conal with a smile, 'but one of the most outlandish I have ever heard. Because the idea of St Colman's actually trying to do St Jarlath's a favour in football is beyond the beyond. If you understood the bitterness that divided both schools over the years, there is just no way they would plot to aid one another. But I think they felt differently in Longford.'

The official 1982 championship photograph was taken in front of the college one afternoon when the foliage was in full bloom. Today, it looks fresher than its twenty-two years. The cup has been spit-polished and the jerseys washed and pressed. It was most likely the last time that group sat down together as a team because, after a tumultuous few weeks of examinations, the senior boys would leave St Jarlath's College. Sitting to Rory

O'Dwyer's right is a skinny boy with a dark fringe and a mischievous face: you can just tell that after the photograph was taken, he would have been off that bench like lightning. Leslie McGettigan, at the age of fifteen, was the youngest player to feature in a Hogan Cup final and one of the few boys in the history of the competition to feature in three successive finals.

Nearly twenty years later, McGettigan remembers this time as 'the happiest three years of my life'.

He had entered St Jarlath's through a family connection. His brother Paul married a sister of Jimmy Duggan's, the celebrated Galway football player and Jarlath's alumnus. When Leslie crashed disastrously in the Inter Certificate, his parents thought boarding school was his only hope of salvation.

'I was kind of surprised just how quickly I came to love the place,' he recalled.

'I think I was fortunate to attend there at a time when the staff were just terrific. Like, I would have regarded Fr Oliver as a friend. He was my French teacher and when I arrived I would have been way behind and he just had this way of encouraging and helping me catch up without really making a big deal of it. And then on the football field he was just a brilliant trainer. Obviously the whole week revolved around the football and I loved that. On a Wednesday, you had a half-day and on the notice board was posted the "A" team and the "B" team for the week. That was how you found out how you were progressing. And you could not get the dinner inside you fast enough so you could go and see if you had made the "A" team.'

McGettigan lives abroad now, but when he is in Ireland, he invariably finds that he returns to Tuam. The centre of the town has changed but, in his mind's eye, the hot spots remain. Cafolla's was where things happened for Tuam boarders in 1982.

It was there they hung out with the Mercy girls on the

pretence of having to go up the town for a haircut or a pair of shoes. Some study nights, depending on who was supervising, it was possible to arrange to meet a girl and spend a couple of hours in the local cinema. Most nights, though, they spent trapped in the dormitories.

'It was a new thing for me because we had so much time on our hands, we ended up talking in a much deeper way about stuff than you would have in a normal outside environment. Like, we would have sat up half the night chatting about football and women and philosophising about life, thinking we were real whiz kids that had it all sorted out. What I really learned in Jarlath's was how to share. Everybody was thrown into this place together and you looked out for people. I don't know how many Sundays lads took me out to eat with their families when my ma and da couldn't make it down. But Tuam kind of felt like home. Like, I was sixteen years of age and if you got down the town for an hour after school, there would be local men there who would know your name. And when we won the Hogan Cup, the homecoming nights were just magic.'

No school has ever won three Hogan Cups in a row. McGettigan's generation came closest. The team of 1982 was a gifted one but in 1983 St Jarlath's produced a truly mesmerising team that somehow got caught by three goals against Coláiste Chríost Rí in the final in Croke Park. Nothing was expected of the 1984 team. Only McGettigan and Mark Butler had returned from the previous year. McGettigan was deeply disappointed when Butler was made captain and although he never discussed it with Fr Oliver, he concluded that it was not based on any prejudice but on the fact that Butler had attended the school since first year.

'They created this vice-captain thing the same year just to camouflage it a bit. I was cut up, no doubt about it, but once the season began, it was forgotten about. But we had a young team that year and no one thought we could go anywhere. That's what made it so satisfying.'

They beat St Patrick's Maghera – a team that included Henry Downey, the future Derry All-Ireland winning captain – by 0-10 to 2-3. McGettigan pitched in four points. After the homecoming, the school organised a disco and invited pupils from the other town schools to come along.

A brother of Pat Holmes, the future Mayo player and manager, drove down for the party. McGettigan is not quite sure how, but before the night was through, about four of them ended up in Tingles nightclub in Ballina. They awoke on Holmes's brother's floor the following midday and concluded they were going to be murdered once they got back to the school so they hung around the town for the day. Around dusk, between evening meal and study, they stole back into the college and presented themselves in the dormitories for roll call. To their amazement, nothing was said. Three weeks later, term over, they exited St Jarlath's and were free to spend all the nights they wanted in Ballina.

Gradually, the team lost touch. The photograph is their epitaph, the shrine that distinguishes them from so many other promising football teams that passed through the college. Connacht titles or Hogan Cup final appearances do not cut it. Only the national winners go through the ceremony of posing together in the grounds, exemplars of a tradition.

Three years ago, McGettigan was passing through Dublin airport, about to leave Ireland, when he met an old acquaintance who had a vague notion that there was a reunion celebration in St Jarlath's. He made further enquiries, immediately got on a flight to Shannon, drove to his brother Paul's house in Corofin and was back in the college by nightfall.

'I was delighted but I was half-annoyed I could have missed it. I started givin' off to everyone about not keeping in touch.

But I am as bad myself. It's strange, every time I drive through Tuam I get a shiver of excitement and being in the school that evening took me back. Fr Oliver was there and I had not seen him donkey's years, probably since I'd left. It was just like seeing an old friend. It wasn't like you'd imagine meeting an old teacher – the handshake and the usual. It was a fuckin' hug.'

No man features in the photographs as often as Oliver Hughes does. His appearance has altered little through the decades, a neat athletic figure with a tidy hair parting and a reluctant smile. He took charge of the football team in the late 1970s and then passed control to Joe Long, who delivered a Hogan Cup in 1994. Thirteen of that team would advance to the Galway panel that won the All-Ireland senior football championship four years later. Oliver returned to St Jarlath's after spending his time as a seminarian in Maynooth, an experience that still makes him shudder.

'It was an extension in practice and ethos of St Jarlath's with all the old coldness reinforced,' he said. 'It was a brutally impersonal place. You were not bidden the time of day.'

After a brief spell as a curate out in the majestic wilds of Leenane, he was summoned back to his alma mater at the age of twenty-six. His return coincided with the arrival of lay teachers like Joe Long and the staff of that period almost consciously strove to move away from the last strands of doctrinaire education.

'You would make a point of poking fun at the pupils, of laughing with them and trying to put them at ease. And they would be asked if they had enough to eat, enough milk and things like that. And the regime of discipline was waning at that time anyway. I think it was probably a much easier and less intimidating place for students by the 1970s.'

Football was a six- and seven-day a week preoccupation during that time. Each evening, Oliver conducted training out on the main field, raced in for a shower and then began driving the 'day' pupils home on epic jaunts across the back roads in the Galway countryside. Several priests would make the runs. Even then, cars were relatively precious commodities in many rural households and if the boys wanted to play football, they needed a lift home.

'Parents appreciated it, yes. But I think they also probably regarded it as a service the school provided. And to be honest, we almost thought of it that way ourselves. You would do it without thinking. And the boys were thankful; it meant a lot to them.'

The banter in the car on those evenings, the talk about an upcoming match or an incident at training or just normal schoolboy gossip were as much a part of the scene as the laps or shooting drills.

'They were simply enormously fulfilling days. I never resented the hours involved, never felt taken for granted. I just enjoyed the whole spirit of being responsible for these teams.'

And yet there was a time when he questioned the worth or meaning of his choice – never his vocation but the philosophy he tried to bring to his everyday work with children. Countless times in recent years, Oliver Hughes has read articles and watched discussions on RTÉ in which the Church, the entity to which he devoted his life, was reduced to nothing but a frothing beast in a white collar that had scandalised and terrorised the country. When story after story of physical and sexual abuse came pouring out over the national airwaves, crimes perpetrated by men who wore the same collar as he, certainly he felt confused and vulnerable. When he spoke with friends, they couldn't understand why the archbishops weren't moving swiftly to address a problem that clearly ran deeply. He couldn't understand why nothing was done. It was a tough time to be a priest, but at least in St Jarlath's they felt removed because they looked around them and saw that they ran a happy house.

Then one morning a phone call came from a solicitor to

announce that a student who had attended the school in the 1980s had filed a case against the college chaplain of that period. By the afternoon, the television cameras were at the gates.

'We were sick and devastated. We just presumed that this would close the school.'

The case went to court and the chaplain pleaded guilty and, for a long time, Oliver Hughes did not feel comfortable enough to walk through Tuam wearing his collar. It did not matter that these were the same streets through which he had led All-Ireland winning teams on so many fine May evenings. All had been poisoned.

'People would have found it impossible to understand how we could have worked with this man and not have suspected. But it never even entered my mind. I mean, priests in particular are so bloody innocent or naïve when it comes to things like that – it would have just been completely inconceivable and alien to me that someone I knew could do anything harmful to a child. And this was the chaplain, the most trusted position in the school, someone I saw as better than me.'

The saving grace, though, was that throughout that sleepless term in 1995, the students still looked him in the eye. Nothing had changed; he was still the principal, still the football legend. He was, evidently, still somebody they felt they could trust. It made him more self-conscious, though. For years, he had been in dressing rooms with his teams when they were changing clothes and in the showers afterwards without ever giving it a thought. He felt like rebuking himself, felt like a bit of a simpleton moving in complicated times. Small things spoke volumes for the direction in which the educational climate was drifting. Windows replaced wooden doors in the teaching offices. Where once he would put his arm around a homesick first or second year, now he hesitated. He held back. An air of precaution descended on the teaching fraternity and it will not lift. But he still put in the same hours in the school and when he began coaching football again in the late 1990s – because there was nobody else prepared to take the post – he made a point of wearing his collar on the sideline at matches.

In the parish house in Corofin, Oliver is just a few miles away from St Jarlath's but he has departed the place in a way that distance cannot measure. It is hard to translate just how completely an institution as relatively minor as a college can come to be the dominant force in one's life. For Fr Oliver, Jarlath's was supposed to represent nothing more than it did to thousands of other kids – a house of rules in which they spent their adolescence. Instead, he came to preside there and he regards it with a complex affection, as an imperfect place that had its share of men and women who tried their best and continue to do so. It is easy to jumble times there. In the Fifties, his boyhood pals used to throw meet-me-later notes across the wall to the Mercy girls, and on nights when boys prepared to sneak out, there was a keen sense of anticipation across all the dormitories. Being caught meant expulsion.

'But if you were clever enough and brave enough, you could get away with it. There was only one dean on so it was possible then just as it was in my time as president.'

Oliver never sneaked out but he secretly admired the few who did. His own exit last May was more ceremonial and now he is in a different world. Irish society has changed greatly since his brief period as a young curate in Connemara. The days of sponge cake and tea presented in every house the priest might choose to visit are dead. He is conscious of how desperately short on time young families are nowadays and wonders aloud if and how he will get to meet all his new parishioners. To call on a rushed Tuesday evening on young families with meals to prepare and kids to tend to and soap operas to watch would cause them inconvenience. Already, the local club, Corofin – a modern giant of Galway football – has come to enlist his expertise, but he isn't sure how deeply he wants to get involved. His record with St Jarlath's is the stuff of folklore in the west of Ireland and he has had offers to manage at all levels. Although he is deeply respected as one of the shrewdest match coaches and tacticians around, the game never consumed him like it does others. Those hour-long conversations about a player or a team always bored him. For him, it was never really about the skills of the game as much as the company. Football was just another expression of teaching, of communicating through a method that at its best was more exalted and clearer than any other way he knew. It was all about learning from the youngsters, whose optimism could make him feel as if his role in life was worthwhile. And he misses that.

'Take this afternoon,' he says, raising his hands in gesture in the middle of his pleasant and understated living room in Corofin. 'A year ago, I would be supervising lunch in a dining room teeming with kids and would be either taking care of paperwork or maybe preparing for a game. Today, I'll go down to the kitchen there and prepare my own little bite. And that change is ... traumatic.'

Tom Murphy, the great Irish playwright, did not attend St Jarlath's and spent his boyhood consumed with envy of those who did. During his boyhood in Tuam, he attended the Christian Brothers' School from 1948 until 1951 and regarded Jarlath's as the bastion of privilege and opportunity. St Jarlath's represented the good life; he imagined that behind its walls were evenings of providential feasts and enlightened discussions and endless fun. Any hardship that he experienced growing up in modest circumstances on the Galway Road was, he believed, the complete opposite of what Jarlath's boys' experienced.

'They just seemed to have it better. There were strong class distinctions then and the assumption was that anybody who attended St Jarlath's was of middle class while the poor went to the CBS. And of course that meant better educational opportunities for them. In my class at the CBS, there were forty-two boys in the class and five of us managed to scrape a pass. We couldn't all have been that stupid. St Jarlath's also had the opera which was quite an event on the social calendar around Tuam. This was further evidence of their natural advantages – I had a reasonably good singing voice at that time but there was no place to exhibit it and impress the girls in the town. And there was an element of mystery about the Jarlath's boys – they were only ever seen around town for a few hours on a Wednesday or a Thursday. And this was probably one of the reasons why the local girls tended to fancy Jarlath's boys, which made it even more intolerable. So we would have regarded them with latent resentment and jealousy.'

Although the football rivalry between the two schools was fierce and too close to call during some decades, it was hopelessly lopsided during Murphy's brief stay in the realms of Irish education. Some of his most vivid memories are of participating in spectacularly crushing defeats at the hands of the St Jarlath's boys. For some reason, a score line of 5-47 to 0-3 clatters around at the back of his mind, although he can't be sure if a game actually ended on that specific result. But there was that sort of chasm between the teams. And it was not as if the St Jarlath's players tried to rub salt into the wounds they inflicted on their less illustrious counterparts. Murphy often got the impression that they simply couldn't help scoring that much.

'They were a big school by comparison and would have met us early on in the colleges' competition. We could recognise that some of these players were truly talented athletes and I think they were above the braggadocio.'

For even before Murphy became conscious of the explicit differences between the local school and the closeted, vaguely frightening boarding school, he was aware of St Jarlath's

football. He was still in national school when the first Hogan
Cup was won in 1947 and he got caught up in the general
excitement.

'There would have been real pride among everyone that this
was St Jarlath's of Tuam and that was always the case when the
school won football titles. Everybody appreciated the
significance of those wins and they transcended the begrudgery.
And of course, we had local boys that would have contributed
to those wins. Sean Purcell was like a god in Tuam. He still is.'

Today, Purcell lives on Bishop Street. He had left St Jarlath's
to pursue a career as a teacher by the time Murphy entered
secondary school and so their paths never crossed on a football
field. Murphy followed Purcell's orbiting star from a distance.
He is one of the most decorated footballer players to have
played the game and was voted, along with fellow Galway man
Enda Colleran, onto the Team of the Millennium.

What Purcell remembers most clearly about St Jarlath's first
ever Hogan Cup is the cold.

'The snowfall that year began in February and lasted right
through until May. I never experienced anything like it since.
There was no green to be seen for months, the landscape was
entirely changed. It must have been six feet high in places in
the town where it drifted against walls. All the bushes and the
shrubs were killed and you were just constantly cold.'

The weather, however, did nothing to disrupt the training
pattern devised by Fr Michael 'the Doc' Mooney. They trained
on the frozen, snow-covered field, learning to run and solo the
ball with the snow numbing their ankles and soaking their
socks and leaving the ball wet and heavy. Scoring a goal was
impossible because the velocity of a low strike died in the
snow. The boys resorted to wearing gloves and long johns
during the months of March and April when it was still truly
bitter out. Purcell was the only 'day boy' on the 1947 team and
he used to shudder with relief when he departed for the relative

comforts of home while his team-mates traipsed inside for another evening of lamentable food and icy dormitories.

Having been beaten by St Patrick's Armagh in the inaugural Hogan Cup final – the great Iggy Jones scored a record 3-4 that day – St Jarlath's were desperate for atonement the following season. That was one of the reasons why no allowance was made for the weather. Jones had left the Ulster College when the teams met in Croke Park on Sunday, 11 May. Purcell travelled with his team-mates in cars driven by the priests, and the team stayed in a hotel near Croke Park the night before the game. At that time, the students did not travel but were permitted to listen to a live broadcast of the game in the main hall in the college. The lack of goal practice did not impede upon the St Jarlath's team as they won a terrific game by 4-10 to 3-08. Purcell landed three late frees to finish what had been a ceaseless challenge from St Patrick's.

Asked about these scores as he sat in his living room, a black-and-white photograph of the Galway three-in-a-row team in front of him, Purcell got a bit embarrassed and shook his head and replied, 'Ah, I don't remember much about it. I may have. I don't remember. 'A week later, though, I got on the Galway junior team that was playing a game against Mayo. And they had this lad Henry Dixon, a big strong player who was just back from England. And Henry never gave me a kick of the ball the entire game. I will never forget it. And he was completely fair but it was just a whole new scene. I couldn't get near the ball, Hogan Cup or no Hogan Cup.'

Purcell did not see many of his 1947 classmates after he left the college.

'There was a culture then that when you got to fourteen, you left school and caught what was known as the ten past three – the train for Holyhead. The priorities and expectations we had of life were very different then. It was grim. I think I had it easy in comparison to the lads that were boarding. They spent a lot of that year hungry and cold and I heard stories that made me glad I was not inside the place at night-time. The place was football crazy then as well, but at the heart of it, football was a release, it was fun. There would have been many talented footballers who simply did not have the opportunity to play on after school. Vincent McHale, our captain, died a few weeks ago. Peter Solan is gone and Mick Flanagan. There aren't too many of us left. But they were good boys.'

There was to be no Hogan Cup for St Jarlath's college this year. The Senior A team were defeated by St Mary's in the Connacht semi-final. Nobody had any complaints. In late May, the school's first-year team played their final in Corofin, also against St Mary's, coached by the great Galway wingback, Sean Óg De Paor. St Jarlath's were ferociously strong and inside the first twenty minutes rattled home four goals against the city team. Before long, the score ceased to matter and the boys just played for the sake of playing. It was a bright day, one of those intensely summer lunchtimes that seem to precede the examination season, and teachers like Ray Silke, Galway's All-Ireland winning captain of 1998, and Tommy Davin stood on the grassy bank in shirt sleeves watching the match. Afterwards, the young St Jarlath's fans stormed the pitch, flags and banners raised as in the days of old. Conal presented the cup to the boys and posed for photographs. Hopes are high for this gang of boys. It is believed they can bring the thirteenth Hogan Cup title to Tuam.

Oliver had been expected at the ground as he was anxious to see the latest generation on the field. However, he was celebrating a wedding in the local church just across from the football field in Corofin. As the bus with the schoolboys pulled away from the ground, a white stretch limousine was parked outside the church, spotless and shining with darkened windows that reflected the outside world.

5

The Gaynors of
Kilruane

Camogie season awakens deep in the provinces, in small-town GAA fields with groaning turnstiles and stone walls for powder rooms. The defending All-Ireland champions Tipperary began this year's championship against Galway in Ballinasloe, and although the day was fine and the ground warmed by direct sunlight, the registration numbers of the cars parked outside the ground seemed the best way to identify the teams. There were no hamburger stands, no hawkers with flags or hair braids. There seemed nothing of the tremulous atmosphere of championship. Although it is a growing sport and makes a splash every September when finals lauded for flair and competitiveness are played out on live television in Croke Park, in reality camogie exists in the underworld. A dedicated fraternity follows camogie through the seasons and Ballinasloe was the place for the misanthropic fan of Gaelic games, with rows and rows of stone-cut benches sitting in glorious isolation. At a rough estimate, five hundred people watched Tipperary beat Galway by 4-11 to 1-11 in a game that was far closer than the scoreline implies.

'Five hundred?' queried Ciara Gaynor remembering the afternoon. 'Was there even that many?'

The Tipperary player has become familiar with the individual names and faces of those who have followed the county camogie team through her five seasons. It is a small, tight and knowledgeable group comprising mainly family, friends, former players and those who simply follow the game. Ciara's father sits among them for most games and this day in Ballinasloe was no exception. Len Gaynor is a name that rings sonorously through Tipperary hurling lore and, as her own star rose, Ciara had to deal with the perceptions of being her father's daughter. Like all the Gaynor children, she grew up vaguely aware that her dad had a past that was wrapped up in black-and-white film of classic hurling matches and in the gold standard of three All-Ireland medals that were never on prominent show in the house. They heard other people talk about his triumphs on hurling fields more than he ever spoke himself but by travelling with him during the seasons when he trained teams all over Tipperary, they learned of his love of the game and came to share it.

All the Gaynors could hurl but Ciara has been the one to reflect her father's excellence. Her ascension to the first rank of camogie players coincided with and contributed to Tipperary's evolution into the definitive force of modern camogie. At just twenty-five, Ciara Gaynor has played in five All-Ireland senior finals and won four medals. She is recognised as one of the most significant players of her generation. She is a defender, like her father. Back in 1999 – it seems almost misted in time now – she managed to distinguish her father in the crowd although there were 15,000 people in Croke Park that day, enough to make her knees tremble. Len remembers that for the closing minutes of that match – an old fashioned end-to-end epic that wrought screams of sheer terror from the stands – he had to relay the happenings on the field to his wife, Eileen, who had her head buried in her hands. He was surprised himself that day at how completely moved and overjoyed he was to see his daughter wearing the blue and gold jersey of his own youth and giving a brave and clean demonstration of centre-back play in Croke Park. When the final whistle went, he was overcome in a way that he never had been during the tumult of Tipperary's All-Ireland hurling seasons of 1965 and 1971. 'You go from match to match and year to year just wondering at it all,' he said of watching his daughter playing the sister sport of hurling.

When the whistle went to signal Tipperary's first ever All-Ireland win, Ciara separated herself from her celebrating team-mates and ran over to the stands to where her parents stood, and embraced them. The newspapers carried a picture of the moment the following day. 'Of course, his eyes were all watered-up,' she remembered. They recognise in each other a mutually hot temper and an unbending stubborn streak but, like most daughters, she charges her father with being a softie at heart. Len does not keep any footage of his own playing days and confesses that he would probably be appalled at himself if he watched them. Ciara has heard many times from neighbours and GAA men who would awkwardly describe to her a memory they have of her father during the heat and dust of a lost hurling summer. 'I know he was supposed to have been very fast and brave and tough,' she said.

Len appraised his daughter's game for a long moment before offering a comparison. 'To be very honest, I think she is better. She is more skilful that I was for sure. She has a different style, very comfortable and easy on the ball. Nothing ever rushed. I am sure she probably got one or two things from me all right. There wouldn't be much surrender in her anyhow. But she is a better hurler.'

For both Gaynors, hurling and camogie are about the pulse of competition and about winning but also about who they are as people. The pride and sense of achievement they take in winning All-Ireland medals is unspoken, not something that tends to come up often at the family dinner table. They share the trait of being deeply serious about their sport without taking themselves too seriously. Occasionally they row about something that might have happened on the camogie field but rarely for long and never lastingly. He is careful about offering advice, never wanting to sound heavy-handed or superior but his is still the first ear she seeks when she has doubts about the game. Although Len retired from inter-county hurling in 1974, he is still smitten by the occasional opportunity to puck a ball around in the back yard. When Ciara is at home, it is a common enough occurrence because her direction is frequently perfect and he can avoid jolting his old bones chasing under trailers or cowsheds. Kilruane is where the game started for the Gaynors and, now that the family has laid steadfast roots in and around the north Tipperary parish, it is where Len is happy to confine what remains of his energy for the game. He is chairman of Kilruane McDonagh's and father of a household that still, on special occasions, is liable to break into an impromptu game of hurling out the back. It is on those evenings that Len Gaynor considers how big a part chance plays in it all. And he thinks about that letter.

The most extravagant landmark in Kilruane is Lucky Bag's pub, a salmon-coloured building that has been the social focal point of the village for as long as anyone can recall. The Gaynor name has been associated with the parish for countless generations although Len's grandfather broke with tradition by moving to the Silvermines parish in the late nineteenth century. In 1899, Michael Gaynor was born, making him a perfectly ripe age for active duty in the War of Independence twenty years later. He fought through those barbaric years of burning and death, with the North Tipp Brigade, and once a freedom, of sorts, had been attained, he promptly fled the new country.

He spent some time in San Francisco before sailing on to Melbourne, where he met a local girl with a name that made him wistful: Eileen Murphy. They were not affluent but had attained a comfortable standard of living in the fashionable suburbs when the letter arrived. It was from Michael's grand-uncle Patrick, a bachelor who had kept the family farm in Kilruane. In careful hand, he invited his grandnephew back to claim the land and take over the property, allowing that he had reached the age where the responsibility had grown too much for him. The Gaynors had five children at this stage, and Eileen was accustomed to daily contact with her own family. Michael, equally, had become used to considering the place of his youth from the unfathomable distance of the southern hemisphere. It was on instinct rather than on sound reason that they made the decision to leave, telling themselves that they would return to Melbourne if the Irish farming life was not to their liking.

They were six weeks at sea. When they arrived in Kilruane, it was not to the palace of their dreams.

Eileen Gaynor was used to modernity. She travelled to the other side of the globe to find a house with an open hearth, no electricity and no running water, inhabited by a likeable but quiet man locked into a worldview that was completely alien to a young Australian woman. Many years later, she used to tell the story of buying a wet-battery radio shortly after arriving in Ireland just to create some cheer in the house. One afternoon when the children were at school and Michael was out righting the farm, it was just herself and Patrick in the room. Some love song of the day was filling the living room with a dreamy saxophonic melody.

'Isn't that a beautiful song, Patrick?' she asked.

'Ah, musha, Mam, I would rather hear an oul bullock bawling,' he replied.

Patrick lived just about long enough to see the farm he had tended all his life begin to thrive again. Whether its new occupants would stay or not was settled by the outbreak of World War II, which removed the option of crossing the ocean again. Len was born during wartime, along with the remaining two youngsters of the family. Eight children and the ceaseless demands of farm life diluted whatever allure Australia may still have held for the couple.

'I suppose my mother must have had a Melbourne accent but we never noticed it because she was just our mother; it was what we were used to. I was never conscious of this Australian background at all even though my older brothers had clear memories of living there. It just never came up. But what intrigued me at different times was that my mother used to receive these letters with all kinds of stamps and she would sit in the kitchen reading and be in floods of tears. It was obviously bad news from home but we were too young to fully grasp it and could never understand what this was about at all.'

Len remembers his childhood in Kilruane as Elysian. Because he was caught in the middle of a large family, he was probably spared the more heavy demands of domestic work. But he remembers the stamina and discipline of hand-milking cows, the rhythm of squeezing the udder long after his fingers had cramped up, like his brothers had shown him. There was always something going on either at the farm or in the village. Hurling was an everyday occurrence. They hurled in Matt Peter's field or on the roadside, tacking on strips of metal cut from shoe-polish tins in order to protect the heel of the crook – Len was ten before he received his first 'proper' hurl. The game had always been strong in the locality with a club called De Wett's, named after a Boer War general who had led a famous victory over the British, being the forerunner to Kilruane. When Len was learning the game in the early 1950s, competitions were organised and the magnetic radio commentaries of

Mícheál O'Hehir gave the game an omnipotent quality and filled their childish imaginations. When Michael Gaynor purchased the family's first car, a Ford Prefect, trips to the Gaelic grounds and Thurles were made relatively easy and so Len saw in the flesh the heroes of the airwaves: Tony Reddin, Christy Ring.

Len absorbed his earliest hurling lessons playing in evening games with his brother and other boys from the locality who took neither size nor age into the equation. It was clear that Len possessed ability that was beyond the average from an early age. His father accommodated Len's ambitions without ever explicitly encouraging them. When he was sixteen, he got the loan of the family car – a Beetle by this stage – to drive down for county minor trials in Borrisokane. He made the team but the day was ruined when the car spun in a puddle on the road and smashed into a pillar. He continued along the road, ignoring the unhealthy sounds coming from the engine and when he got home, he sought out his father in the yard.

'Put a bit of a dint in that car,' he admitted and then busied himself in the shed.

His father looked at him and walked off to inspect the damage.

'That's some bit of a dint,' he yelled. The car was beyond salvation. But he was still given the keys to attend training or games when there was nobody to drive him. After Len got selected for the Tipperary minor team, he remembers his father's complete surprise when he informed him he would be playing centre-back for the Munster final. 'That's a very responsible position,' he said and shook his head.

Michael Gaynor never saw his son playing for Tipperary. He had fallen out of the habit of attending the big summer games some years earlier and it was not in his nature to double back on that path because his son was playing. He was, like a lot of men of that generation, reserved and undemonstrative, although Len does not believe his personality was afflicted by his experiences during the Civil War years.

'He rarely spoke about it and I am sorry now we did not draw more out of him. Every now and again, one of his old comrades might arrive for a visit and, if they were having a glass of whiskey, it would come flooding out of him but we were too young to really take the most of it in. We know he was wounded in the shoulder during the Civil War and that he did time in prisons in Belfast and in Limerick. He was there the time Nenagh creamery was burned down and he spoke about that sometimes. But I think the break he made for Australia put some distance between him and that time. He wasn't bitter about it or anything and he had his pension and his medals. See, when he came back, he could start afresh and I just think he felt that the war was something that had happened, a closed chapter and was best not talked about.'

Neither was Len's hurling. Eileen Murphy went to all of Len's games even though she never fully grasped hurling. They left Michael at home listening to the radio. Generally he listened in silence. A neighbour told Len that one time when Mícheál O'Hehir's commentary went 'and Len Gaynor has the ball, he's running ten yards, he is running fifteen yards, he still has it', his father stood up in the kitchen and yelled, 'Would ya hit the bloody ball!'

It didn't bothered Len that his father never made the journey to see him play because he understood, intuitively, it was not out of a lack of pride or interest. It was just the way things were.

'I know he was delighted by whatever success came my way and that he felt proud. It was just never spoken about.'

Speech was superfluous then, even within the enclosures of Tipperary hurling. Len Gaynor broke into a storied senior team in 1964, a youngster among strong, opinionated men. He was his father's son and knew when to keep his mouth shut. The godfather of Tipp hurling then was Paddy Leahy, an austere, universally respected man whose word was gospel. Len often wondered why Leahy selected him above other promising youngsters of that time and attributes it to his attempts to join training one night despite having his arm wrapped in plaster of Paris. Leahy ejected him and thundered at him for being a fool but he probably recognised that the stunt wasn't for show, that Len was genuinely hoping to train despite having broken a bone.

A year later, he played wingback on the Tipperary team that won the All-Ireland but every outing was a lesson. In the final against Kilkenny, they were eleven points down at half-time. Gaynor headed back to the dressing room in mortal terror of what lay ahead. He expected all kinds of oaths and recriminations, an unholy row. But when he came into the room, he found a haven of peace. The day was dreadful and the Tipperary men took their seats and began wiping themselves down with old towels. Len was dumbfounded. For ten minutes a meditative calm prevailed and then Theo English sighed, stood up and said, 'Right lads, we'd better get down to business now and beat these fellas.'

That was precisely what happened. It taught Len a lesson for life and he never forgot the unspoken confidence – he recognised it much later on as the certitude of champions – that travelled through that room. Only in later life did he realise how rare it was and how privileged he had been to share in it.

There was a macho element to hurling then. Before that 1965 final began, he was assigned to mark Kilkenny's spell-binding forward, Eddie Keher. It was a significant responsibility for a new player but Paddy Leahy was convinced of Len Gaynor's mental strength and speed. As they were leaving the dressing room, a veteran Tipperary hurler grabbed him by the lapels and shoved him up against the wall.

'You're marking Keher out there today,' he said. 'You stop

him scoring and we will win. It doesn't matter if you don't touch the ball. Stop him and we will win.'

After that induction, the scale of Croke Park and the ceremony of the day held no fears. His emergence in the Tipperary team coincided with a fierce rivalry with Kilkenny. The period is often remembered for an incident in the 1967 final when Kilkenny's Tom Walsh lost an eye. Players from both teams were deeply affected by the incident but the games between the counties afterwards were characterised by diamond-hard exchanges.

'It was a different game. Lads weren't as fit and you could be sure your man would be a lot closer to you than is the case now. You had to be brave. That was the one thing at that time. If you showed any type of cowardice at all, you were gone. In everybody's eyes, even in your own family's eyes. It was the one thing you didn't do – you just couldn't show the white feather. And you didn't. There would have been the odd one that wouldn't have made it because they hadn't the bottle but not many. It wasn't awful dirty but it was hard. Lads were always jostling and sent flying but it wasn't that mean. Anything that was coming, you could see it coming. But players were able to protect themselves. It was a sign of a good hurler that he had his hurl in close, like a shield. Not that lads would try and take the head off you but, if you knew how to look after yourself, you could avoid the injuries.'

Len Gaynor was lucky. He has the usual facial scars to show for his decade of hurling in the furnace of the Munster championship but he never broke bones, something he attributes to his mother's faith in vitamin tablets and tonics years before they were in vogue. His working life was hectic then but there was never a question of missing training. After he married Eileen in 1968, he knows there were entire weekends that he seemed to spend either farming or travelling to and from Tipperary hurling meetings.

The couple have seven children but their first child died at birth. They had driven through the night to the Coombe hospital in Dublin because Eileen had started to experience difficulties.

Len waited outside the delivery room and early in the morning he was told the worst.

'They brought me in to see the baby. He was a perfect, beautiful little boy. I started crying and the doctor kind of hit me a rap on the chest and warned me not to let my wife see me in any state after all she had been through.'

They left in a daze, seeking solace back home in Tipperary, and it was only a few days later that they were informed that the burial had already taken place somewhere in Glasnevin Cemetery. Nobody could tell them precisely where. Len still finds it difficult to speak about that time. The reason he brought it up was because about a fortnight later the Tipperary selectors arrived at his door, ostensibly on a condolence call, but the conversation soon turned to hurling. The county was, inevitably, playing Kilkenny the following week and they were keen to have him back. It was important they said. Almost on automatic, Len Gaynor agreed to play. The only detail he carried off the field was of somehow getting his hurl to stop a 21-yard free towards the end, an intervention that turned the result in Tipperary's favour. The emotion of the game broke him and when he got back into the dressing room, all he could do was to bury his face in a towel before crying hard. The rest of the team would have been aware of the personal tragedy but either did not make the association or could not broach it at that moment.

'What's wrong with you?' he heard. 'Where did you get the belt?'

It was a different era: remorseless and stoic. The attitude was that you moved on.

'People did not understand at the time. Things like that were all bottled up. It was unhealthy but that was the mindset.'

But the Gaynors would not forget. For fifteen years they persisted with enquiries and, after years of paperwork and letters, they established where their child had been laid to rest. They called him Patrick and erected a gravestone and reclaimed him, and when Len Gaynor talks of his family, it seems natural and right to remember the couple's first-born. The joy of the other children helped to soothe that early grief and the Gaynor household evolved into a loud and boisterous, outdoorsy and happy place.

When Ciara was nine, like almost every child in the country, she used to pester her parents for a pony. Sometimes the request came on an hourly basis, sometimes more often. Every Saturday, they used to drive her over to the stables run by the parents of Eimear McDonnell, another future Tipperary camogie player.

Because the family had land, and one more animal wouldn't make much difference, they decided to get her a pony. Twinkle. In two years, Ciara had outgrown it and one afternoon Len took her to see about getting a bigger horse.

'We bought him near Dromineer about five miles from home,' Ciara remembered. 'We had no trailer or anything like that so I was insisting that I would ride him home. Even in the stables, the harness was a bit loose and Dad told me he could see me falling and falling the whole time. He was a bit difficult but I fell in love with him straight away, I don't know why. But that day I wasn't strong enough for him and he kept turning back on the road going home. So Dad had to come over and he was wearing these big top boots that were way too big for the stirrups. He got on the horse and went tearing off up the road. So I was left to drive the car – this was just a little back road. I was crawling along and he had warned me that every time I met a car, I was to pull into the side of the road and turn off the ignition, like I was just a passenger waiting. I think it took us about four hours to get home that evening.'

She was tomboyish, a trait she claims has stayed with her in adulthood. Much as her father had done, she learned how to hurl a ball playing with older brothers and sisters and around the fields in Kilruane. Camogie was just gaining prominence when she began to get interested in competitive sports but she played a couple of seasons on the Kilruane under-twelve and under-fourteen hurling teams, the only girl among boys. That fact did not trouble her in the slightest; it was the boys from opposing teams who were bothered, initially by their reluctance to play tough on a girl and then by the realisation that even when they did they were getting skinned anyhow. On one occasion, a boy from the other team was keeping a conspicuous distance between himself and Ciara and was soon being pressured with calls, 'mark yer man, mark yer man.'

'The poor lad didn't know what to do. I suppose he felt awkward or whatever and Ciara was just exploiting the space – she was in the forwards and was cleaning up,' Len said.

An uncle of Len's was watching the game behind one of the goals. When he heard the calls to mark the roaming Kilruane man, he turned and growled, 'That's no man, that's a girl that's beatin' yez.'

When Len had the time to hurl about the field with the children, he probably noticed quite early on that Ciara definitely had the ineffable something. They could all strike a ball and both David and Lenny were fine hurlers at under-age and senior level. Ciara had a full complement of gifts though – a good eye, steady hands and she could strike the ball smoothly off either side. He never dreamed of her going on to represent the county and was not inclined to push any of the children in that direction. Although he remained deeply committed to the game, he never preached about it to the children. It was something to be enjoyed. When Ciara's aptitude was reflected in the local newspaper notices and her selection onto the minor team, no one made too much of it.

'Ciara took it in her stride. She was happy and we were delighted for her but we never made too much or little of anything or anyone in the family. Like, when she was a child, there would be a lot more made of her not eating her dinner than of something she might have done on the camogie field earlier on in the day.'

Len always had an interest in coaching. He trained the Tipperary minors in 1973, roaming the sidelines for the curtain-raiser of that year's Munster final and then returning as a player for a game that was immortalised by Richie Bennis's late free that gave Limerick their first provincial championship since 1955. Throughout the 1970s and 1980s, he built a successful career managing at club and county level and got into the habit of taking his children with him to grounds across Tipperary and Clare. Because of that, Ciara had a hurl in her hands almost every day.

'We loved it,' she said. 'Like, you got to hit around on the sidelines at training and we got to know the players. And I suppose it taught us what Dad knew about the game and showed us a side that wouldn't come out at home. Before some of the club games, we would have our heads glued to the dressing room door trying to hear what he would be saying to the teams. And you would pick up tips, definitely.'

When Ciara was seven, Len was manager of the Kilruane team that reached the All-Ireland senior club final. The club had been consistently strong in the 1970s but was considered to be in decline when it swept Munster out of the blue, with a great tussle against Blackrock of Cork in the decider. The All-Ireland final was against Buffers Alley of Wexford in Croke Park and it was that period that gave Ciara Gaynor her first taste of the possibilities and scale of the sporting world her father was involved in.

'I can't say I remember much about the game, it was more a constant feeling of excitement around that time. There was a special train laid on for supporters going up and I suppose when you are seven, just heading off on a train when it is still dark is exciting enough. But because it was full of Kilruane people, it felt as if it was actually our train. And then the novelty of being in Dublin – O'Connell Street, and I am sure we went to McDonald's – all made an impression. Then the team won so there seemed to be no end to the fun because the celebrations back in Kilruane were like nothing we had ever seen. I just remember bits of it – bonfires and people cheering but it all seemed very magical.'

She followed him during the periods when he trained the Clare senior team and later his native Tipperary. He had various spells in charge of his native county. After the 1971 team's All-Ireland triumph, the winning just stopped. Tipperary had gone from 1916 to 1925 without a Munster title but other than that the honours had come thick and fast. But then came a crisis that began in 1971 and only ended in 1987. That era was characterised by nerve-ridden decision-making: management teams were selected and dumped at alarming speed so there was rarely any continuity in the system, a flaw that made it impossible to instil faith in the players. For a county accustomed to success – Tipperary had won twenty-two All-Ireland titles up to this point – the situation was deeply harrowing. Len cannot recall off-hand his precise periods in charge of the county because it felt like musical chairs. What he does know is that the criticism was precise and venomous during that time. When he managed Clare in the 1990s, his team came up against his native county in the championship. Clare, of course, won and a few days later a man came up to Len Gaynor on the street and called him a traitor. After all his years playing and coaching in the county, the remark was like a knife wound. In the years when he was with Tipperary, the sports pages of the local newspapers were heavy on analysis and unforgiving of disappointing results. There were days when it got to Gaynor, but at home, he never made much of it.

'I suppose the children would have heard the odd thing said and probably saw the papers the odd time but I don't think they ever saw it bothering me.'

He was at the helm for the 1984 Munster final that was lost to Cork and in 1997 when Tipperary lost the Munster final to Clare by a single goal. The counties met again in that year's All-Ireland final after Tipperary qualified through the novel 'backdoor' system but lost out to Clare in a thriller that finished 2-13 to 0-20. Some of the guys he had coached years earlier in Clare left the field victorious that day – the captain Anthony Daly had broken through to the Clare team under Gaynor. Len was fond of him before that match and remained so afterwards. When everything was said and done, sport was about honour and being able to look someone in the eye. He was disappointed but never bitter and his commitment, the hours of driving and talking on the phone and worrying about players, was reaching a full stop. By then, Ciara's potential as a camogie player had become apparent and what she achieved at the end of the 1990s was like a tonic after the extremes of hurling management. Through her, Len learned what he never had time to consider before: the joys of simply being a spectator.

The Ballinasloe game held mixed fortunes for Ciara. The team won easily but, for the first time in her career, she was sent off in the last minute after receiving a second yellow card. Galway had a free about 25 yards out and she positioned herself to meet the trajectory of the ball if it was hit low. The shot came like a bullet and walloped off her; she swung to clear and got tangled up with the Galway girl; in frustration, she pushed away. It was a tough enough dismissal but Ciara Gaynor was more annoyed at herself than anything. She was down on her own form, although throughout the second half she had been in comfortable control of her sector, sweeping up the ball and delivering three strikes downfield that yielded the scores which broke the game open. Afterwards, she left the ground fairly rapidly, the incident still gnawing at her but, like her father, she does not dwell on the negative and was able to laugh at herself a few days afterwards.

She was disappointed in the way she reacted. So was Len – although from where he was seated he had not seen how the ball had rapped against her just after the free was taken. They both knew the situation was avoidable and Len didn't chide her about it; she is a senior player now and is adept at criticising herself when the need arises.

When she was at school in St Mary's in Nenagh, camogie was simple and glorious.

She was with a bunch that were talented at the game and they created a bit of a stir locally, featuring in *The Nenagh Guardian* regularly and generally ascending to the ranks of queen bees in the playground. She always had her heart set on studying veterinary medicine but fell short in the points and against her better judgement opted to pursue it through a course in Carlow. From the beginning, she was miserable there, disillusioned with the course and not all that enamoured with the repetition of college life.

'I went back one weekend after being home and I remember not being able to find my purse. I was totally down on myself and I had bills to pay off something and I searched high and low for this purse for the entire day. I knew I hadn't left it at home but I rang anyhow and Dad was there and he must have kind of figured I wasn't myself and asked me what was wrong. And I got upset and just said that I hated it there and he said, "Come home, just leave it." Mum and Dad were always great like that – they never pressured us into doing anything. I went home and thought about what I wanted to do.'

The following autumn, she began training for the Garda Síochána in Templemore. It was perfect because it was only a short drive to the field at Thurles, but after graduating, she was stationed in Sundrive Road in Crumlin. For a country girl and a camogie player in a station full of Dublin lads whose interest in the GAA began and ended on Hill 16, it made for a stark change of circumstance. She travelled from the city for training in Thurles every Tuesday and Thursday evening and again on Saturday mornings. If she had been working nights, she would often clock out at six in the morning and drive straight down the road. Her team-mates would arrive to find her sleeping in the back seat of the car and used to leave her for as long as possible. The old stories about GAA players using the garda life to roll off to training on the permission of a conspiratorial wink from the Super were unfounded.

'Maybe it used to be like that. But I used to take leave for training. It was the only way to make it. Everybody in Sundrive was really supportive of the demands or whatever and they would pretend, anyhow, to be interested, but there were no special favours.'

Her three years in Dublin were the most difficult in terms of camogie. The station was fairly busy and there were times when she turned up for Tipperary sessions physically drained. The fact that their championship experiences were so rich eased the hardship. But she often considered the dedication of the more senior players like Deirdre Hughes and wondered at their perseverance through the years when Tipperary was winning nothing. After three years, she got transferred to the Castleconnell Station in Limerick. Nenagh has become home. Although she missed her colleagues in Dublin, her sporting life was instantly less of a strain. Working as a garda still means shift work, however. It doesn't invite the healthiest of lifestyles. Sometimes dinner hour arrives at two in the morning, other times not at all. During April and May she often feels her fitness

St Laurence O'Toole's girls' NS football team, winners of the Cumann na mBunscol division 3 title, Croke Park, 2002.

Courtesy of St Laurence O'Toole's GNS, Dublin

St Jarlath's first-year team, 2004.

Paddy Downey, former Gaelic games correspondent for
The Irish Times.
Courtesy of Paddy Downey

William Rock, the Custodian of the Ball in Croke Park
for many decades.
Courtesy of Joe Rock

Crossabeg-Ballymurn senior hurling team, 1992.
Courtesy of Crossabeg-Ballymurn GAA Club

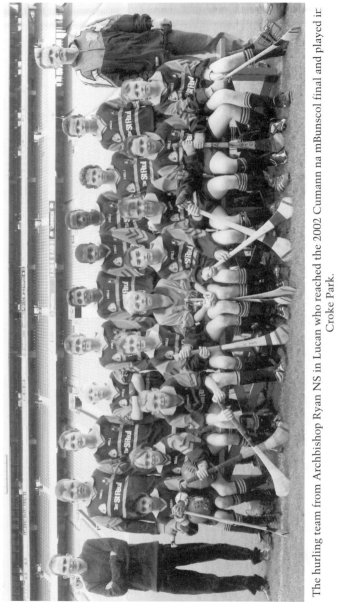

The hurling team from Archbishop Ryan NS in Lucan who reached the 2002 Cumann na mBunscol final and played in Croke Park.

Courtesy of Archbishop Ryan NS, Lucan

Christy Ring and Louis Marcus during a break in filming in 1960.
Courtesy of Louis Marcus

Len and Ciara Gaynor celebrate Tipperary's victory over Cork in the
All-Ireland camogie final, Croke Park.

Courtesy of Sportsfile

Donegal manager, Brian McEniff, after winning the 2003 All-Ireland
senior football quarter-final replay against Galway.

Courtesy of Sportsfile

Leslie McGettigan, New York manager, speaks to his players during the Connacht senior football championship 2003 in Gaelic Park.
Courtesy of Sportsfile

Frank McGuigan playing for Tyrone in 1984.
Courtesy of Sportsfile

is poor in comparison to the other Tipperary girls and begins to punish herself accordingly. She is conscious of the short lifespan that holds true for most camogie players: last season, Tipperary introduced a fourteen-year-old, Claire Grogan. The sport mirrors the trends in football and hurling but to a more extreme degree. The instances of epic careers are growing increasingly rare. Because Tipperary have had such a rich run of success, it has been easy for girls to persevere with it.

'I know it's probably not politically correct to say so but it is probably generally true that physiologically it is harder for girls to keep playing as long as fellas do anyhow. Particularly after children come along. But it has been great in Tipperary – only Maeve Stokes, who was one of the players I looked up to coming into the team, has retired in my time. It is easier when you are winning. And it is a weird thing but every girl on that team seems to get on with each other. We are such friends at this stage.'

When Ciara started out, any questions she was asked for radio or television interviews invariably related to her father. It took a while for her talent to be viewed in a self-contained light. She never minded anyway: it was all promotion for camogie.

She knows a fair few of the Tipperary hurlers – Mark O'Leary, who scored 2-1 in the All-Ireland final that the county won in 2001 – is from Kilruane. When they chat, she sometimes marvels at the constant spotlight they live under. Small remarks and even looks can communicate the fact that everything you do gets noticed. The price for the excitement and honour of playing on shimmering days in crowded sports theatres is that you come to feel like public property. The camogie scene is private in comparison to the vast numbers of people that Tipperary hurling games attract but, even so, the profile is rising. One night last winter, Ciara went into an off-licence in Nenagh to buy a bottle of wine. It was post-season;

the only sport she was engaged in was fox-hunting. She never apologises for enjoying the winter – it can be wet and cold on the beat in Castleconnell but it is also an opportunity for late-night meals without any guilt and Friday nights in the pub.

'This what the Tipperary camogie players are at now?' enquired the vendor as he wrapped the wine in a brown paper bag. 'Wouldn't say the Cork wans are at that, now.'

Ciara battled to release a pressure valve on the famous Gaynor temper. She strode off into the night and the wine didn't last all that long. But it is a small price. Len always says that playing for the county is an honour. When he got his first games for Tipperary in the 1965 league season, these unsigned letters began arriving from New York. They were addressed to: Mr Len Gaynor, The Greatest Hurler Ever, Thurles, County Tipperary. Len lived thirty miles from Thurles but the postman knew the intended recipient. They were always short and contained, in faltering pen, words of praise and advice. Sometimes a two-dollar bill was enclosed. There was never a return address or a signature. Len felt privileged and a bit sad about them. Months later, after he had plucked up the courage to venture some conversation in the dressing room, he mentioned the letters to one of the senior lads. 'From yer man in New York,' his team-mate said with a nod. 'Sure we all get them. Have been for years.'

When the team were invited to tour the American city in 1971, he often saw an elderly man at the functions organised by the American county board. He was none too wealthy looking, and Len and some of the other players figured he was their writer. But he never approached them and they didn't like to ask. Some years after that, the messages just stopped.

Hurling was good to Len. He saw both coasts of America and played in Wembley stadium. He hurled with and against his idols and met many men he considers friends although he meets his former team-mates now only if they bump into one another in the crowd at games. When Eddie Keher began to write books on hurling, he called down to Kilruane to interview his former marker and confirmed himself the immaculate gentleman that Len Gaynor always credited him as being. They remain close.

Len's own inter-county career ended abruptly. One October morning, he was reading the local newspaper and noticed that his name was not included in a list of panel members for the first Tipperary training session. He called one of the selectors on the assumption that it was a mistake.

'Ah, no, actually. You are gone.'

The previous year, he had gashed his hand badly on the farm and was out for about a month. He came back to the game too early and played terribly in his first match and that probably mitigated against him. But they would never have even bothered telling him that he was considered past it had he not made the phone call himself.

'That was the way then,' Len shrugs. 'There was no mercy. But I had a lot of hurling behind me.'

He hopes and believes that Ciara's departure will be the opposite: self-determined and gradual. But they are both keenly aware that the seasons aren't endless.

'I remember Deirdre Hughes saying back in 1998 when a few younger girls came in not to expect anything easy,' Ciara says. 'Maybe we were showing signs of cockiness and were just expecting to win. I feel really lucky to have come into this team when I did. Like, every single one of those All-Irelands was special to me. I don't think anything will ever compare to the few seconds when we heard the final whistle after the first one. The thing is that every year feels like it is getting shorter now and I can't believe we are back into the championship again.'

Len's workload on the farm has become lighter over the years. Sometimes the main bane of his life is the club where it all began, Kilruane McDonagh's. He does not have a chairman's soul: too much mediating and pen-pushing to be done. Last year, the club cost €53,000 to run, an absurd figure for a club just about surviving on the senior scale. There is a good under-age structure in the locality and, in the long term, with new families moving into the parish, things look bright. But he finds himself worrying about the senior team, sometimes lying sleepless for half the night.

'You often hear people say that in the Fifties and Sixties hurling was all we had. The thing is, that was true. The effort it takes to keep it going in strongholds like Tipperary now is unbelievable. And if it drops one iota, it will be gone. Because people have so many choices now. And hurling is an expensive game and you can get knocks in it you mightn't get in other games. You need to give a lot of time to hurling too. You do. Unless you are at it before you are ten, you are done for. For the likes of me as an administrator now, to provide that facility is a big task. Kids expect a certain level of organisation and standard now or they won't turn up. And they are right. For years, we were all happy to swan along expecting hurling to do fine because that was always the way. It's only lately we have woken up to ourselves. Like, they are talking about spreading hurling. That would be a great thing. But I think at the minute we will do well to keep it going in the strong counties.'

Travelling to the All-Ireland hurling championship games and watching Ciara playing with Tipperary is, for Len a means of getting away from the bread and butter of club existence. This is the centenary year of the Camogie Association so the championship is of added significance. Len and Eileen will travel to all the games, proud parents like all the others.

'You never get used to it. It is an incredible thing for us. I think even if I had never played, it would mean a lot.'

Ciara's brothers and sisters dip in and out of her championship season when time permits. They all have busy lives.

'The most you would get from the brothers is, "from the start", or "first ball". Nothing major. But they mean well,' she says.

Now that she is secure in her game, now that she has accumulated the top honours many times over, Len feels that enough distance has passed for them to discuss her game. Often he finds he has no advice to offer.

'I would still wonder why she did this or that during a game. We would have chats about it, just the two of us. But generally, I suppose I am happy with her philosophy towards the game.'

Ciara remembers an evening years ago, when the whole clan was out in the yard, their father stopping to tell them of a match he played late on in his career, maybe at junior level, for the club. He was in at full-forward and a high ball came in. He made to catch it as the goalkeeper came out and then let his hand ghost away at the last second so the ball passed by everyone unseen and into the net. It was just a trick and he was telling it for laughs but it was also a tip. Those were the little ways he imparted what he had known about the game.

Nenagh is an ideal distance from Kilruane. Ciara still keeps a horse at home and teases her father that he has become her *chef d'équipe*. Her brothers Lenny and Brian aren't fond of horses so it is often Len who tends to Joey's feeding and cleaning out the stables. It is a fair trade. Even when Ciara was a teenager, her parents trusted her with the running of the farm so they could get away for a weekend break the odd time.

On championship weekends, she loves just roaming about the house or heading across the fields, clearing her mind by taking in the familiar. It is pretty much the same countryside that awaited her grandparents when they returned in 1939. Officially, they have left the house but because all the children have settled locally, the home place is rarely empty for long. There is no such thing as the quiet life.

Len Gaynor looks back on his hurling life with quiet satisfaction.

'What I feel is that it is a tremendous honour to have played hurling for the county. It is a privileged thing, I believe that and I think that it demands a certain level of behaviour. But at the same time, I feel I am no different, no better or worse than hundreds of lads that played for Tipperary over the years. It is nice talking about hurling and the people in the game. It is nice to tell your story. But sometimes you wonder have you a story to tell at all.'

Ciara just wants to keep on playing. There is no better feeling than being lost in a game. There are days out on the playing pitch when she is instilled with the feeling that she understands exactly what makes her father tick.

'The Gaynors are the kind of people – well, we have our moments like all families. But we would be the kind that would always be there when it matters.'

6

They Came From Far and Wide to See Him Play

Christy Ring died twenty-five years ago. On the anniversary of his death, on 2 March, his family gathered for a private Mass and commemoration in Cloyne, where the Cork man was raised and is buried. Since his sudden passing – on a humdrum Friday afternoon when he was walking past the School of Commerce in Cork city – the Ring family has been stoical and dignified in the remembrance of their most public and adored member. Christy Ring is lauded as perhaps the greatest hurler of the twentieth century, by hard, shrewd hurling judges who often felt blessed to share in Ring's thrilling and incomparable union with the ancient game. Ring was – is – like a god to those many men and women whose honeyed years coincided with his own. The longevity and brilliance of his hurling life were enough to separate Ring from the great contemporaries who both loathed and revered him. But those who know insist that it was the grace of the man as well as his deeds on the field that distinguished him. Although Mick Mackey of Limerick also has considerable support as the greatest ever to play, it is generally accepted that Ring the hurler was unique and untouchable. But he was also a father and a husband and a brother and that is how he is remembered – in still and uninterrupted grace – twenty-five years after all of Cork, in tearful and broken disbelief, allowed the legend to end all others to take his leave.

A few days before Christmas last year, I met Paddy O'Sullivan at the memorial for Ring in Cloyne. Not from a hurling county and six years old when Christy died, I wanted to try to know more about a man whose name has become a metaphor for incomparable hurling achievement but whose vivacity and colour and style have become less fathomable over the ages. There is very little of Ring to study. There are newspaper reports that cover his great games over three decades – he played for so long that it must once have felt as if the passing of time could not violate Ring. There is a short and splendid film made by Louis Marcus in 1960. Val Dorgan, the celebrated *Cork Examiner* journalist and a Glen Rovers' teammate of Ring, wrote a book about his friend in 1980. The Ring family was not happy about that at the time; Paddy Downey of *The Irish Times* had been chosen to write Ring's official story. Compelled by reasons of his own, Dorgan pressed ahead and produced a quirky and impressionistic but deeply fond and respectful portrayal of Ring. The very first paragraph – perhaps one of the apocryphal tales that have blossomed about Ring – is among the most moving.

'Christy Ring was a lone figure on the field in Croke Park, deserted by the crowds after the 1978 All-Ireland final. In the fading light of the September evening he searched about with little confidence for a presentation watch which fell from his wrist when, as a selector, he rushed out to greet the Cork team that had beaten Kilkenny in the All-Ireland final. The watch was given to him for twenty-five year's service with Irish Shell and he had worn it for the first time that weekend. He told nobody at the time about his loss, and never did find the watch. It was the last time he walked Croke Park, on which he had won eighteen Railway Cup medals and eight All-Irelands. He died on 2 March, 1979, aged fifty-eight.'

It seems somehow apt, the ageing Ring searching in the shadows for something irretrievable on the very playing field where his brightness could not be dimmed. Anyone who has ever been fortunate enough to stand alone on the field in Croke Park on an evening after the crowd has gone knows how haunting the place is when empty.

Paddy O'Sullivan arrives at the appointed time. An uncle of the present Cork full back, Diarmuid O'Sullivan, Paddy is hewn from the same fearsome combination of flesh and granite. Some kids are playing a football game in the shadow of the elevated cast-iron portrait of Ring – based on a photograph where he leads the Cork team in parade – in front of the gateway to the pitch in Cloyne. Paddy clears the boys with a shout and boots the ball into the field behind. The kids slink off and Paddy throws his eyes to the heavens. It is a scene he has been through before. A little square was built around the memorial, with benches where people can sit and rest. The memorial is placed at the exact site of the house in which Ring, born on 12 October 1920, spent his boyhood. The street was called Spital Lane, its residents known as Spit Laners, and today it is just a couple of minutes' walk from where Willie John Ring, Christy's only surviving brother, lives with his wife on St Colman's Terrace.

'We are in the right house, now,' Paddy says, smiling when he greets Willie John, who shows us into the sitting room where Ring used to call to talk with his brother at weekends. Ring's presence is in the living room yet, with a framed photograph of a Cloyne championship team dating back to

1939 and in Willie John's own features – pleasant, blue-eyed and fiercely discerning. Although he has spoken rarely about his brother's feats, he has a perfect recall of those twenty-four seasons of hurling and the fifty-eight years of living. What I want to know is if Willie John believes that Ring is remembered as he might be now that the music has long stopped and the game of hurling adapts to the vicissitudes of the new millennium, when nothing or nobody seems sacred.

'I think so. I think so,' he replies after thinking for a time. 'He is still mentioned even though many of the best men are gone. I met Ned Power there at the last county final and he said to me one thing – you would want to play against him to know how good he was.'

On the table in the living room, Willie John has laid several documents and images of his brother. There is a photograph of a smiling Ring about to depart for America, a postcard of the memorial where the pared silhouette of his likeness is cast against a blue sky, and a plain photocopied list of Christy Ring's playing record. This catalogue, Willie John says, is the proof. This is the legacy.

'When we were growing up in Cloyne, we played every evening but we had no pitch at the time. Christy was very competitive growing up, the same on the street here as in an All-Ireland. If a man struck him, accidentally, well he forgot it. Because he did not think you could carry that into a game. And hurling was tough at that time. He was able to look after himself. The lads of today – and I am not condemning them – but I don't think they would last for eighteen Railway Cups. Christy played in Railway Cups with lads who were not born when he started. He loved it. He believed in fitness through hurling, hurling, hurling. I remember one Saturday we were sitting above in our sister's house and there was a priest coming through with a mini-bus of young fellas. Cork had played Tipp a few weeks before and Christy had got some belts, like.

'Anyhow, they brought Christy out to shake hands and the priest said, "Well, they got Christy, but weren't they dirty?"

' "I see nothing wrong with them, Father," Christy said.

' "Ah, now Christy, you couldn't call them gentlemen," the priest said.

' "I tell you one thing, Father," he said. "Gentlemen don't win All-Irelands."'

Willie John is laughing at the story and then stops suddenly and says: 'Another thing the priest asked him: "When will you ever think of giving it up?"

' "That's a very simple question, Father," says Christy. "When I think I know all about it."'

The depth of Ring's respect for hurling appears to have been immeasurable.

The US historian Shelby Foote once remarked that the Civil War general Nathan Forrest was born to be a general as surely as John Keats was born to be a poet. So it seems to have been with Ring and hurling. His immersion in the game was so natural and selfless that it is impossible to imagine his having existed away from it.

He played the game at the highest levels as long as his body would physically permit, declining an entreaty from his club-mates at Glen Rovers to play in the 1967 Cork county final against St Finbarr's. By then he had undergone the metamorphosis from the classically handsome teenager – blond, intense, elusive – who burst upon the Munster hurling scene just as the lights went out all over Europe, to the stocky and more familiar incarnation with receding hair and sleeves rolled high on ferociously powerful forearms. In all those years, he never lost the lightness or the grace although his mature bulk safeguarded him in the more ruthless attentions that his gifts warranted from opposing defences. The glories came almost immediately, with All-Ireland medals in 1941, 1942, 1943, 1944, 1946, 1952, 1953, and 1954. From 1942 to 1963, he failed to win a Railway Cup medal only three times. And through those bountiful years for Cork hurling, Ring's magnetism and genius were a show within the show. He had a reserve of charisma that binds the handful of true sporting virtuosos, creating the sensation that when he was in the theatre of play, anything might happen. Some of his more startling moments, never captured on film, have been celebrated and retold by generations too young to witness them.

There was the goal in the 1946 All-Ireland final when Ring, with black and amber jerseys closing in on him, embarked on a solo run some seventy yards out from the Kilkenny goal. The noise in the stadium rose in tandem with Ring's easeful acceleration, as it became clear that he was not about to content himself with a point. The exultant finish was both economic and lavish – a balletic sidestep through Kilkenny's flailing cover and then the calm, effortless stroke beyond the helpless goalkeeper.

It is said that the applause in the stadium at that moment was general. Two years earlier, Ring had broken Limerick in the Munster final replay with another wonder goal from nothing and some ten years on, in the 1956 provincial showpiece, he again destroyed logic and Limerick with three goals and a point in the last five minutes of the match. The fifty-five minutes during which Donal Broderick, his luckless marker, had frustrated him, went up in smoke. There was to be no All-Ireland for Ring that or any subsequent year as Wexford denied Cork and Ring what would even today have been an unrivalled ninth medal. Yet his legend was further embellished by the melodrama of that September day. The 1956 All-Ireland final is celebrated for Art Foley's famous save on Ring three minutes from time. Cork were two points down and Ring, brooding and quiet for a good deal of the afternoon, ghosted away from Bobby Rackard, took possession on the opposite wing, turned infield and suddenly and electrifyingly had the fate of yet another season in his grasp. Although Foley's save was originally declared miraculous, there has since been some revision on its technical difficulty, an acknowledgement that Ring was impaired from striking the ball with his customary unstoppable velocity. But it almost certainly won the final for Wexford.

Just after Foley repelled the shot, Ring's momentum carried him through and he descended upon the goalkeeper in a manner that appeared to be aggressive. Then, out of the blue, he shook Foley's hand.

'It was a very unusual thing, particularly for such a competitor as Ring,' remembers Paddy Downey, who was as enthralled as everybody else in Croke Park that afternoon.

'Art told me many years later that Ring said, "You so and so, you will win it now."'

The gesture moved the Wexford team and afterwards Nick O'Donnell and Bobby Rackard took the unprecedented step of carrying the defeated Cork man on their shoulders. Downey remembers it as the most astonishing and magnanimous act of sportsmanship he ever witnessed.

'They did not carry him right around the ground or anything because the crowd had come onto the pitch but it was the most incredible sight to see.'

Some minutes later, O'Donnell paid a final, memorable tribute to Ring, planting a kiss on the Cork man's cheek, a remarkable show of affection among a taciturn generation of men. Funny, for all the great and brave moments that Ring enjoyed on a field and that were never filmed, there is a famous photograph of this tender, fleeting post-match moment. Fans have gathered around Ring and it is clear that O'Donnell has just stepped into the frame and surprised the Cork man with this firm and sudden kiss. Ring evidently had no time to react in astonishment or otherwise. At the instant the photograph was taken, his eyes are closed and he looks tired.

Although he hurled on for Cork for another seven years, the ninth All-Ireland medal eluded him just as the first eight had fallen at his feet. An unforgettable tribute that Paddy Downey wrote of Ring a week after his death contains the passage: 'Curiously, I remember most clearly of all the day in 1963 which marked the end of his inter-county career. It was a day of June sunshine and Cork were playing Clare in the Munster championship at Thurles. As we waited for the teams to appear the word came to the press box on the sideline that Ring was off the Cork team. Within minutes you could sense that the news of his absence was spreading through the crowd and the low murmur all round seemed like one voice uttering disappointment. And as we stood for the anthem with the light wind billowing the flag against the white clouds and blue sky, I knew by some instinctive foresight that Christy Ring would not again be seen wearing the red jersey of Cork in a championship game in Thurles or in any other ground.'

The premonition was correct. Ring did not play that day because of the tragic passing of his infant son, Nicholas. Although he was forty-three, there were botched attempts by the Cork selectors to deliberate upon his services for the 1964 championship, and when Tipperary's John Doyle equalled Ring's record of eight All-Ireland medals in 1965, there was further talk of an encore for the 1966 championship. Val Dorgan was among the most vociferous of supporters for the return of Ring in his pieces for the *Examiner* and eventually the selectors named Ring as a substitute on the team to play Waterford in the Munster final. Ring declined the invitation through a letter he dropped through the door of the Cork county board. He was still giving testimony to the health of his hurling abilities with displays of periodic luminosity for Glen Rovers. It was in memory of one such afternoon that Paddy Downey chose to end his tribute to Ring many years later.

'There was an epilogue still to come. I saw his last big game for Glen Rovers outside the boundaries of County Cork. It was the Munster club final – against Mount Sion of Waterford, played in Limerick on Easter Sunday, appropriately the fiftieth anniversary of the Glen's foundation. Even then with pace failing at the age of forty-six, he was still a thunderbolt. He revealed his age only when the spurt to the ball was more than ten yards. Otherwise, he went through the whole gamut of his skills; the dazzling stickwork, the lightning stroke, the dainty pass and he scored a goal and a point.'

There seems little doubt that he was still good enough in that shimmering summer of 1966 – in the *Irish Times* report of that final, Downey believed that Ring demonstrated 'all the artistry that would not have surprised us twenty years ago ... he is still far and away the best forward in Cork.'

Be that as it may, the power brokers of Cork hurling never did call upon Ring again. There would be no ninth.

It was Paddy Tyers who persuaded Ring to commit his skills to celluloid. Tyers, who hurled for Waterford and had kept goal for the Cork footballers, was working in the Gael Linn office on Patrick Street across the road from where Ring was living at the time. A series of instructive films on Gaelic football had already been commissioned and filmed, featuring contemporary greats like Kevin Heffernan, Frank Stockwell and Sean Purcell. Tyers, charming and easy-going, convinced the reticent hurler of the potential of the film and he agreed to watch the football films.

'He offered a few funny remarks about the technique that was shown,' remembers the director Louis Marcus. 'But he was immediately alive to the possibilities that the project held for both himself and the game.'

Marcus was only twenty-five then and one of only three film-makers in the country. He possesses some wonderful photographs of the filming in progress. Marcus is wearing a duffel coat and heavy-rimmed glasses and looks like a figure from the New Wave of French cinema. Standing beside the camera is Ring, striped white socks pulled up to the knee, the sleeves on his jersey rolled as if he has just been transported from some distant and timeless supernova afternoon on the field in Thurles or Croke Park. It is reminiscent of the scene in the corny baseball romance *Field of Dreams*, where a vision of Shoeless Joe Jackson appears among a group of dreamers desperately trying to escape the smallness of their own epoch.

Today, Marcus lives in Dublin and remembers the experience of filming Ring as one of the most valuable of his working life. Once Ring warmed to the task, he talked flowingly and hypnotically about hurling. Sitting on a desk in Tyers' office, he began to instruct Marcus on the theory of the 21-yard pointed free. Control was everything, he explained, not speed. He rolled a sheet of paper tightly in his wrist and asked the men if they wanted to throw the ball into the wastepaper basket, would they fire it hard or lob it gently in?

Ring was interested in Marcus's role as the film director but believed that in order to understand fully the repertoire of strokes, he would have to master them. So the young film-maker got a series of lessons on lifting the ball, on checking the ball from the ground, on checking the ball in the air, even on doubling on the ball in the air. Ring's one concession was to allow the film-maker to retain the grip he used playing golf. He believed that altering the grip at that stage in Marcus's life would be more of a hindrance. Then he gave the lesson.

'I was surprised and thrilled in a way. But worried too – because if I had failed, what would happen the film? But after fifteen minutes at the most, I was carrying out each stroke. He let me off the sideline cut because he felt that would be too difficult for me. I suppose I was self-conscious at first but you lose that because Christy was so intent on the game. This was the greatest player of his day and probably ever but, you know, I think he regarded himself as a servant of hurling. The last skill we practised was doubling on the ball in the air and that took time. But I remember I jumped as he instructed and the ball came in, and Christy, standing near the goal post said, "He has it this time, Paddy." And sure enough, I struck it cleanly. He saw it before I knew it.'

They filmed Christy at the Mardyke in Cork over a bitterly cold winter that sometimes yielded snowfalls. Watching the black-and-white film that he made those forty years ago brings Marcus back and he anticipates the variety of clean strokes and perfect, nonchalant control as if he had filmed them freshly just hours ago and was in the editing room for the first time. There is one sequence where Ring is taking 21-yard frees at an angle, over and over, the ball following one sweet unalterable trajectory every single time. It ends with Ring turning to the camera, and Marcus remembers him saying, 'You would hear someone in the crowd saying, "Ring just got that inside the far post." But he didn't know I was keeping it so far from the near post.'

Ring was forty years of age when the film was made and even on the simple black-and-white film, his splendour is compelling. It is, of course, merely a distillation of the skills that Ring called upon during the midsummer heat in the great arenas, a vast technical and natural array that he used with great speed and nerve and daring. But even without the colour of the pulsating crowd and his storied contemporaries breathing hot murder upon him, even without another prestigious title at stake, his presence on the ball is transfixing. Like John McEnroe returning a backhand at Wimbledon, like Jesse Owens in full flow or Ali dancing on canvas for the gallery or like Michael Jordan switching the basketball from right to left hand in mid-air, Ring looked perfect when he was doing what he did best. Pause the film at any point in which Ring is demonstrating any skill and his form is godly; balanced and coiled to move and flowing, the movement from beginning to end is a joy to behold. Although Marcus believes that in some private way Ring was glad that his demonstration of skills would be preserved, he was intent on communicating the basics as clearly and accessibly as possible. So, occasionally, when the ball bounced deceptively as it was passed to him, he demanded that the movement be filmed again even though he had adjusted with barely perceptible speed and completed the skill perfectly.

'But Christy, that was great.'

'No, no. That was exceptional. There is no point in using that. That is not how you teach hurling.'

He introduces each skill briefly, in clipped, formal language that is suggestive of an early cookery show. All is reduced to the simplest theory. For the first task, lifting the ball, he repeats the precise angle at which the hurl should be placed, raised to stun the ball into the palm of the poised left hand across which the hurl is immediately drawn as a shield. He completes the movement in the blink of an eye.

'He had analysed every theory. And I quickly came to have colossal respect for his intellect. Christy was a relatively uneducated man who was highly intelligent. He never spoke much about general affairs but, when he did, he was very shrewd. He had a complete independence of mind, and I think that if he didn't know much about a certain subject, he would come to no conclusion about it.'

There were some days when the weather was too bitter to film. Then, Marcus and Tyers and Ring would go to the Fountain Café on Patrick Street where Marcus listened in fascination as Tyers quizzed Ring about every aspect of hurling and the two men would relive small and vivid details of matches that even then carried a twenty-year vintage.

'Of course I didn't have the background knowledge but it was easy to recognise that this was somebody with a rare and incredible attitude to his given pursuit. He used to explain about the great scores of his that became legendary. To him these were not extraordinary feats – it was the times that he believed he should have scored that he kicked himself about.'

One exchange from these café sessions became famous among those who knew him. Tyers, listening to Ring calmly discuss one of his own more outrageous scores joked, 'God, Christy, you are modest, aren't you?'

'I am,' replied Ring steadily. 'Being modest isn't saying you're no good when you know you are. It's knowing how good you are and what your shortcomings are.'

Sometimes, the trio would go along to The Oyster – one of the swanky restaurants in Cork – just to make an occasion of it. It was here that Marcus came to appreciate how manifest the cult of Ring truly was. He was walking in the presence not of mere celebrity but of a man truly revered. The manager of the restaurant fussed and purred over the group. The waitresses were excited and flustered in their attentions. 'More rolls, Mr Ring?' 'Can I take that for you, Mr Ring?'

The more that Ring's fame and influence is considered, in an age before either television or self-aggrandisement, the more extraordinary it seems. It was not just a case of the man being a hero in his own city (not that Cork, O'Faoláin's city of cynics, is an easy place in which to achieve heroic status). This was a man who earned his living driving a lorry for Shell yet who commonly received offers of reckless sums of money from both Dublin and London newspapers to commit his thoughts to print. On a visit to the States, Ring was offered $10,000 just to become a silent partner in a pub that would be named after him. The Cork man found the idea amusing.

'The Yank asked him if he could put his name on the door,' confirms Willie John, 'and Christy turned around and told him that would have been breaking the rules. It would never have entered his head, like.'

His reluctance to engage the press stemmed from both a

natural shyness and an equally innate wariness. Paddy Downey secured an early interview with Ring in his first months working for the *Gaelic Weekly*. They met at the gates of Shell in Cork and spoke at length. Afterwards, they became fast friends.

'I have no idea why,' confesses Downey. 'The only thing I can think of is that I was from Cork.'

One year, John D Hickey ran an imaginative series of articles in the *Independent* entitled 'That Game I Will Remember', where the stars spoke about a particularly important match. He headed to Cork and eventually tracked Ring down near his flat on Patrick Street. They talked for a while and then Hickey made his proposal.

Ring smiled and said, 'John D, boy, I remember them all.' And that was the end of the interview.

The more elusive he became, the more fascinating the newspapermen found him. *Sports Illustrated* ran a piece on Ring and, during a well-publicised visit to New York in May of 1966, Red Smith of *The Washington Post*, who would become the dean of American sportswriting, was among the newspapermen who waited to meet him in the Times Square Hotel. According to Dorgan's book, 'He would look, they assumed, like a man suited to pound a beat in Hell's Kitchen. Then they met him. Christy Ring is slightly bigger than a scupper of Guinness. He has small compact features, bright blue eyes and thinning blond hair. He does not talk much and when he does it's well to listen sharply, for County Cork softens and broadens his accent, blurring it for American ears.'

Inexplicably, his employers at Shell never seemed to grasp fully the untapped value of this employee. The request for two weeks off so a film could be made of his hurling skills was met with bemusement. However, the penny seemed to have dropped when their lorry driver was the star turn at the premiere of the film in the Savoy in Cork. It dawned upon them that the company would be better served if Ring was a sales representative.

'They were sitting on a goldmine and they didn't realise it,' agrees Willie John. 'Eventually, they made him a salesman – Christy said to them, "I am staying in Cork." Ah, he was happy in the job. It suited him. Like, he was a terrible shy fella and that never left him. When he went to see matches then, he would go with normal local fellas. He never forgot them.'

He was a loyal employee and saw no contradiction in the ordinariness of his working week and all the exultant Sundays when the whole of Cork, and sometimes all of Munster, looked upon him as someone divine and not completely understandable. It was as if he had the pride and the ego and the ceaseless thirst for better days without any of the conceit that goes with it. Still, with a family to support from the early 1960s, Ring's total and genuine disinterest in the many lucrative approaches tendered to him tells us something of his mindset. He was not a wealthy man and lived no extravagant lifestyle. Squash was his leisure pursuit and he practised it with the same appetite for victory that he hurled with. Although he turned up for a golf outing to mark the founding of the Hurlers' Association, he confided in Downey that he did not really approve of the game as it was selfish and kept one away from family for too long. Drink never interested him.

'It showed one thing – and it's not to praise him – but the determination he had was something,' said Willie John.

'You know the way you would have fellas buying pints for you after games and throwing drink at you. He wore the pin and so have I for fifty years. But sure that wouldn't stop lads – a lot of times the pin is there for show. He never had a problem with people smoking but the temptation would have been unreal. And I will tell you one small thing – my father [Nicholas Ring] died at forty-five years of age. He called us out one day and said, "Whatever you do, lads, do not smoke." Well, Daddy was terrible heavy on the Woodbines but they would not have known anything about the health in those days.'

Ring was apparently low-key and reserved when it came to socialising. He kept in touch with Downey mainly through letters. There is, however, an unforgettable passage in Dorgan's book recalling a visit to the house of Ring's former Glen Rovers' team-mate, Josie Looney, then settled in New York. Amongst tight friends, the atmosphere was relaxed 'and Ring was high on hurling. Shoulders hunched, head thrust characteristically, blue eyes gleaming, Ring shook a massive fist at Looney and demanded: "Can a man sing about himself?" In a light ballad voice with lots of expression, he sang us Brian McMahon's celebrated ballad for Christy Ring.

"We'll have a good cry tonight," said Josie Looney's wife Mary.'

Mrs Ring, Willie John's wife, brings in tea and fruitcake and apple tart. Her husband is recounting a story concerning Seamus Bannon, who played for Tipperary against Cork in the 1951 Munster final.

'He was twenty years younger than Christy, I suppose, but he was a decent enough fella and he shook hands at the throw-in of the ball and he says, "Christy, I hate being honest," says he, "but this job must be done and you won't be seeing much of me today."

'And Christy said "It's all right, Seamus, it's the ball that counts and you won't see much of that either!"'

Another afternoon, possibly travelling to a Railway Cup match, Ring and Bannon were debating the art of cutting the ball.

'Next thing, Christy said stop the car and he took a ball and he cut it nearly as high as the trees, man. And Bannon said he would not have believed it only that he saw it. And Christy said to him, "When you go back to Tipperary, tell them the grass grows no better than it does in Cork either."'

Ring was a killer for the one-liners. There are several variations on the story of when he visited a stricken Cork player – possibly Josie Hartnett – on the eve of an All-Ireland final to commiserate and say a few kind words. In some versions, he visits by himself.

The most lavish has the entire Cork team solemnly lining up to murmur heartfelt words of pity to their fallen comrade and finally Ring comes up, shakes his friend's hand and vows, 'Could have been worse. It could have been me.'

'But if he said anything like that at all,' laughs Downey, 'it would have been meant as a joke.'

It is highly probable that he did visit the hospital regardless of what was said. Seamus O'Brien, a former Glen Rovers' teammate of Ring's told Downey that when he went up to John of Gods to dry out one year, Ring visited twice a week without fail. He would arrange to finish work early, then drive to Dublin and talk – about hurling mostly – for a couple of hours before travelling back to Cork again for work the next morning.

'It shows the charity of the man,' says Downey. 'I heard another lovely story about him to way back when I was in the polio division of a hospital. When Ring was very young, he used to do a line with a camogie player. When they went out on dates, they often took two hurleys with them. Anyway, she later married somebody else and fell on hard times and Ring would give her the odd hand-out financially – and probably anonymously.'

On the morning of the 1953 All-Ireland final between Cork and Galway, Downey was in the middle of a lengthy convalescence for tuberculosis in the Richmond Hospital in Dublin. The prospect of the final had him in a state of high excitement. As it transpired, the match acquired a notorious place in the hurling canon for events that had nothing to do with the quality of the hurling. Cork won a rancorous game remembered for the felling of Mickey Burke, Ring's marker, who suffered facial damage from a blow. Late that night, while leaving the Gresham ballroom, Ring was punched in the face by a Galway player. The next morning, the tensions had not abated and in the dining room of Barry's Hotel where both teams were staying, Ring was again struck as he was eating breakfast. This time, a general row broke out, during which blows and bitter words were exchanged. It is said that Ring stayed seated and remained perfectly still – possibly out of shock – while pandemonium reigned. That was the reason the 1953 All-Ireland is remembered.

However, around noon on the morning of the game, Downey was told that he had visitors. Hospital regulations were extremely strict during the period and the ward lived in mortal terror of falling foul of Sr O'Neill, the matron.

'But this morning, this lovely sister named Ms Russell, I think Frances was her first name – a true saint – came in and said, "Paddy, I can't let these visitors in but I'll tell you what, I will guide them around to your window."'

So Downey made his way over to the window and standing below were Tony O'Shaughnessy of St Finbarr's and Ring. Downey was momentarily amazed but later realised the appearance was not really out of character for Ring. They began discussing Cork's chances in the match.

'I think that in moving across the room I must have pushed the bedside locker out in front of the doorway or something but the matron spotted it. I remember catching sight of the big white cuff and blue sleeve as she came charging into the room. We had only been speaking for two minutes at this stage. She threatened to have me expelled. And then she saw the two heads below! Well. "Get Away. Get Out of This Hospital. How Dare You!" She was furious. And the two boys were gone in a flash. They were running. I am not sure if she knew who Ring was. But she wouldn't have cared.'

Incident followed Ring. With his fame and reputation transcending the hurling parishes in the 1950s, it could not have been otherwise. He was taking the ancient game to an unimagined level of expression and achievement and even in counties where hurling did not matter, Ring mattered. Among his peers, that caused complex emotions. If the defeated Galway men of 1953 regarded him with singular hostility, his presence in a Cork jersey inflamed generations of Tipperary folk as well, particularly on Sundays when he was literally unstoppable. He ended several classic games with deep welts and cuts and bruises. Defenders dealt with him unsparingly, driven by a mixture of adrenaline and respect and, most pertinently, a fear that they would have to play close and unflattering witness to the next immortal goal. Ring became accustomed to heavy treatment and adept at dealing with it. He was no angel. In one league match against Waterford in 1957, he came off the field with a broken wrist and three goals to his name and demanded that they return him to the raging front lines where he vainly tried to play on through the pain. And the next summer, he ventured out against Tipperary with heavy padding on broken ribs and managed yet another crusading hour, defined by yet another irrepressible surge on the goal which was the murmur in pubs throughout Munster by sunset. A goal that is now remembered only by the elite few – those who saw and who heard it first hand.

Ring was hit hard and returned the belts; that was the law of self-preservation in hurling during his era.

'All his games were hard,' says Willie John. 'Every last one of them. He was great to make openings for other fellas as well – he would draw the second man before making the pass. I remember Mickey Byrne, the Rattler, saying that when Cork beat Tipp in Limerick one year, the teams must have both been rooming in the same hotel. Christy played well the same day, like. And Mickey met him afterwards and said, "Ringey, we will have to shoot you. We tried everything else with you." Christy could look after himself.'

But he took grave exception to an accusation that spread like wildfire after the Munster final of 1961, that year's instalment of the Cork and Tipperary rites of passage. The match was unbearably tense and subsequently not the most flowing: Tipperary, in the flush of a bountiful period, prevailed by 3-06 to 0-07. Ring, the soul of the Cork team for the previous twenty years, was switched into centre-forward in the company of John Doyle, the man who would equal his personal collection of eight All-Ireland medals. Soaring towards the peak of his own indomitable game, Doyle had age and momentum on Ring that day but the Cork man, at forty years of age, was loathe to yield anything. The pair's initial race for a ball led to a tussle which ended when Ring reportedly pulled across his man in a rash and doomed attempt to get the ball. The men crashed heavily to the ground and players from both teams rushed towards the talismanic duo. When the dust settled, Tipperary's Tom Moloughney lay hurt on the ground and many who witnessed the game felt certain they had seen Ring hit him across the head with the hurley. Certainly, that was the view in the press box and John D Hickey went to print with that opinion, which was later broadcast on RTÉ radio by Seán Óg Ó Ceallacháin. Although Mick Dunne wrote the same thing in the *Irish Press*, the decision was taken in Burgh Quay to remove Ring's name from the report. Moloughney had been carried off with his injuries and by Monday Ring had publicly denied that he was responsible. Ó gCeallachain, who had relied on the proofs of the newspaper reports, immediately apologised but Hickey, convinced that Ring was culpable, held out. The Cork County Board prepared to issue legal proceedings against the journalist's employers, Independent Newspapers, and when

Hickey showed up at the Cork Athletic Grounds to cover the county senior football final, he discovered that he was barred. Other journalists, including the badly compromised Val Dorgan, left in support of Hickey. For a few tense weeks, an all-out battle of wills loomed between the Cork Board and the National Union of Journalists. Ultimately, the affair just petered out. Hickey quietly retracted what he had written and the legal case was dropped.

'It was a messy business,' says Downey. 'I remember when the actual incident started, Ring must have done something to Doyle because Doyle was leaning over him and shaking him. They were separated and while this kerfuffle was going on I saw a Tipperary player running up the field and then I got distracted. When I looked back, Maloughney had gone down. And Ring was very upset for getting the blame. He was adamant that he never hit Maloughney and he didn't either of course. I have it on tape from my researches that it was Pat Fitzgerald – he told me so himself.'

Ring was deeply upset about the rumour and at how widely and quickly it was embraced as fact. Willie John remembers when he called into the house during those evenings, it became the inevitable and only topic of conversation.

'He sat over in that chair there,' says Willie John pointing towards where his wife is sitting, on an armchair near a low, smoking fire, 'and swore many times that it wasn't him. Kavanagh the poet was after winning a libel case against the newspapers about that time and we were all telling him he should go down the same road. But that was making Christy miserable. He said he did not want any money. He said if it came to it, he would give it to charity.'

The Taoiseach, Jack Lynch, happened to arrive in Cork City on the afternoon that Christy Ring, his great friend and team-mate from the red-and-white halcyon days, died. He learned of the news in a manner that is darkly cinematic. It could not happen in Ireland today: the State car stopping on Brian Boru Bridge so the leader could pick up a late-afternoon newspaper; the vendor acknowledging the Taoiseach like an old friend and rolling up the newspaper for him. Then leaning into the window and whispering, 'Wasn't it terrible about Ringey?'

And Lynch simply murmuring, 'No, it can't be true.'

The strangeness of the day is heightened by a story that Paddy Downey discovered some months afterwards, one he has seldom spoken of. On the street where Ring fell for the last time was a schoolteacher, Patricia Horgan, who saw him collapse and came to try to revive him and whisper the act of contrition in his ear. Although the man's face was recognisable, it was not until she went home and heard the news that she realised it was Ring that she had happened upon. And then the young woman heard from her mother that twenty-six years earlier, Ring, incredibly, had acted as her benefactor. Walking her pram along a tight slope near the Cork Athletic Grounds, Mrs Horgan was startled by two cars coming towards her on the steep track. The hurlers were training in the ground that evening. The second of the cars, its driver obviously unsighted at that moment, made to squeeze past the first car, endangering both the young mother and the infant. The occupant in the first car realised this and drove sharply across the path of the second car, forcing it to stop. Mrs Horgan, shaken and relieved, recognised the first driver as Christy Ring. As she relived that story for Downey, she could not get over the fact that her daughter, the infant on that forgotten day, should have been the first to attend to Ring as he slipped away.

Out in Cloyne, that Friday was the evening of the local GAA dance. Paddy O'Sullivan remembers that he was almost going out the door when the sad news hit the village. Urgent phone calls were made to decide whether or not to cancel the evening.

'In the end we felt we had to go ahead with it. Some people

would actually have been arriving when word broke. Ah, it was one of the saddest nights I ever experienced. Needless to say nobody felt like eating or dancing. All the talk was of Ring. We could not believe it.'

At fifty-eight, he was not young in sporting terms, but because he retained such voracious energy and because his hurling life was characterised by a seductive brand of genius and class, Ring must have seemed to friends and admirers like a man somehow above the limitations of ageing. That he could be gone like a fresh gust of wind was beyond their immediate grasp. Paddy O'Sullivan had met him the previous Saturday at a garage on the road to Ballycotton, which was popular as a car wash at the time. Paddy, twenty-five years of age then, was sprucing up his first car and when he arrived, Ring was there, working the hose on his own car. They talked for a while about everyday things, O'Sullivan suppressing his own awe.

'He was as fit a man as you could meet,' Paddy says. 'That was what made it so hard.'

Willie John says he cannot remember how or when he heard the news: those immediate engulfing and highly public days left him in a daze.

The more you read the coverage of the funeral of Christy Ring, the stronger the impression you get that people felt that Ring's death brought a sudden and cold end to some fundamental triumph of their own.

That tone comes across in Lynch's graveside oratory.

'As long as young men will match their hurling skills against each other on Ireland's green fields, as long as boys swing their *camán*s for the sheer thrill of the tingle in their fingers or the impact of ash with leather, as long as hurling is played, the story of Christy Ring will be told – and that will be forever.'

Tens of thousands of people gathered in Cloyne on the day of funeral. It was reported that 25,000 people lined the roads when his remains were brought to Our Lady of Lourdes Church in

Ballinlough on Saturday evening. The crowd that turned out for
the funeral was significantly larger, too many to account for.
Paddy O'Sullivan acted as a steward that day, standing near the
graveside. It felt as if the entire population of Cork City had
gathered in the village and around the hinterland of Cloyne.
The atmosphere was heavy with the hushed sound of tens of
thousands of people grieving.

'The church was thronged and people spilled out of the doors
and onto the gravel paths and out the gate onto the street,'
wrote Paddy Downey in *The Irish Times* on Monday, 5 March
1979.

'It was a warm sunny morning and the sun enriched the
stained-glassed windows with its warm blues and reds above
the high altar. And on the south-side it glinted through the
coloured panes of green and blue and mauve, lighting up the
grey heads of hurlers who were Ring's contemporaries.

' "Lord, have Mercy on your servant, Christy." We listened to
the prayers but our minds wandered to Thurles and Limerick
and Croke Park and all the other grounds where we had seen
him in vibrant life, thrilling the thousands with his incomparable skills in so many games. "May angels meet you in
paradise." '

The warriors who had duelled with Ring down through the
long, bright years of grace and fury stood close at hand in heavy
coats and with backcombed hair. Mick Mackey was there and
Rackard and O'Donnell were among the Wexford mourners.
Theo English, Jim Devitt, Tony Reddan and Tommy Doyle –
who claimed the unique feat of keeping Ring scoreless in two
consecutive games – were prevalent among the many who
travelled from Tipperary. The cream of talent from Clare,
Waterford, Clare and Galway were all present and throughout
the crowd were his team-mates from the 1940s, the 1950s and
1960s, and the young Cork hurlers for whom he had been a
selector from 1976 to 1978. Many of them shared in the task of

shouldering Ring's coffin towards the family grave. Afterwards, Paddy Barry, the captain of the Cork 1952 team, spoke for the rest when he said, "We carried him at last."'

Those furthest from the funeral ceremony lingered for hours and hours afterwards, waiting for the chief mourners to leave and for the crowd to lessen gradually so they could pay their final respects. One man was heard wondering aloud if Parnell's funeral had been like this but nobody could answer.

Over four years later, on a gentle May morning, a smaller gathering marked the unveiling of the memorial. The bronze figure, sculpted by a Breton artist named Yann Goulet, stands at nine feet high and was inspired by Louis McMonagle's well-known photograph of Ring leading the Cork team in the parade before the 1954 All-Ireland against Wexford – his last perfect September as a player.

Mrs Rita Ring, Christy's widow, was there along with their daughter Mary and son Christy. Jack Lynch unveiled the memorial. 'How then, apart from this splendid memorial can we perpetuate his memory?' he asked in his address. 'First of all by ensuring that hurling, that noble field game that is truly ours, is cherished and developed to strengthen the fibre of our people.'

The applause echoed off the high, decorative stone walls that framed the memorial and the site where the great hurler had taken his first unsteady steps. Willie John Ring built those walls.

This is not the country that Christy Ring lived in. Oh, he would recognise Cloyne all right, a lovely and unpretentious town built on a sloping crossroads and famous for its eleventh-century tower, looming above the GAA field where Ring spent countless hours. Although he hurled almost all of his adult life with Glen Rovers, he never lost his love for Cloyne and came back to the old home from the city practically every Saturday to visit his mother Mary and his brothers and sisters. After

Nicholas Ring passed away, Christy and his brothers, Pad Joe and Willie John, assumed the role of earners, Christy taking an apprenticeship in a garage in Midleton. The protective streak remained in all of them and Christy tended to small tasks for his mother and, when she died in 1953, he did the same for his sister, Mary Agnes, who lived in the family home. The field, though, was always his enchantress.

'We used to play a match every Saturday above at three o'clock,' says Willie John. 'I was in charge of them at this time. Christy would come along and talk to the lads and play if there was just a game amongst ourselves. I remember before one Munster final Johnno Coyne coming along and saying, "Jesus, is that himself out there and him playing against Tipperary tomorrow?"'

That was the enigma of Ring, content to lose himself in the blissful ordinariness of home and family and work for every day of the week but Sunday, when he answered to a greater and exquisite calling. He wanted nothing from the game other than to be its most compelling and poetic advocate, to show the audience of the sport what he believed it to be about. And to win at it, of course: like all great athletes, loss feasted upon him. But those low moments were vastly outweighed by the many afternoons of winning he enjoyed with Cork. And though Ring understood that his gift held fascination for successive generations of people, that it cast him in an extraordinary light, he never let it alter his serene concentration on the game or his unbending sense of self. This was a man who casually and automatically refused to contemplate making money from his standing, a man who shied away from the early shafts of media shine, a man who experienced what it was to be adored and accepted it without ever cheapening his essential humility. He was a man of rare self-possession.

'And men who are fathers and grandfathers now will tell their children and grandchildren with pride that they saw

Christy Ring play. The story will pass from generation generation and so it will live,' continued Jack Lynch in that eloquent graveside oratory when he struggled to keep his composure.

But this is not the country Jack Lynch knew either and it is no longer common for stories of any kind to leap from generation to generation. Folk tales do not get passed through mobile phones. The time is coming when there will be nobody left to vouch with passionate, first-hand memory for why Ring mattered so richly and abstractly to the hundreds of thousands who followed him through the middle section of the twentieth century. Or for why he fascinated quite so thoroughly or why virtually every person who met him alluded to a presence, a slow-burning, attractive and vaguely unsettling aura.

Or to tell of how, after some of his finest scores, he would succumb to elaborate and wildly joyful jigs, as if the field beneath him had turned to hot coals. Or of how he posed for team photographs with a distant, restless look in his eyes and a half smile, as if his spirit was already caught up in the white heat of the coming game. Or how coldly his choice words stung when he wanted to convey his displeasure. Or how, driving team-mates home in the evenings after games, he could be enticed into singing a song. Or of how, after realising his eighth and final medal in 1954, he fell flat on his back in Croke Park, reeling and pacified, the great crowd in thunderous mood and the clouds moving swiftly over the stadium. Not enough will be told.

Has there been neglect? In America, they believe that baseball holds all that is venerable about the past. That is why the icons – Ruth and Cobb and DiMaggio – of that bat-and-ball game cast longer shadows with each passing decade and why Red Smith's prophetic last line in his last ever column – 'I told myself not to worry. Some day there would be another DiMaggio' – looks all the more wistful. America refuses to let its sporting exceptions diminish with the political and social details of faded decades. They are remembered and fêted and re-explored like great works of art.

Although Ring's name remains sonorous and potent, the reasons for celebrating it grow more ethereal.

'Well, part of the problem is the paucity of the visual record,' says Louis Marcus. 'His time coincided with a period when film was expensive and a novelty and there is just so little archive footage of him. Or of those who followed him. They came from far and wide looking for Ring to do something unbelievable and they were rarely disappointed. How could a great figure like that be remembered except in conversation? When the past is remembered, his name will come up. The problem is that now, less and less people around have seen him play in any shape of form, so what is there to say? Because at the time, his very name meant magic.'

Perhaps in a perverse way it is appropriate that in an age where everything is exposed to film we should have to make do with the few broken and scratched reels of film of Ring that have survived. The greatest of all the Native Americans, Crazy Horse, was alone among the leaders of the Oglala and other tribes in refusing to allow his photograph to be taken. He feared that the image would capture his soul and though he died on the remote plains of Nebraska just a couple of decades before Ring was born, he left absolutely nothing tangible behind. Yet he survives to this day as a triumph of the imagination; even now, artists are chipping a 240 foot sculpture into the side of a mountain in South Dakota, a work of art that has been ongoing for four decades.

Ring, of course, has his own monument, perfect in place and scale. But more could be done to remember. It seems reasonable to state that Christy Ring, through no invention of his own, was among the original heroes of sport, thrilling Irish society just as profoundly as DiMaggio engaged his sporting public in

New York City. Ring was the GAA's first and only true superstar, years before the concept gained currency.

There are signs, twenty-five years after his death, that a Ring revival may be imminent. The recent television documentary, broadcast at Easter 2004 was a valuable celebration of his feats. Perhaps Louis Marcus's film could be translated into a freshly packaged DVD, to be sold along with a coaching manual. And there has been no official biography as yet. It would have to be written by a Cork person, of course. And there are many hoping that Paddy Downey will yet complete his planned book on the master in the not-too-distant future.

As the afternoon changed to evening and the Christmas bulbs appeared in the windows along the houses on St Colman's Terrace, Willie John talked a little of the modern game and of the most recent All-Ireland final featuring Cork and Kilkenny. He spoke highly of Kilkenny but did not believe they would make the three in a row. Christy regarded his brother as the shrewdest analyst of the game and Willie John speaks as passionately and easily of the current generation as of those he trained and watched some sixty years ago. He has his fears for the game and believes that some of the basic skills are slowly and surely vanishing. On summer afternoons, he turns on the television and winces, growing annoyed as players make the same mistakes he watched them make twelve months earlier. He wonders about coaching, about how the youngsters are taught.

Eventually, we said goodbye. Mrs Ring said always to be sure and call – that the door was always open. Willie John showed Paddy some work he was doing on the neat garden and then he stood politely in the chill by the black gate until we were out of sight. Paddy took me across to the Cloyne clubhouse. He searched in the twilight for the right key. It is a classic clubhouse – odd bits of silverware, notes for long-abandoned meetings pinned to a green baize board, stacked chairs and a kettle. He wanted to show me an oil portrait that Christy had agreed to pose for. It was hung on the rear wall behind the chairman's desk and was expensively framed. It is the only one of its kind; posing went against everything that Ring held dear to his nature. But he must have assented to do it for Cloyne, for home. It is the familiar Ring expression, pleasing, strong and slightly formal and detached. Paddy joked that it must have been the longest the man had ever sat still for.

There was not a sinner about as we walked up the street, leaving behind us Ring's great likeness marching silently and eternally in the weakening light.

7

Spirit of the Bronx

Hard, shiny ice coats the sunless corners of the streets around the subway station where the number four train creaks to a halt. It preserves the verdant reaches of Woodlawn cemetery and is bunched in glistening, cobalt packs all along McLean Avenue. In the summer, this sprawling Irish-oriented suburban street in the Bronx is known as 'the Strip'. Its bars and restaurants teem with Irish kids leaving for and coming from work, Irish kids hanging out in the relentless and intoxicating city heat which smells of petrol fumes and spices and beer and baked bread. They come to have the summer of their young lives. Maybe 2,000 summer workers descend upon this Irish quarter of New York every May, living the dream. Woodlawn draws them like a magnet; it has connection and familiarity and those not independent or sure enough to stake a claim down in Manhattan get a taxi here from JFK, sometimes with an address or a phone number in their pocket. The accents and sights soften the distance from home. Girls come to wait on tables or keep bar, lads come as novice builders and often as football players moonlighting as novice builders. Sometimes, kids come with nothing clear in their minds other than a vague desire to experience the otherness that they have heard New York offers, to melt in the glamour of just existing in the most famous city in the world. If you can do so and still buy Kerrygold butter in the shops, then so much the better.

'You want to give these kids a leg-up,' explains Leslie McGettigan. 'You see some of them walking up and down the street and they haven't got a clue. Like, it costs $1,200 for the student visa package and flights. That's a lot of money for parents to fork out. Then the rent here can be astronomical in summer and places are tougher to find. It's the same with work. You can be down a small fortune before you get work. I'll tell ya, I would let no kid of mine come out here unless I knew who they were staying with, where they were staying and where they were working. But then kids go home and blow the whole thing up to their friends because they don't want to look bad instead of just telling it for what it is. And so more keep coming. They keep coming.'

Leslie is drinking a coffee from Dunkin' Donuts and sits in front of the fireplace of a bar he owns on McLean Avenue, called Fagan's. On the hot and roaring nights of midsummer, Fagan's is a beacon, but it is a fine place in winter also, cosy and atmospheric with a jukebox hammering out modern classics. Leslie is a cult hero around his hometown of Letterkenny, so naturally enough the Donegal gang drink here, along with lads from Galway and Kerry. February is a nothing kind of a month in Woodlawn. On the streets, it feels like a seaside resort just coming out of hibernation. The community has just taken a buffeting in one of the harshest winters to settle upon the state in modern times. The air is still crisp and grating on the lungs and when you drive through the winding residential streets, with big American Sedans and Buicks parked in front of pretty wooden house fronts, the snow is still in evidence. The ground is frozen hard, making it impossible to play football. In fact, being outdoors at all was up to recently an unpleasantly chilly experience. So February is a drag but it is also an optimistic month. Leslie knows that as quick as a finger click, Spring will announce itself and the air will moisten and warm and then this section of the Bronx will be full of hustling transients from the old country, looking for fast dollars and adventure. It is a never-ending cycle.

Leslie doesn't blame them. After all, he came here too. McGettigan's story is wrapped up in everything that New York–Irish life and the GAA stand for. See him as he is now, lean and sallow skinned with short black hair that he wears spiked. He has that burnished, fresh look of a middleweight boxer that got out at the right time. Not that McGettigan ever needed to box; on the football field, he was a purist. He was mercury.

That giddiness he had in St Jarlath's College, it never left him. To his mother's disappointment, he rejected a place studying Arts in UCG, appalled at the prospect of another three years bent down studying the words of dead men and women. Leslie always found it more fun when you could talk back. He sought out life with the natural ebullience that all scoring forwards have: Gimme The Ball and I'll Score. That was his mantra on the field of life. The problem was he chased too much, bouncing through places and ideas without ever pausing for breath. In 1985, one year after he left St Jarlath's, McGettigan played senior championship for Donegal against Monaghan, marked by Fergus Caulfield. It never struck him as odd or unusual that he had made it so young; he was half surprised that Brian McEniff hadn't given him a shot the year of his Leaving Cert. His skill and precocity saw a lot of offers put in front of him at a young age. From 1985, he was courted on both sides of the Atlantic, spending three months in Chicago, summering at home and then moving on to New York. It was fun and frantic and helped him avoid having to make decisions about himself. Fun was the spur, and because he was unsettled at home, the American scene provided a nice winter income and a better time than Friday-night pints at The Grill in Letterkenny. Only now are the consequences of those muddled days clear.

McGettigan was a constant presence on the county under-21 team from the age of seventeen, but when he was made captain in 1987, he was lured back to Chicago a month before training began.

'I can safely say that not once in my life did I get a decent job in Ireland. Around that time, Jimmy Duggan [the Galway footballer and Jarlath's old boy] got me an interview with Irish Permanent and I was recalled three times. We were all full sure I would get it and I was looking forward to it but, for whatever reason, it didn't happen. I was disillusioned with the country, really, after that and I suppose me coming out here left a sour taste with the boys at home. Still, I was full sure I would be called back later in the championship.'

He wasn't and the team that McGettigan was to have captained won Donegal's second ever All-Ireland title while he worked on a site off Lake Michigan.

Scour the official annals of the subsequent years and McGettigan's name features frequently at both club and county level on both sides of the Atlantic. In 1989, he began working in a bar in the Bronx but travelled home regularly enough to take part in the 1990 Ulster championship for Donegal. He was on the bench for the 1991 Ulster final when Donegal were ransacked by Down and he flew from Dublin convinced that the beaten team was finished. Everybody felt that way. For the first time in his life, he thought hard about things. Engaged to be married to Elaine, he took stock of his situation.

'I was flittin' between here and back home like an asshole and I wasn't getting ahead of the game.'

He was still only twenty-seven and commanded a place on the fringes of the Donegal championship team without ever reaching peak fitness. He was doing as Leslie did, burning the candle at both ends, getting by on skill and charm. Enough was enough.

Brian McEniff put a phone call through, as McGettigan knew he would, on New Year's Day of 1992. The Bundoran man cooed and cajoled and listened and accepted McGettigan at his word when he was told there was no point in calling any more. The resonant click of the receiver being replaced left him cold but at least he had clarity. At least he had decided where the future was.

And then, of course, it happened all over again. That summer, through reports and phone calls back home and later on satellite television, McGettigan heard and saw through a kind of appalled fascination that Donegal were just refusing to be beaten. A miracle victory with fourteen men against Derry brought a fifth Ulster title and then somehow they stuttered to a first ever semi-final win against Mayo in a really mediocre game and the word was they would be cannon fodder for Dublin in the All-Ireland final. But God, they were in an All-Ireland final. The county, he was told, was one big, mad carnival. In GAA terms for McGettigan, that fact was like the Second Coming. And he had just renounced his faith.

'There was about twenty-five of us that knew each other from football here in New York and we all went back,' remembers McGettigan over a Marlboro Light. It is darkening outside and Mike Scott is singing on the jukebox about Brigadoon.

'Did the whole thing, headed to Letterkenny and partied around Dublin for the weekend. But if I told you I felt good watching that game that day, I'd be a fucking liar. I was sick. Like, I was proud that the boys had won it, as a Donegal man. But as a football player, I was hurting so much that I felt sick.'

There are endless metaphors for the moment – the guy who burnt his lottery ticket and so on. McGettigan looked at Declan Bonner kicking that famous, timeless point in the last minutes of the game and could remember greeting the scrawny, uncertain ginger-headed boy from the Rosses when they were both kids on the U-21 scene and Leslie had confidence to burn. When Leslie was the man and a casual word from him meant something. And although there was no guarantee that McGettigan would have been on the 1992 team, there was certainly a possibility of it. He is entitled to believe that when he hung up on McEniff that 1 January, he wilfully closed the door on an All-Ireland medal. It was literally the chance of a lifetime.

'That Sunday night, myself and Charlie Mulgrew, Joyce McMullan and Matt Gallagher went drinking. Everyone was celebrating and we just got away for awhile, the four of us. Like, in front of everyone else, I kept the face up, made out I was delighted but they knew I was hurting. I was able to show it in front of them. Months afterwards, I read Barry Cunningham saying in the *Donegal Democrat* that he just wished I had been around for that season after playing down the years. That meant a lot to me, just to know that you were kind of part of it in the minds of a few boys.'

There are moments when, uninvited and illogically, the pang of not being on the field that grey September day will pierce McGettigan. He might be driving to collect his girl from school or having a coffee or talking on the phone to home and something will trigger it. He is accustomed to it now, used to the fleeting pain that comes and goes like a phantom nerve. In a sense, it has become a comfort. It reminds him that choices are everything.

There is a restlessness at the soul of New York GAA and it has been that way from the beginning. The organisation in the American city and the GAA authorities at Croke Park have always had a troubled relationship. Neither entity ever fully clarified what the other meant to it. In familial terms, New York is the tearaway son with a glimmer in his eye who the local sergeant delivers to your door drunk and rowdy at 3 am. Again. And the kid throws a roguish grin at you, the parental authority, an expression that is hard to resist because it shines with a generous spirit. But because rules are rules, the kid's allowance is cut off. And New York sulks but never for long. On it goes.

There are easy assertions made about the New York GAA scene. Traditionally, the games at the mythical passion box that is Gaelic Park are portrayed as a maudlin recreation of what the ex-patriots miss most about Ireland. Generally, the organisation has been regarded as maverick and unaccountable. Locally, the faraway lure of the big city skyscrapers and the promise of easy greenbacks is seen as a whorish and callous way of draining small Irish clubs of their best players by rich city teams intent on winning the New York championship. By those players who are sought after, New York is the rare perk in an association where perks are buried if not explicitly forbidden; it is where you get treated like a star. And nationally, New York is perceived as the misfit that gate-crashed the party so often that it ended up on the guest list.

Elements of truth exist in all these simplifications. But it is impossible to pigeonhole Gaelic games in New York. Like the very fact of Irish life in the city, it is too complex and deeply ingrained for that. It was to New York, after all, that Michael Cusack and Maurice Davin looked when trying to promote the organisation in 1888.

'The Gaelic Athletic Association is now an accomplished fact and it has reached a point at which it can be developed into an institution most beneficial to the country,' Michael Davitt wrote in the *Freeman's Journal* that August.

'Mr Maurice Davin's project of invading America and Canada with a force of fifty of the picked athletes of the GAA is the second practical step towards the inauguration of international Celtic festivals. The foundation of the GAA was the first.

'The fifty athletes will be dressed solely in Irish manufacture and will be in every way an honour to Ireland. An immense reception awaits them in America and they are certain to uphold the athletic fame of their country in their contacts with competitors on the other side of the Atlantic.'

As theatre, this tour was applauded, drawing crowds at venues all along the Eastern corridor, but financially, it was ruinous. Seventeen of the elite Gaels were so impressed by the banquets and lifestyle they witnessed while on the road that they declined to return home on the *City of New York* liner and instead joined the legions of Irish immigrants in the city. The tourists were given a grand farewell at Tammany Hall and, two years later, the Gaelic Athletic Association of America was set up. In spirit, it mirrored the original version back home but, from its inception, it retained an independent streak that has prevailed, leading to colourful clashes with central council over the decades.

Even today, it is easy to see what Davin visualised when he looked west. The Irish were pouring body and soul into the great cities of America and there was the population and energy and money to make the spread of Celtic culture a genuine possibility. It does not take a great stretch of the imagination to see how football and in particular hurling might have caught on before baseball became America's pastime. As early as 1890, hurling featured in the old Madison Square Garden. And by 1913, the Irish paper, *The Advocate*, carried this account of a culture clash in its 3 April edition:

'On last Sunday afternoon, while the Sarsfields were practising at 34th Street and 2nd Avenue, a gang of baseball players came along and demanded the Sarsfields get off the field as they wanted to play baseball. The Sarsfields didn't see things in this way and stated to a Mr Jackson, who was leader of the baseball team, that they had spent a lot of time and money fixing up the ground. This did not satisfy Mr Jackson and they commenced to bat the ball around the field with lightning speed until suddenly and most unexpectedly it came into collision with the face of one of the baseball players. This, of course started a little excitement and the baseball players armed themselves with bats and ordered the hurlers to get out at once.

'As the mêlée raged, it was noticed that the baseball gang were soon nursing what were considered serious wounds. It only took a short time to put the trouble makers wise to the fact that hurleys, when handled properly, are much more dangerous than baseball bats and those who were able started to turn for shelter as quickly as possible and this led one watching youngster to describe the latter events as a marathon race.'

Although arrested, the Sarsfields boys were released that evening by a captain William Heffernan, who not only assured the Irish lads they could practise on the clearing when they wished but that he would also afford them police protection when they wanted to do so.

It is a minor and vivid episode but carries the core traits of issues that would remain pertinent for the GAA in New York: a separateness from the indigenous culture, a fiery reputation and a scarcity of the one thing the old country had in abundance – green fields.

Because of that, Gaelic Park, the home of New York hurling and football, has attained a global stature. It was first named Croke Park, but when central council objected to the name being sullied on a site that sold alcohol, the proprietor, John Kerry O'Donnell, changed it to its present name. Gaelic games have been played there since 1927. The place is not spectacular. Rather, it is the opposite but its very existence, unwieldy and ramshackle and proud, right in the heart of the Irish Bronx, tints it with a certain majesty. You enter through a big old-fashioned bar and social room that leads onto a gently sloping cemented hill down towards the field. The pitch itself is a celebrated oddity, pinched for space along the wings, with a sanded baseball mound in one corner and a subway track built overhead (the place belongs to the Metropolitan Transit Authority). Often on match Sundays, the train rattles leisurely towards the northern suburbs of the city, its occupants surveying the entertainment below with casual interest. Over the years, the sight of the subway track over Gaelic Park has become one of the most instantly recognisable and emblematic affirmations of Gaelic games.

In time, and perhaps unfairly, the park would be nicknamed 'The Bloodpit of the Bronx' by one New York sports columnist. But the significant thing is that the place and its games were mentioned at all. There was a time when the arrival of the big native stars to the Big Apple caused a stir in the mainstream media. It was the legendary Arthur Daly of *The New York Times* who nicknamed Cavan's Peter Donohoue 'the Babe Ruth of football' when he scored 0-08 in the famous 1947 All-Ireland final that was played at the Polo Grounds. Yet the Irish games in the city were making headlines long before that, sometimes for the right reasons and on other days for outcomes that were not so perfect. Dan Parker of the *Daily Mirror* had this to say when he attended a game at Yankee Stadium between Cavan, the All-Ireland champions, and New York on 3 June in 1934. The first game between the sides had ended in a 1-07 draw and in the second half, the players went at it.

'As the fighting warmed up, the county Cavan fife and drum corps lads, deciding it wasn't a private affair, leaped over the wall of the grandstand and were out on the field in two beats of a bass drum, some of them trying to hold the fighters and others taking sides with their beleaguered compatriots from Cavan. The battle was decided in Cavan's favour till Tommy Armitage and Johnny McGoldrick swung into action. Then the Cavan men started to drop like arches in a policeman's parade. Tommy, a former fighter, laid low a half dozen Cavan boys in front of the press box and Jimmy McLarnin, who looked on from a press box across the field must have envied him.

'As the battle was raging fiercely on a hundred fronts, the gate near the left field bleachers swung open and like a troop of Cossacks, the Mounted Police, who had been on duty outside the park, galloped into the battlefield at full speed. A few limped off, holding a shoe in one hand – an emergency weapon pressed into service in the heat of the battle.

'Postmaster General Jim Farley who threw out the first ball left just before the war broke out or he would have been asked to throw out the first batter too. Then the game resumed and everything was just lovely for the remaining five minutes of play. New York, which held Cavan to a 10-10 tie in the opening game of the series won the Jimmy McLarnin trophy by taking yesterday's game. The way they handled their fists entitled them to a cup with a boxer's name on it. The Irish are poor business men or they would have staged their free for all two weeks ago and thus ensured a sell out house yesterday. As it was there were only 16,000 fans in the park, several of them non-combatants.'

Such brawls became the stuff of myth and have garlanded New York's reputation as a roughhouse when it comes to Gaelic games. And there have been incidents but none more (or in truth as) violent as those that occurred across the fields in Ireland. From the early days of organised playing, the game existed in two tiers in New York. Clubs were formed, loosely based on county affinities, and played each other in a local championship, similar to the structure in every county in Ireland. But there was also a desire to pit the local best against the best in Ireland and – particularly when transatlantic flights or boat trips were rare expeditions and television belonged to the future – more keenly, a desire to see the cream of the game in New York.

The hurlers of Tipperary were the first Irish travelling party to play officially in New York in 1926. Both the hosts and guests were mutually enamoured and, as was the case with Davin's American Invasion, a number of Tipperary men decided to stay on permanently. Eoin O'Duffy, whose experience of Bronx life was tainted by the bitter chorus of boos he received at Celtic Park (the original New York home for Gaelic games) from the resolutely anti-treaty diaspora, came home complaining that the Americans were acting with no regard for the GAA's central authorities.

So when the GAA sanctioned the footballers of Kerry to travel the following September, written promises to return were extracted beforehand. As it was, this historic tour was bathed in controversy. New York, flooded with immigrants at the time, had a particularly fine football team anxious to test themselves against the standard bearers of the Irish game. Fotry thousand locals showed up at Celtic Park to see New York win 3-11 to 1-07. Among the home stars were Martin Shanahan of Wexford, Mayo's Paddy Ormsby and John Tuite of Louth.

A day later, a report appeared in the *Irish Independent* quoting a cable from the Kerry manager, Fr Dick Fitzgerald, saying 'the game was a very poor example of Gaelic football in a field too small for any real evolution. Kerry never tried to play and say they never mean to play what is called Celtic Park again.'

The remarks were tantamount to a diplomatic incident. The local GAA organisation was deeply offended by the comment and the return game at the Polo Grounds was all but scratched. Only the smooth counselling of John Joe Sheehy from Kerry enabled the fixture to go ahead, which New York won again, 2-06 to 0-03. In the end, the teams were forced to meet a third time when the tour promoter, a Mr Tim Sullivan, embarked on a midnight flit with tens of thousands of dollars. The final game, hastily arranged, paid for the Kerry boys' voyage home and once again ended in a home victory.

That visit set the tone. Always, the New York association and its Irish guests have loved and hated one another like brothers. Both sides carried conflicting emotions towards the other. New York folk always (and do today) consider it an honour to be visited by the Irish teams and traditionally cover the cost of flying them over and then fête them with expensive dinners and late nights. But once the speeches are over, they crave something deeper than token respect. Over the years, various incidents and diplomatic slights have dented the New York sensibility. In 1937, John Kerry O'Donnell was so affronted by the lack of a welcoming committee for the New York–Kerry team that had arrived in Ireland to play a series of friendly games that he refused to leave the SS Columbus. He sailed for America again without once setting foot in Ireland.

Rarely, if ever, did the hospitality laid on to visiting New Yorkers ever touch that which was taken for granted by touring Irish parties. For long periods over the twentieth century, the GAA permitted New York to play in the league in the sense that they would play the winners of the hurling and football competitions for bragging rights. The quality of the New York teams mirrored the health of the Irish economy. When Ireland was booming, the state of the games across the water dwindled. But often, New York was ferociously strong. In 1965, John D Hickey opined that they had probably the second finest hurling team in existence after Kilkenny. A motion to permit the ex-patriots to enter the championship the following year was rejected at Congress. The year 1970, however, changed everything. Cork, the All-Ireland hurling champions, came to Gaelic Park and played a torrid two-game series that ended up on a score-line of 5-21 to 6-16 to the visitors. After the final match, referee Clem Foley was attacked seriously enough to suffer a broken jaw as he made his way to the dressing room. Although the visiting GAA president, Pat Fanning, did not overtly refer to the incident at the post-match reception, officials and the media entourage were enraged. When the New York team visited Ireland some weeks later, central council announced that defender John Maher had been suspended for life from the association because of his involvement in the assault on the referee. The New Yorkers were equally shocked by the timing and heavy-handed nature of this development and went through the motions in a warm-up game in O'Kennedy Park in New Ross, losing 5-08 to 2-06. There was no central council figure at the game to greet the visiting team.

'As guests in this country, we feel we are snubbed,' said New York board president Mr Sean O'Hanlon. It was decided to withdraw from all scheduled games and the tourists left under a cloud.

The GAA general secretary Seán Ó Síochain indicated the mood of the Association in comments made to the national newspapers:

'My reaction is one of complete disillusionment because of the degree of irresponsibility shown by officers who claim to belong to the GAA. Their reactions and their actions over the past three days and their attempt at explaining those reactions and actions condemn them outright and completely dishonours the New York body they represent.'

In the city, the extended GAA community was aghast at the treatment. John Maher bitterly rejected the guilt laden on him for the attack on Foley, and his Galway-based team-mates vowed to stand with him. They refused to line out for their scheduled city games and were duly banned by the New York board. However, both Maher and Galway were later exonerated at a hearing, much to the displeasure of media commentators and central council in Ireland. Patience broke. Tired of what it perceived as New York truculence and its refusal to operate completely under the auspices of the parent association, the GAA moved to sever all ties with New York for at least two years. By 1970, the city game was alone.

It was in the 1970s that Frank Brady bolted from Leitrim. In 1976, he was twenty-six and due to be married and master of a one-teacher school in Glengevlin. The building dated from 1933 and, in the winter, its long, mournful windows were rattled so hard by the wind it drowned out his voice. Still, it was a secure job and the prospects of a principal's post in a bigger school were strong. He was building a house in Lurganboy and playing football on the fringes of the county team. He had security and position; it was not to be scoffed at. In earlier summers, Brady had possessed enough wanderlust to travel to New York as a summer student long before it was fashionable to do so and in this year, he and his fiancée Helen just ended up staying. He flew home to tidy up the loose ends and, over farewell pints, the boys back home told him he was mad in the head and he agreed and set on the urban immigrant trail. Those tempestuous months of 1977 were as far from the eleven o'clock school bell, morning prayers and the dales of Leitrim as life gets. A heat wave hit New York that summer; the disco phenomenon was infectious and the city, in the throes of a financial crisis under Mayor Rich Beem, was seriously flirting with bankruptcy. The famous electrical blackout that summer served as a perfect metaphor of the naked city on the edge. The power was still out when the sun rose the following morning, and Brady remembers walking through Fordham and seeing people almost leisurely back trucks through glass shop windows and then peruse the store like customers, in search of the finest electrical ware or bed linen or clothes. Never before or since would he walk through such blatant anarchy. And to top it all, a real edgy fear coursed through all the boroughs because this was the summer made infamous by the Son of Sam, the serial killer who had taken to executing young women and couples at random.

'That was an absolutely strange time, because every neighbourhood was potentially at risk although I think most of his crimes were in Queens,' Brady recalls over an Irish breakfast in Colleen's café in Woodlawn. It is one of those homely American-style Irish diners, with green décor, implausible amounts of food heaped on white plates and one if not several waitresses genuinely named Colleen. Today, Brady is an unusual combination of Leitrim Gael and university bohemian.

'Young couples and girls in particular were petrified of "making out" as it is called here – I don't know what the current phrase back home is, although it all amounts to steaming up the windows. But no, it was a real constant fear and all anybody was really talking about. The eerie thing was that when they caught the guy, Sam Berkowitz, he was actually living quite close to here, on Pine Street in Yonkers.'

New York was in turmoil for Brady's first winter there. It was the era of the 'White Flight'. In what seemed like an overnight period, the Bronx neighbourhood of Fordham became ghettoised. Landlords, constrained by legislation and a failing economy, could not afford to maintain the buildings they owned and so they just abandoned their properties and the dispossessed and disenfranchised moved in, causing the largely white residents to sell up and move further north. Brady pre-empted this class migration and settled in Woodlawn, about five miles north of Fordham, before most followed suite.

If offered what most people craved above all then – relative safety. But from an Irish emigrant's perspective, the 1970s were an arid decade. Nobody was leaving home, and that was reflected on Sundays in Gaelic Park, when clubs were struggling to field teams. Brady was persuaded to play for Carlow by a guy he met on the plane on the way over and, although he is involved in Leitrim to this day, he played for some ten years for the Carlow side. Once you get sucked into a team, you don't get out too easily.

'To be honest, the scene was fairly grim and pessimistic here during that period. It was an anxious time. I remember we only had three senior hurling clubs – that was a stunning fall in numbers. And it was like *Dad's Army* then – you had guys coming out of retirement years after their final games just to ensure that games got played. It was definitely a period when the GAA here was under threat of dying out.'

The paucity of those times mirrored the last days of World War II, when the depleted male population more or less ended the games. It was then that John 'Kerry' O'Donnell stepped forward, selling a number of highly lucrative Manhattan pubs he owned in order to pump money into Gaelic Park and ensure that the local GAA organisation retained an interest in it. He assumed the position of unofficial godfather of New York GAA, often finding himself in the centre of controversies, but his input during the critical years will remain his legacy. He arguably saved the GAA in New York at that time.

The association that Frank Brady involved himself with had not changed greatly in structure since the first days of Gaelic Park. Local sides augmented their teams with players from home, with offers of cash, summer apartments and jobs. Other big-name players were merely flown in for weekends. Rules were flouted and ignored.

'I was as guilty as anybody else,' says Brady. 'It was an attitude of when in Rome...'

Clubs went on desperate fundraising binges solely to entice a marquee player from home out for a few months or even a single weekend. Meanwhile, New York GAA's epic attempts to secure a permanent home stalled repeatedly on the point of closure. Although the local community is both resourceful and financially astute, the failure to secure a green patch that is patently theirs has dogged them. In 1933, at the height of the Depression, the New York board took the decision to relinquish its interests in a site at Roosevelt Avenue in Queens despite having already invested a non-returnable $22,000. It was a costly error; just a few years later, the owners were able to hire it out for the hosting of the World Fair. In 1991, the Mass Transit Authority (MTA) was taking bids on a new thirty-year lease and because the New York association did not act smartly enough, the field was leased to Manhattan College with the social area staying in the hands of the O'Donnell family. The following season, the Sunday pastime fell into near non-existence when games were played at a makeshift pitch in the outer reaches of Rockland. Attempts to find a home at a development at Tara Circle – into which $130,000 was thrown – and at Ferry Park in the Bronx have all led down cul-de-sacs. Inevitably and almost unconsciously the games have drifted back to Gaelic Park, where Mayo and New York met in the senior football championship in May.

Frank Brady is better versed than most in the puzzle that is the New York GAA scene. There are days when he shares Davin's vision of a robustly healthy native sporting and cultural revolution in the Irish strongholds of the city. On other occasions, he wonders if the association might not just die out. Because New York GAA is a fairly fragile thing. In the deep freeze of America's winter, it is no more than a notional thing, a conversation you have with friends. And then when the thaw comes, it takes just a few guys – the same few – to make manic phone calls and draft up fundraising plans to get the local teams up and running again, always against the odds.

'I worry about who is going to replace those people. The numbers on the ground are small. I mean, in a broad sense, the number of people involved in New York GAA is impossible to quantify. But in immediate terms, a local team can exist on a base group of seven players and two or three officials. You build from there.'

Brady has done his bit. He grafted his way through night school at NYU to secure a doctorate in physical education and has left the menial jobs for a lecturing position he secured in the 1990s. Since then, he has coached at all levels and still takes kids on a Saturday morning at Paddy's Field in the Bronx, a small training facility developed out of waste ground in the 1970s by a Clare man called Paddy Markham. This is the criticism constantly levelled at the New York association – that instead of money being pummelled into the illusory exotica of big stars from back home, it should be used to work on the local population. And it does happen. Even today, there are a few die-hards from the St Raymond's club in an area of the Bronx that has become exclusively European who coach hurling and football to Italian kids on spring mornings.

'It has got better. And there are American-born kids, guys like Kevin Lilly and Terry Connaughton, who excel at Gaelic games. But these lads were brought up in families that were immersed in the association. The reality is that children with no background just fall away after fourteen.'

This is the crux of the problem. Brady and McGettigan meet for breakfast a couple of times a week. Up to a couple of seasons ago, they managed the New York senior football team together. Their visit to McHale park in Mayo for the Connacht championship of 2000 marked a major step forward for the association. They lost the match, as expected, but not any respectability.

'I thought it was a qualified victory of sorts. We learned we were fit enough and what we were doing was good enough but were shy maybe five players. But then we had two players stopped at emigration and it left a sour taste when we went to go to Galway the next summer; guys were fearful. The ironic thing about it was we were beaten 1-15 to 1-05. Leitrim and Sligo only scored eight points against them. That was the team I was most proud of because we could have been on the end of a hiding to infinity.'

As was always the case, home attitudes towards the ex-patriot team varied. Mayo did all but put on a fireworks display over the weekend, but when they visited Galway a year later, they felt as if their presence was regarded as a hindrance. The game was played in Tuam but there was no organised lunch or meal in the town afterwards. The reason given was that there was no place open in Tuam and the players went back to a hotel in the city for soup and sandwiches.

'I remember one of their officials came into our room afterwards and gave the usual platitudes – delighted to have ye and all the rest. One of our guys said, "If ye think so much of us, ye might throw on the kettle."'

For the past few years, New York has been the host team, paying for the travelling costs of Roscommon, Sligo and Leitrim. Word came from Sligo that they were not happy about the idea of playing in Gaelic Park, that they believed it to be little more than a boxing ring with goalposts at either end.

'It all stemmed from a game we played against Roscommon when three guys were sent off, two of those our players. And I suppose the old reputation stood against it. But we had trained guys to play football and hearing that hurt us, it really did.'

Last winter, despite having taken Leitrim to extra time in the championship of 2003, the Brady/McGettigan ticket was not returned to the management post. Such is the Byzantine political world of New York GAA. It is like a contemporary

Tammany Hall so it is best not even to ask, and neither man is particularly bitter about it. But when they meet up and sip coffee, they often talk football and their view on the future of the association differs. Maybe Frank is more romantic. Leslie reckons you keep on paying to import the stars – within reason – or else a community that is growing more indifferent and insular anyway will just stop coming to Gaelic Park, that its fans will slow to a trickle and finally dry up.

The great thing about Gaelic Park is that it is definitively not Croke Park. It is not lush and it is not exclusive. When Jackie Salmon brought Dublin's Keith Barr out for a summer many years ago, the young defender gazed in dismay at this new cathedral, with its busted bleachers and a field that consisted entirely of dust.

'Aww Jaysus, Jackie,' moaned Barr. 'You must be joking. Sure there is no friggin' grass.'

'Son,' grunted the local man. 'Did I bring you out here to graze?'

Anybody can play on Gaelic Park but what makes it unique is that, through the decades, as well as featuring the most basic and ugly junior-league games, the place has hosted all the legends. It was in the Bronx, after all, that Robert Kennedy turned up one sweltering afternoon in 1965 to see Christy Ring, fuller in body but still elegant at 46, score 2-05 in an exhibition match. That day, both gods were mobbed in separate circles. It was in Gaelic Park that the legendary Mick O'Connell took on the celebrated American football player Roy Garela from the championship-winning Pittsburgh Steelers and, attempting all but one kick with the oval ball, he triumphed by seven conversions to six.

And it was there that the Sam Maguire vanished in the heat of celebrations one October night when Feale Rangers of Kerry were on tour. Jimmy Deenihan had been Kerry's captain in the win over Roscommon that September and it was decided to bring the cup to the States. It was left in the clubhouse for safekeeping overnight but when Deenihan returned the next day, John Kerry O'Donnell regretfully informed him that the cup had been somehow stolen, most probably by a delirious Roscommon supporter. Terry Connaughton, a New York GAA stalwart with Roscommon connections, rejected this idea and announced that it had to be still on the premises. In a state of high unease, the boys from Feale embarked upon their east-coast tour without the famous cup and appeared with the World Series and NFL-winning Pittsburgh Pirates and Steelers trophy-less. Only when the FBI was called in did the Maguire inexplicably reappear, with slogans like 'Up Ros' and 'Brook Inn, Brooklyn', suggesting that it had been on a tour of the boroughs.

'I am sorry I ever brought the cup here, I am embarrassed,' declared Jimmy Deenihan. A year after this downright bizarre occurrence, John Kerry had the poise and verve to turn up at congress in Ireland to run for president of the association.

It was in Gaelic Park that New York beat both the 1958 hurling champions, Kilkenny, and the football champions from Louth. The local board spent $133,000, a phenomenal sum then, on what was known as the St Breandán Cup, the latest improvisation to secure games against the fashionable Irish teams of the day.

In 1982, congress relaxed the rules regarding 'weekend' players travelling to play for American teams. This latitude was reversed late in 1983 when it transpired a week after the hurling final, many of those who played in Croke Park starred in the New York showpiece of a fortnight later at Gaelic Park. It was a virtual recreation, like dismantling an old stone cottage in Connemara so it could be transported and reassembled in the States.

Gaelic Park was where John Kerry saw fit to somehow

insult the GAA president Mick Loftus in 1986, an exchange that prompted central council to slap a one-year ban on all Irish teams travelling to the city. Kerry was, as ever, unrepentant. His personality, strong and untameable and proud, seemed to embody the best and the worst of the GAA in New York. Today, more than a decade after his death, New York GAA men regularly lionise him and berate him in the same sentence. Kerry was far from perfect but he was real and substantial and he made things happen.

By the 1980s, Kerry no longer exerted the all-encompassing influence he had in earlier decades, and perhaps sensing this, he got involved in a series of explosive feuds with the local organisation. Sunday after Sunday was cancelled in the summer of 1986 when O'Donnell refused to raise the gate fee from $2 to $3. The entrance cost stayed at two bucks but, a year later, another row arose from the same source. The football final between Connemara and a Larry Tompkins-inspired Donegal team had re-awoken interest in the local competition, evoking comparisons to the boom years of the 1950s. It ended in a draw and before the highly anticipated replay, board president Oliver O'Donnell believed the association should handle the turnstiles while John Kerry insisted that he, as leaseholder, had to appoint the gate keepers. Neither man would compromise and winter settled the matter with a hard and quiet freeze, ending hopes of the replay ever being realised. To those observing from across the Atlantic, it seemed like a typical act of New York self-destruction, mule-stubborn and needless. To the New Yorkers, it was a mere act of principle. It was a refusal to back down, which was always the Irish-American way.

So this is where the games in New York are at now. On a frigid evening in February, they might as well be molecules in Leslie McGettigan's palm as he raps his hand against the table to explain why the scene is so perverse and so precious.

Leslie is funny and generous to a fault and with a casual philanthropic streak to his blood. People interest and warm to him. What he has figured out now is that missing out on the unfathomable magic of 1992 was probably a trade, one of those fatalistic little quirks that magnify as they recede in the distance. The years since have been good to him; the bar is going well and he has plans to open a few more and he has a young family with American accents who seem happy as anything where they are. He has made the very best of his opportunity.

Leslie brings his boy down to Gaelic Park when it's sunny and the child is restless after half an hour. But Stephon Marbury of the Knicks or Derek Jeter of the Yankees are examples of the heroic currency of his generation and Leslie understands that. When you are a kid, your eyes drift towards the brightest stars and it confirms his belief that the GAA in New York is fighting against ever-greatening odds. Through school meetings, he and his wife Elaine have met other parents with no Irish background whatsoever, something that is fresh and nice. Slowly, the horizons of the New World are widening and avenues of choice and decision are opening before his eyes and it is different from when life was reduced to being the slickest forward on the team. It is neither harder nor easier, but different. Yet there is this elemental tug that cannot go away.

'See,' he explains. 'I'm a Letterkenny boy. Always will be. There is not a week where I am not on the phone three and four times to home. Anyone here who tells you they do not miss home, well, they are lying or they have been away too long or else are too caught up in the bullshit that goes on here. Because everyone does, it is human nature. And I am not talking about family or anything that deep. It's just the people you grew up with and that. Lads you played football with. That becomes a part of it. I don't think I could go back now but I would never fully rule out that possibility. When I came over here, Gaelic Park was the place to be. On a Sunday, you went there to play or watch a game or meet a woman. You wanted to play there and people knew you because you played there. It definitely helped me settle in here and make friends and, being honest, it has helped in terms of this business. But I don't know. It is changing. We have had problems with attendance in recent years. People don't really give a fuck. They are just not so bothered. And that's sad.'

The things Leslie sees now worry him. He gets a better interpretation of what Ireland is like now from watching the summer-long residents carousing on McLean Avenue than he does on his whirlwind visits home. Maybe it's just maturity setting in, but he often thinks he sees a core fecklessness, a kind of detachment among many young Irish kids that did not exist in his day. He hears stories from friends at home about the way recreational drugs have taken a subtle and irreversible hold across the provinces and it occurs to him that maybe the Irish Bronx is, in a weird way, now more innocent than home. One thing is sure though. Fewer and fewer kids who spend summers here require Gaelic Park as the sun and moon of their youthful society. As a result, some of them struggle. That is why he believes that the presence of the GAA here can be a comfort blanket. Nobody makes a fortune on the back of the association any more, but they can provide a smooth few months. A really hot footballer, a young lad of strong county-quality calibre, can pocket $5,000, be given an apartment for the summer and a guaranteed job. In Boston and Chicago, the rumour is that the sky is the limit but New York is more modest and sane in its approach.

'If a lad can kick any bit of football at all, there will always be a team looking for a player and that leads to contacts. But even if you don't play, just knowing a few guys, even having their names in your pocket, it can be of help. People do try and look out for kids here.'

It is a funny and at some level a lonely business, the constant breathing of life into New York GAA. For all its flaws, it takes a work ethic and a determination and commitment that is admirable. At present, the association at home has ended the practice of 'weekend' players jetting in and out of summer for one hour of devastating play in Gaelic Park and a tidy cheque at the end of it. However, 'sixty-day' imports are permissible under certain conditions. More often than not, these kids are students who come and leave casually. They promise they will be around until October but come September regularly complain that they need to register back home. Often, clubs pay for return flights solely so their marquee players can register for Third Arts or Business Management or whatever. Once, Irish kids arrived to play ball in New York with a sense of gratitude. Now, it is more like a business transaction; it is a straightforward case of guns for hire. A New York senior club can spend $80,000 a season just to survive in the high-stakes game of roulette. The buzz comes when the championship season is at its height and the cobbled teams have meshed together well and the games are of a decent quality. But then the season ends and the Irish players pack their bags and vanish and the temperatures plummet and it is like the whole thing was a mirage. It must be hard for the Bronx–Irish residents not to feel like saps at times, not to feel like they have been somehow used even though this is a system of their own making. Maybe it is self-perpetuating. In a different life, Leslie McGettigan was flown back and forth for the things he could do on a football field. Now, he hustles to raise money and spends time on the phone paying dues to some youngster from 'Blaney or Carndonagh who is said to have a mean left foot.

'There is a pro- and anti-New York story,' he explains. 'It used to be open season here – the week after the All-Ireland final, half the players would be out here playing. OK. It was a carrot to guys back home. Ask guys who played at All-Ireland level. It was a perk. But it destroyed the game for some of the local kids playing here whose place was taken. Some of them were fucking gone. Some were OK about it, others walked and never got involved again. It was a terrible thing. Then they brought it down to two weekend players. That was good and here is why. A guy lives in the Bronx and couldn't give a toss about Donegal–New York. Then he hears Brendan Devenney or Adrian Sweeney are coming out and he says, right, I'll go along for a look, bring my wife and kids and a friend and have a look. You need a draw, you need an attraction. Every sporting association does. The GAA should allow two weekend guys per team here – provided they are out of the championship at home. That way, the home clubs don't lose out and the dynamic of the local teams here is not altered because it is just two players. Either way, it is an uphill battle. But I mean the general rule here is that no matter who you are, if you are OK, then you will be given a shot. And if you turn out to be an asshole who takes advantage of that, then shame on you. Being generous doesn't shoot me in the foot. You are who you are.'

Frank Brady cannot put his hand on his heart and promise an eternal future for the GAA in New York. He believes it will be so; the natural assumption is that where there are Irish people, there will be games. The Mayo association started preparing for the visit of Mayo for last summer's championship game in October of 2003. The banquet that night was easily the biggest New York–Irish night of the year. When the GAA flexes its muscle, then the great stone canyons of the city still rumble. But those occasions are exceptional. Perhaps on a daily basis there is less need for the old pillar of a Sunday afternoon at a match. Frank could name a dozen or maybe twenty people without whom New York GAA would just collapse. And he wonders who is going to take their place.

On a visit home recently, Brady watched a documentary on

RTÉ about the Irish labourers who migrated to London in the 1950s and 1960s. They sent much of their earnings back home and cashed the rest around the bars of Cricklewood and Kilburn with inevitable consequences, and now many have ended up destitute and impoverished.

'A lot of Mayo men for some reason,' says Brady. 'That struck me. This one guy had this battery radio and he was so attached to it, he was clinging on to it like it was all he had.'

He found that film brutal and heartbreaking and naturally compared it to the New York community that has become his home. Definitely, he has known those solitary, sad-eyed Irish working men who have fallen on hard times but not, he believes, to the wretched degree portrayed in London. The American scene is all unionised and regulated and even the loneliest of emigrants had some sort of pension to depend upon when they finished up. Maybe it is wishful thinking, but he is inclined to believe that the American experience has been kinder and brighter to the vast majority of those who came here over the decades. He suspects that because New York's economy of space has packed the Irish communities tight together there is less likelihood of people falling out of sight. And he also likes to think that the local games helped as well.

At the very least, Gaelic Park always promised the solace of noise and family and sport. It was always good for that much. It never claimed perfection. Rowdiness has often got the better of it. It can be messy and beery and sentimental. But it has a true heart and has probably come closer than any other place to realising Davin's vision of a replanted and autonomous Irish culture. In recent years, the New York association has become more streamlined and closer to the mother association in Dublin. The pitched battle of wills, the power struggles, appear to be over.

But at heart, New York GAA exists in isolation and it

survives purely because people see and smell something worth preserving.

Leslie McGettigan has played on enough fields to know the potency of Gaelic Park on sweltering late afternoons in June. He just wants to keep those days alive. You should hear him talk about the best days, when the old place was packed out and the games were teak-tough but exhilarating. Even on the pitch you could smell frying onions and beer drifting in across the wire and there was a great crowd that you might get at a county final. And as you kicked a point towards the splendid crimson skyline that lit up the concrete and metal sprawl of the Bronx, playing there felt perfect. It felt like home.

8

We Could be Heroes

In St Laurence O'Toole's girls' national school, rehearsals for the Luke Kelly memorial concert were in full swing. It was one of those breathless days of molten city heat that left the footpaths baking and a sense that even the frowning buildings that border the river Liffey were sighing, glad of the dry heat after all the damp and smoke of winter. Because of the sunshine, the windows and front door of the school were open and the childish choruses of famous ballads could be heard on nearby Sheriff Street and Seville Place. Luke Kelly, who grew up in No 4L, St Laurence's Mansions, has remained a beacon of local pride around these streets throughout the bleaker turns of fortune and circumstance. To commemorate the twentieth anniversary of his passing, the boys' and girls' schools prepared to give a concert which was to be held in the last weeks of the term. St Laurence O'Toole's GNS has changed little since it was built 150 years ago, an orange brick building fenced in with wrought iron and two steps leading through its arched front door. Many of the present-day pupils were preceded here by their mothers and grandmothers and so the place is reminiscent of everybody's first school experience: worn staircases, narrow hallways the smell of cocoa and pencil parings. The walls, though, are brightly painted and decorated with art exhibitions and projects. And everywhere, there are photographs of Gaelic teams.

St Laurence O'Toole's GNS has little modern heritage when it comes to Gaelic games and, locked between the railway lines of Connolly Station and the glassy financial citadels that have come to boss the riverscape, the school does not even have a field. Its schoolyard is a narrow triangle of tarmac hemmed in by a wire fence and is so small that the pupils have to go home at lunchtime. Because of the architectural layout of the terraced houses, street soccer was the game that children here grew up with. But in the last three years, out of the blue, the girls in this Dublin school have stormed through the divisions of Cumann na mBunscol. A year after Aodhán Ó Ríordáin, a teacher at St Laurence's GNS, gathered a group of children together for their first Gaelic football session in the community hall, they won the division four final in Parnell Park. A year later, they had graduated to Croke Park for the division three final. All season, they conceded a grand total of one point. Their victory over a school from Monkstown was the subject of a sports report on the main evening news on RTÉ television that night. It bounced in the face of generations of soul-destroying stories featuring the usual list of urban malaise that seemed to have taken a permanent hold in Sheriff Street.

'I was offered a post here in March and I wandered along figuring I would leave in the summer and find something else,' said Aodhán Ó Ríordáin when we met. 'That was in 2000. And I would have had the same perceptions of Sheriff Street as everyone else – that it was rough and all the rest. But you forget that it is also a place with seven- and eight-year-olds the same as anywhere else – polite, well brought up, funny, intelligent children. That somehow got lost.'

Aodhán has the distinction of becoming the first male

teacher in St Laurence O'Toole's girls' school in its history. The first 'sir'.

'And even though we have another "sir" now, I am still "the sir".'

Brought up in Malahide and attending a school with sumptuous facilities, Ó Riordáin played Gaelic football with great enthusiasm but, he insists, not enough skill ever to entice Dublin selectors out to the coast for a look. He decided to set up a girls' Gaelic football team on a whim and was staggered when forty-six local children turned up at the local hall for the first session. He had one football and no experience of coaching the sport. Most of the girls were only vaguely aware of what Gaelic football was about. The first evening was mayhem but the kids scattered to their houses with glowing faces and showed up again next time out. A few weeks later, Aodhán happened to be at a GAA function attended by the then president of the association, Seán McCague.

'I just thought "why not?" and explained I worked at this disadvantaged school and asked if he could do anything. He enquired what we needed. I asked for a set of gear and he replied, what colour? It was fair enough.'

A week later, McCague visited the school to present the team gear. Had the children been informed that this was Seán McCague, the first Gael to travel in space, they would have given him the same polite, indifferent reception. They simply did not know who he was.

'Seán, though, has a primary background himself and he was great with the kids,' Aodhán says.

In 2000, the nascent team continued to work in the community hall, learning the fundamentals of the game and about discipline, with the promise of – some day – playing on a proper field luring them on. In their maiden season of 2001, it was clear that the girls had tremendous aptitude for the sport. One of the characteristics that all the teachers who go to work among inner-city schoolchildren notice is a profound lack of self-esteem. That was one of the reasons Aodhán started up football. He noticed that lessons were approached in the dread assumption that failure would be the ultimate result. Art classes were underpinned by a constant need for reassurance that their efforts were acceptable. 'Common' was the word the children used to describe themselves. As they approached one of the more illustrious schools in their first season as a team, one of the girls confided in Sir that the opposition 'are going to know we are common as muck.'

Those hall sessions were spent convincing the girls that they could be good at the game. Once they lost their inhibitions, they began to play the game with utter fearlessness and reaped havoc on the more genteel schools they encountered. Although participation is sacrosanct at under-age level, the fact of beating children from schools that the girls would otherwise have been intimidated by was invaluable.

'You were starting out with their self-esteem at rock bottom,' Aodhán explained. 'And then when they started winning and beating these happy-clappy middle class Gaelscoils, well, it felt great. I know I shouldn't say that because they are very nice people and extremely sporting. But I love seeing St Laurence's girls' school beating Gaelscoils, I think it's fantastic. Because they always felt like they were not in the club, not in whatever Ireland is meant to be.'

In its golden period, Sheriff Street resembled one of those fresh and roughly energetic Manhattan dockside communities immortalised by Elia Kazan's *On the Waterfront*.

It was never affluent, but the B&I freight ships and coal ships that docked on the Liffey were a steady, reliable source of income – men took number seven shovels to unload the coal supplies that came in at North Wall Quay. There was constant movement along the quays in the 1940s and 1950s, with people heading towards the passenger boats or farmers shipping cattle out. There were at least five pubs along Sheriff Street, none of which languished.

The old cottages originally housed the British Army and, today, the street names bear the titles bestowed upon them by the Empire. Some of the original Sheriff Street residents could remember little jail cells in the back yards. By the end of World War II, those houses were straining under the burden of growing families and, in 1956, the Sheriff Street flats were built, with 456 separate dwellings.

Gerry Fay, who today has a post office and general newsagent's at Seville Place, remembers the flats when they were new and pristine and a source of optimism among the community. He went to St Laurence O'Toole's boys' school with Luke Kelly. They played football together under Brother Francis and on Sundays, they headed up Gardiner Street towards Croke Park, skipping in the solemn steps of countrymen in peaked caps and jackets and ties. They knew of a gap in the wire where they could squeeze through and watch the big championship games on a Sunday. Kelly was strong at sports and played soccer as well as Gaelic. When he was around sixteen though, there was a fire in number 4L and the Kelly family was relocated to Whitehall. There is a photograph of that St Laurence's team, of which Gerry Fay was captain, hanging in the school today. Even in the black and white image, Kelly's russet colouring and freckles are unmistakable and he looks astonishingly fresh-faced and young. Gaelic football had a strong identity in the community at that stage through O'Toole's, a staunch city club which competed in both football and hurling and had a celebrated pipe band. In the 1920s, O'Toole's was the most overt symbol of parish life. It is said that when the players from Tipperary and Dublin raced in terror from Croke Park on Bloody Sunday, it was in the houses of the O'Toole's players around Seville Row that they sought refuge. The Cumann na nBunscol movement was founded at 100 Seville Place, the headquarters of O'Toole's, in 1928. Eight schools took part in the inaugural league and then the Ard Stiúrthóir of the GAA, Pádraig Ó Caoimh, extended the invitation to play the finals in Croke Park. It has been a privilege unique to Dublin schoolchildren ever since.

The demise of the club coincided with the advent of containerisation, an innovation that made the unloading of dockside materials much more efficient. It also decimated the need for a locally based labour force. Just like that, the main source of income to Sheriff Street was choked. It was a working-class community stripped of purpose and Fay reckons that things fell apart as quickly as the late 1960s. It was then that the banshee screech of tyres became the common sound of night and, truculence turned towards violence and the more extreme manifestations of poverty set in. The local schools were vastly overcrowded then and most children did their best to ease that burden by leaving at the earliest possible opportunity.

With the national economy floundering, Sheriff Street silently took its hits. Families that had been in the community for generations noticed, with some disquiet, that Dublin Corporation was relocating residents from other troubled areas of the city to their neighbourhood. That created a sense of disharmony which was heightened when other long-time residents took advantage of the FitzGerald administration initiative to encourage corporation-housing dwellers to purchase their own property. Several, having lost faith in Sheriff Street, left. The usual litany of ills – unemployment, alcoholism, drug abuse, teenage pregnancies – had afflicted the place by the 1980s.

'There was a period,' says Gerry Fay, 'when it became a bit of a Hell's Kitchen.'

It was during that decade that Fay had to fight with a

community group to prevent a proposal to erase Sheriff Street
and redevelop the land. He was at a function one night at the
Green Isle Hotel when a comedian on stage made a passing,
derogatory reference to Sheriff Street. What astonished him was
that everyone in the room understood the meaning. It was the
first time he realised how desperate the public perception of his
home place was. Still, he wasn't alone in wanting to see it
preserved. Street marches were held and slides were presented
to illustrate that Sheriff Street, for all its problems, had the
heartbeat of a firmly rooted community. It had five schools
through which four generations had passed; it had a credit
union, a boxing club, a youth club, a church. It was real.
Finally, sanctuary was granted and, in the 1990s, PJ Drudy of
Trinity College fronted the Sheriff Street Group, and bright,
expensive buildings replaced the ghostly dereliction along the
ruined docks of the Liffey, and slowly life on the long street of
red-brick cottages became calmer again. The flats went.
Although the 456 units were declared structurally sound, many
were in appalling condition and they were sold, for the paltry
sum of £2.4 million, to a private interest in 1994. There was a
general sense of relief when they crashed down but also a pang
of nostalgia because the flats were also a symbol of older, better
times on Sheriff Street.

It was against that backdrop that the present generation of
St Laurence O'Toole's girls grew up. When Aodhán Ó Ríordáin
came to teach in the locality, he was struck by how family-
orientated it was.

'The street is like the living room here. You come along
some mornings and can see kids sitting out in their pyjamas
because sometimes the houses are crowded and also because all
these children grew up together, as did their parents and
grandparents, in many instances.'

Because of that, the revival of Gaelic football in the area
created a connection between school and home that formal

education could not. At the same time as Aodhán started training his team, Ciara Harte spent her Friday evenings coaching hurling and football in Luke Kelly's alma mater.

'We just started training in the yard,' she recalled as she kept one eye on her class. 'I think the first evening we had twenty boys. We started out hurling – Fintan Walsh from Cumann organised a scheme where everyone could buy a hurley for a fiver so, for the first term, all the boys were walking to and from school with their hurls. But because we only had the yard and because all of these boys are soccer fans, we decided that football was a more natural sport to start with.'

The CBS is a bright and airy modern school located on Seville Place.

In the computer room, Carlos Donovan, Kofi Kelly and Gerard Brennan, gathered to talk about the 2002 season, when they enjoyed an astonishing run of success against schools from more privileged areas of the city. Against the odds, they too got to the final in Croke Park, which was played on the same afternoon as the St Laurence O'Toole's girls' match.

'We got hammered in the final,' confessed Kofi. 'The other school were class, they were. They were lethal. They were way bigger than us. But Croke Park was great. The dressing rooms were unbelievable. We had a green pitch inside with a net in it. And the grass was class compared to Fairview. But then we had to watch the girls win their match.'

Most of the players on the 2002 team were only in fourth class when they reached the final against schools with much greater numbers. Ciara Harte has constantly tried to explain that part of playing sport is learning how to lose. Like Aodhán Ó Riordáin, she battled to try to raise the self-esteem of the children. The boys tended to be full of bravado in the beginning but it was hollow. Only when the sense of team developed and they realised that they could legitimately expect to do better than the other children they encountered did the first rays of genuine confidence appear. The natural rivalry between boys and girls of that age meant that Kofi and his team had to watch the girls' glory-run in a kind of benign sufferance. The girls were their neighbours: they grew up kicking soccer together or at least trying to disrupt the games of soccer that the girls organised.

But the sensation of both schools reaching a final in Croke Park stirred the community in a way that other school-related projects could not. Although the great monolith of Gaelic games is the most imposing piece of architecture in this part of the city, the more recent generations of Sheriff Street children have had a curious relationship with it. Some had been with their fathers. Some had not. Most of them felt it was the preserve of people from the country. On that afternoon in May, however, the Sheriff Street residents turned out in force. Grandmothers of the players, who would never have troubled themselves with Croke Park in their own youth, roared as if witnessing this final was the culmination of a lifetime's dream.

'It was all a bit crazy,' says Aodhán. 'I remember when we won and the final whistle went, one of the fathers came racing down from the stand and started hugging me. I kind of got carried away myself. And then another father took the grass and mud that had got caught on his girl's football boots and he sealed it in a cellophane bag to keep. He still has it.'

That night was one of jubilation: it was a homecoming. The relationship with their street remains intensely local. Last year, on a school trip to France, Aodhán was struck by how indifferent the girls were when they arrived in Dublin Airport. They did not cheer when they drove in through Drumcondra, nor when they reached O'Connell Street. They stayed quiet as the bus passed along Amiens Street and turned into Seville Place. Only when they went under the bridge and caught sight of St Laurence's Church and their own school did they start cheering. So Croke Park was outside their world and the sight of their game on television was beyond comprehension. The slot dedicated to the triumph in the main evening news was recorded and then played and replayed.

On the morning we met, Aodhán excused some of the sixth-class girls who played on the 2002 team from class and replayed the RTÉ report again. It was clear that the three players, Emma Byrne, Stacey Grimes and Stacey Watson, knew every syllable by word. But their eyes still lit in anticipation of seeing their friend, her face painted green, pulling a funny expression and waving at the camera, and then the action shots of the match.

Emma, probably the best player in the school, was the most quiet and watchful of the three. To begin with, they offered a rehearsed series of answers they rhyme off for all visiting adults.

'Twelve.'

'Sixth.'

'Soccer.'

'Cos you have to handpass it.'

'Thought it was funny.'

'Thought we wouldn't be able to play it.'

'Cos of all the rules.'

But the two Staceys are natural impresarios and, after a respectable amount of time, they began giving a guided tour of the school. They explained the meaning of the crest on their jerseys designed by one of the school's former students, Natalie Delaney. The reason the school colours were green and white was that the school caretaker, Tom McDonald, had suggested those colours that the O'Toole's team had worn long ago. When the girls took to the field in Croke Park, Tom told Aodhán later, he shed a few tears. They point out the various stars of that 2002 day, some of whom have left for secondary school in Marino or Killester or King's Inn or Larkin College.

The girls have this motto: 'Always Play with Pride'.

'Do you remember the first day, sir,' asked Emma, 'when you

asked us, "What do you play with?" and someone shouted, "A football"?'

A wall of photographs was also dedicated to last year's trip to France. The team played against a local French school in both soccer and Gaelic. To their consternation, they lost at soccer.

'They were hacking at us,' said Stacey Grimes.

After the rules of Gaelic football were conveyed to the bemused French, a further game was organised and revenge was mercilessly enacted. After she scored a goal, Stacey Watson turned to her marker and said: 'This is our game.'

The good and bad points of France were discussed. The girls were adamant that the food was a disgrace. Nobody had tried frogs' legs.

'But,' Stacey Grimes remembered bitterly, 'we had to have carrot soup.'

'The McDonald's was good, though,' consoled Stacey Watson. 'It's the exact same as over here.'

The highlight of the entire tour was a visit to Stade Français to see Zidane and Henri play for France against the Czech Republic. Jason Sherlock is about the only Dublin player the girls can name check, but they are well versed in the heroes of English and European soccer. The metamorphosis to creatures of the Gaelic scene is slow and although they sometimes go along to see Dublin play in the summer now, Gaelic football remains a sport to be played rather than watched. But on foreign soil, it was their birthright. Everybody had been impressed with the Eiffel Tower, although they were only allowed as far as the second level.

'We were told it was because we were too young,' said Emma, shooting a baleful look at Sir.

'That was just a big lie,' said Stacey Grimes crossly. 'We weren't too young. Sure there were babies up on the top.'

We moved on through the corridor, the group of us, to a mural that depicted all the local Sheriff Street features, from the church to the flat. All of the girls have memories of the flats, which were knocked down before they made their First Communion.

They have mixed feelings about them still.

'When you went up the steps, you had to stamp your feet because of the rats.'

'But they were good too because everybody was around and it was good fun.'

'It was very old and very dirty. Everybody was around it and was playing.'

'It's all private buildings and apartments and banks and all. A Spar. See where the park is? That's where the flats were.'

'I'd say Ma and Da were kind of sad because that's where they lived but happy cos we got somewhere better to live.

'We didn't. Because we were in a one bedroom for a while.'

This summer will be the last the girls spend on Sheriff Street before their lives broaden with the secondary-school experiences. The connection with Gaelic football will remain, though. Last year, Aodhán and a number of parents in the community set up an under-age club affiliated to O'Connell's Boys' Club and St Joseph's. They train or play games on Friday evenings at under-fourteen level, meaning that the girls still have a connection with the club after they move on to secondary school.

They took to the city leagues with much the same result as they began in Cumann na mBunscol, wiping out established teams like Ballymun Kickhams and Na Fianna and Clontarf. The Na Fianna game was won with a goal in the last ten seconds and, after it was scored, the players jumped on each other like in the Premiership.

'They are still mad soccer heads,' Aodhán laughed. 'You can't knock it out of them.'

Children from Marlborough Street, East Wall, the Liberty House flats and Rutland Street began to play with the club.

They won the division three county title and Emma was then selected on the Dublin under-fourteen team. They have high hopes of success when they move into the under-sixteen bracket.

Neither Ciara Harte nor Aodhán Ó Ríordáin considers themselves to be a Gaelic games fanatic. In essence, the sport is a means of communication. What they share, though, is a deep sense of pride and concern for the children with whom they work, a genuine altruism that has nothing to do with career or salary. The funny thing is that Sheriff Street and Seville Place are perhaps the last places in Ireland to cling on to the traditional view of the teacher as a figure to be respected. And it may sound preachy or worthy but you can't listen to these teachers talking about 'their kids' for very long without feeling humbled.

'I enjoy it, see,' says Aodhán. 'If I didn't, then I'd be the right martyr. But the honest truth is I get as much of a kick out of it as the kids.'

None of this is to suggest that Sheriff Street or the CBS is a paradise regained. Although the walls of St Laurence's are brightly painted, the building is simply too dark and old to be suited to modern education standards. On miserable, wet mornings over the winter, Aodhán or one of the other staff members occasionally found a discarded syringe in the yard. The culture of leaving school early is still deeply ingrained. In the boys' school, the class projects deal with darker material than is probably the case in most Irish national schools, explaining in stark terms the consequences of alcoholism and of using drugs like cannabis or heroin. One project shows a picture of a man who is evidently homeless. The children imagine the life he led before that point: they think he had a job and a family and a good life but that he just got lost.

Gerry Fay believes the community is gradually recovering from the deletion of its former existence. A number of students from the area are studying in Trinity but continue to live in Sheriff Street. Ciara and Aodhán are hopeful that at least some of the kids from their class will follow that path. But for now, it is enough to see them happy, at least on their watch.

After the impromptu tour of the school finished, we looked for a suitable place to take a photograph. It was Stacey Watson who suggested the front steps.

'That way,' she said, 'people will be able to see our school sign.'

Archbishop Ryan National School is located on the edge of consumer country, just a few minutes' drive from the Liffey Valley Centre in west Dublin, one of the über-malls that have lit up Irish suburbia in recent years.

Gaelic games are a relatively new pursuit in Archbishop Ryan but because of the work of staff teachers like Joe McDonagh and because of the close affiliation with the local GAA club, Lucan Sarsfields, it has enjoyed a degree of early prestige. The size of the school – over 600 children are registered – is part of the reason. But the school's success in the Cumann na mBunscol division four hurling final last year was bound up in the abilities of Sujon Alamjir, a Bangladeshi youngster who has already established a reputation as a young hurler of note.

Sujon is one of 212 foreign national children attending Bishop Ryan NS and was the pre-eminent figure in the team's triumph in Croke Park against Our Lady of the Wayside, Kilternan, in May of last year. He was one of five foreign national children to play that day.

'I think it was as early as our second-ever training session that you could see that Sujon had an aptitude for the game that was beyond the other kids,' said Joe McDonagh one lunchtime over a sandwich in the school staff room. 'He played cricket in Bangladesh so his hand and eye co-ordination was advanced.

Initially the emphasis was on ground hurling and just his touch, his eye for the ball, hitting on the ground, doubling on the ball, the ease with which he moved right and left and then his natural athleticism just made him stand out. He was by far and away the best.'

When we met in the computer room – seemingly the conference location of choice in the national school system – Sujon was, as promised, a brilliantly sunny and easy-going child. Because of his aptitude for hurling, Sujon is accustomed to notice but he deals with it all as if amused. Dami Ajike, a solemn, polite Nigerian boy who speaks perfect English, and Ibraham Chaudery, from Pakistan, also played on last year's team and they joined him for the reminiscence. But Sujon led the way.

'It was a great game. Last year, we had a very good team. We played games like in the champion's league and then beat Kilternan in the final. I know I scored two goals and five points. And good goals – I made solo runs and then I scored. I don't take the frees – Cormac [Reynolds] who plays with me in midfield takes the frees. Cormac is a great player.'

John Ring, the vice principal in the school, who sat in on the conversation, can't pinpoint when foreign national kids began enrolling, in the school but it wasn't before 1998.

'I just remember that one September we had a few obviously non-Irish kids in the very junior classes and then more children kept appearing. I imagine we have one of the highest percentages of foreign national kids in the city now. And I think it makes us very lucky, to be honest. Because the local children were very open and receptive to the idea and it has been a great learning process for everybody. But now it is just a natural thing. Sujon, for instance, would be an icon among all the children in the school at this stage.'

Of the three children, Sujon claimed to have been the least fazed at the upheaval of moving to Ireland. Dami, who has never been to his parental homeland of Nigera, spent his early years in London. The hardest thing about Dublin, he said, was finding somewhere to live. The family moved to Cabra and then to Lucan and are now living in Blanchardstown. Ibraham readily declared that he had been terrified at the thought of coming to live here.

'I thought it would be wet and full of big, rough boys.'

And perhaps it was, but mostly on Gaelic fields. When Sujon turned up one weekend morning to play with Lucan Sarsfields, his birth certificate had not yet arrived from Bangladesh, so the trainers placed him with a group of under-twelve children.

'Then his birth certificate turned up and we realised he was born in 1991 so he was a year younger than we had thought,' remembered Liam Ryan, a Kilkenny man exiled in suburban Dublin. 'So he had been impressing among kids that were a year older than him, which can be a fairly dramatic gap at that age. He had this tremendous skill, but as well as that, there was a real positive aggression to his game that doesn't come naturally to most kids. Like, children at that age group tend to take steps backward to clear the ball and we try and encourage them to take on their opponent and step into the space. With Sujon, it was the opposite. He was always going forward, always looking to drive. You had to sit him down and explain the benefits of stepping back. We would use Brian Whelahan as an example whenever Offaly were playing on television.'

But in the Corn Aghais, the trophy dedicated to the 1916 Rising patriot, Thomas Ashe, Sujon's 'go-forward' inclinations were more than enough to set the tone of the game. Archbishop Ryan NS has a video of the game courtesy of their Kilternan opponents. They played across the width of the pitch and so the video shows the huge wall of the Hogan and Cusack stands as the game goes on, which seem even bigger in scale when empty. The supporters from both schools are gathered behind the respective goals, but they fill only a few rows and their voices echo around the stadium, as if the hurling is being played on the floor of the Grand Canyon. Although the announcer, a girl from the Kilternan school, is obviously commenting from her local perspective, she maintains an impressive level of impartiality throughout, even when Sujon begins lording over affairs.

As he had suggested, the two goals he scored were indeed worth the admission price – had there been one. Because of his height and skin colour, Sujon would have been prominent anyway, but after about five minutes into the game, the extent of his accomplishments become apparent. They were certainly not lost on the commentator, who began to refer to 'number nine' with growing trepidation. Much of the game passed with the players chasing the *sliotar* on the ground, but every so often Sujon would dip to pick it up and then simply accelerate away from the crowd. All of his scores were taken with great ease but the last goal was out of the ordinary. He ran half the field carrying the hurl with the kind of nonchalant use of wrist that makes the hurling critics purr. When three Kilternan defenders – tired now of seeing him zoom into their orbit – gathered around him, he turned one way and twisted another before finding room for his shot on the turn.

By then, the result was a formality but children being children, they continued to play their hearts out. You can see Dami darting around the left wing and Ibraham comes in as a substitute in the second half.

'We were brought on a tour of Croke Park once,' said Dami, 'but I never thought I would play there. It was unbelievable being in the dressing rooms and pretty scary coming out onto the field. But my mum was there to watch.'

When the whistle went, the Archbishop Ryan team celebrated with abandon, with Sujon the focal point of attention while the Kilternan children trooped back to their coach.

'They wore the jersey proudly,' concluded the commentator, 'and the school should be proud of them.'

Because the video belonged to the defeated school, there was only a brief shot of the Archbishop Ryan children receiving the cup. But later, at a function for the beaten team, a man who is presumably the principal gave a touching speech to the children about how privileged they were and what they had achieved by playing in Croke Park. He told them, while they sat sipping Cokes and listening politely, that it was one of the great days of their lives, something they would never forget.

'That school,' he said, referring to Archbiship Ryan, 'is made up of children from many parts of the world that came to live in Dublin. It hasn't been easy – families uprooted that came to live here, settling in school and learning to play hurling. They didn't all come in at baby infants. Now, we can admire them and I know you'll admire one player above the rest. Hopefully, that boy will go on to play hurling at post-primary level.'

What he said struck a chord and reinforced the often-forgotten fact that the teaching fraternity continues to pump so much lifeblood through the heart of Gaelic games. He was right about Sujon: this summer, he continued to post notable scores for Lucan Sarsfields. Sujon talked fondly of the Dublin players and the Kilkenny hurlers. His personal hero is Conal Keaney of Dublin but he admits to holding a torch for DJ Carey. He has Carey's DVD at home and practises hitting a ball off the side of his house every day, just like the master. In July, he was nominated for a place in the DJ Carey summer school in St Kieran's college, a four-day course that is sponsored by the Leinster Council to help develop the skills of the most promising children in the province.

'More hurling against children of a similar ability is what he needs,' said Liam Ryan. 'Sujon is one of those kids that could do well at any sport but hurling is his game. He just has it. They are certainly aware of what he can do in the south Dublin league anyway With his ability and his enthusiasm, he can hopefully go on to greater things over the years.'

Dami started school in Lucan in September and was optimistic about his intentions of maintaining his hurling career. Ibraham, with a shrug and a grin, assented that he might keep playing as well. Sujon had no doubts.

Pat Ryan hoped that more and more foreign national children would keep turning up for club training on Saturday mornings in Lucan.

'In all big urban estates,' he said, 'people don't get to know each other until the children come along and start dragging their parents to one another's houses. It is the same with people moving into the country. The GAA really has a great opportunity to lead the way when it comes to integration. At this stage, we would know Sujon's parents and brothers and sisters just from dropping him home or calling around for a few quid for membership. It was a natural process. He is one of ours, really and truly. And we won't be letting him go.'

The staging of the Cumann na mBunscol finals in Croke Park is one of the GAA's more beautiful oddities. It is like holding a senior infants' Nativity play in the Abbey Theatre, with full costume and lights available. Walking around Croke Park in the off-season is always a strange experience but it is even more disconcerting when the stadium is turned over to little people. The place seems absurdly vast and cavernous and the whole exercise shouldn't work but it does.

People like Gerry Grogan do untold work to sell, in a sense, a way of life through Gaelic games. Every May, the finals of the various divisions are run off and every single team is made feel as if its members are competing in an All-Ireland final. The dressing rooms are pristine, the pitch immaculate. A raised platform is placed in front of the Hogan stand so the captain can raise the cup and deliver his or her speech. Given the furious debate about whether other sports should be played in

Croke Park – whether the world's finest rugby and soccer players should be permitted to grace its turf – there is something slightly humorous about the way that it is converted into a playground of dreams every May.

Many of the children who play Cumann na mBunscol finals are not serious about their sport at all. They end up playing because their best friend played or because the class they happened to belong to possessed unusually gifted players like Sujon or Emma. Children are realists when it comes to the laws of the playground and understand implicitly that some of their peers excel at games and some don't. And they are truthful enough with themselves to acknowledge which category they fall into – a skill that often eludes adults. For those not destined to shine, it is enough to share in the experience and to enjoy the games. In later life, interests beyond sport will consume them.

But as the Kilternan principal said, the fact of having played in Croke Park will remain one of the burnished moments of their childhood, a thing to wow their own children with. And it will also heighten the probability of their maintaining some sort of affection towards the GAA.

And already, it has begun to dawn on those who work in the promotion of Gaelic games that numbers matter. Beyond the perception that the native games must battle with the twin evils of soccer and rugby for the minds and souls of the young, there is a more fundamental realisation that the chief distraction is life itself.

Children do not heed or need the call of Gaelic fields as urgently as they did twenty or even ten years ago. If you talk to people who devote their time to coaching children, it is not other sports that they fear but general torpor and restless indolence and a growing obsession with gadgetry. There are a million different ways of impressing peers nowadays; scoring goals or being the toughest hurler on the block is just one.

You listen and see the glossy advertisements promoting

this great cultural institution of Gaelic games and the accompanying homily about the mysticism of the parish and you wonder to whom they are reaching out. It is a tired and outdated yarn, particularly for the children of Dublin city who play Cumann na mBunscol. The parish is an alien concept to many children and becoming the town or village warrior, wearing the fabled jersey, no longer holds the same weight.

There are many hurling men, names that illuminated the end of the last century, who are gravely worried that the sport is within a few generations of fatal decimation.

More than most sports, hurling demands a degree of fortitude and lonely discipline that leaves the convenience generation cold. The hothouses of hurling continue to produce its stars but although the sport has never been more visible, there has been a marked failure to broaden its appeal.

And against that, the culture of volunteerism is disappearing. Even as the pride of the jersey is a hoary old cliché, so is the notion of putting it back into the game. A well-known hurling coach told me that he believed the biggest threat to hurling and Gaelic games was golf. Think about it, he insisted. Most of the game's best players go straight to the golf course when they retire from the game. There are fewer and fewer willing to pass the knowledge on to the next generation. The mass practice of Gaelic football places it on safer ground but the traditional cycle of the game being passed through generations of school-goers has quietly been eroded in many places.

On the epic, celebratory days of the All-Ireland finals, it can often be forgotten just how delicate the GAA cosmos is. If a relatively small number of people who work anonymously and constantly behind the scenes at encouraging children to play Gaelic games just suddenly decided to stop, it would not take long before the empire began to crumble like a deck of cards. Its oxygen comes from the same sources and, for many years, the educational system has been an invaluable supply. There will always be teachers who continue to throw their energies into coaching games, but they number fewer and fewer. In every school, it is the same people, season after season.

Their names are never in lights. They never receive many thanks. There is nothing in it for them other than the happiness they see in the faces of the young. That is what keeps them coming out, winter after winter, year after year, that and imagining how joyless it would all be without the games and the laughter.

9

Bringing it All Back Home

See him in all his grace, the limping man. From where we lurk in the stands, it is hard to overlook him moving purposefully through the players, their loose running and kicking and ironed shirts of red and white merging like liquid around him. This is a Saturday evening local-league game, so there is not a great crowd. The junior players who have just finished their game leave the changing rooms and gather in the stand in an adolescent bunch, their hair shining with gel, drowning the parched taste in their mouth with ice lollies although a formidable April breeze is coming in from Lough Neagh. Around them is not so much a crowd at all as distinct clusters of people: families, girlfriends, children, football men talking and smoking, and those of us on our own. Tyrone football, the contemporary ideal of brilliance, is what brings everyone together. On the field, the referee is blowing his whistle with impatience and we watch the man in beige jacket and trousers delivering last words to his players before moving stiffly towards the sideline, favouring his right leg in a manner that might be theatrical were it not so unselfconscious. Strangers could never imagine the spells of true beauty that this man cast here on the football field in Ardboe or what his name means or why men of a certain generation cannot bring themselves to say it without shaking their heads. But anybody local will know. Ask them about this man with the ruined leg walking among the football team and they will tell you, astonished that you could not know that it is Frank McGuigan...

To know where Frank McGuigan is from, you have to go back. Not just through the years but on back to the lough shore. It is a drive through undisturbed country. Some four hours before the Saturday evening league game, that is where Frank takes us, laughing, in his four-wheel drive, as the road becomes a track and then a winding lane riddled with puddle-filled craters.

'I remember us flying along this here on bikes and every last bone in your body would be rattling. Serious speeds, now.'

He pushes his modern-day transport along at a fair rate also, happy and on familiar ground. About two miles outside Ardboe, the hedges grow high and unkempt and secretive so that it feels like we are driving towards dense woodland rather than the shining expanse of Lough Neagh. As his car rounds a corner, Frank points to his right to the half-collapsed black stone walls of a cottage hidden behind drooping branches and weeds.

'An oul couple used to live in there. Nice people too. They were the people who lived closest to us.'

He has retained the schoolboy's feel for local cartography, able to recall a story for every hollow and hill and tree in an area he has not passed through for a couple of years. When he lived here in the late 1960s, he used to walk the four-odd miles to the main Ardboe road every single day to get the bus to the grammar school in Magherafelt. It was fantastic in the summer months but in December, when it was pitch black at half past four and there was no sound once the school bus carried the cheers and screams away in the distance, it was a different matter. But he never missed school: any attempt at skiving off prompted a card home from Magherafelt. So he walked this narrow shaded road in all seasons, exposed to its various natures, its thrills and its wintertime spooks and goblins. After the derelict cottage, the car turns another corner where the track stops abruptly. Ahead of us is rough grass for about thirty yards and suddenly, through broken trees, is the silver veil of Lough Neagh, peaceful and epic in scale after the tight, hooded roads and visible from shore to shore. Just before the open ground, there is a muddy track, shrouded by trees and hedges and fading away to the right of where Frank is sitting in the driver's seat.

'Up there is where we are from,' he explains, looking out at the path of mud which seems to lead nowhere at all. 'The house is still there, about a hundred yards up. You can't see it from here. You'd hardly get up there now.'

He accelerates gently and the golden jeep moves slowly onto the open land. He turns off the ignition and sits for a moment in the atmosphere of authoritative quiet, water lapping close by and the low, urgent hum of insects echoing the sounds of his boyhood.

Tommy McGuigan fished the lough all his life. Eels are not the commodity they used to be for fishermen in this part of the world but thirty years ago they were a standard livelihood. There are still a few boats tied to a rough jetty but nothing in comparison to when it was the predominant cottage industry. After trawling with nets was made illegal in the 1970s, Tommy McGuigan and his sons would feed lines down to the bed of the lough, as fishermen had done for centuries before them, one man snagging bait onto the rows of hooks which were weighted by stones.

'This was often done at night-time as well. Like, people have

CBs and safety equipment and all kinds now but then there was nothing. You would head out for about three-quarters of an hour and the shore on the other side would seem no closer. It could get rough enough and a lot of these men could not swim a stroke.'

The boat would glide slowly out towards the middle of the lough as the line was dropped down. In the morning, they returned in boats to draw the lines in again. The more skilled fishermen had a method of taking the eel and knifing it over a barrel in one swift, mysterious movement. Frank McGuigan fished for eel for a single season – his sixteenth year – after he left school, and he hated it. It was not his scene. But he loved the lough.

He walks across the grassy shore and stops at a large, smooth rock which is an oddity because it is alone – a virtual feature in its own right amid the dense greenery.

'This stone is where the football started,' Frank explains. 'It would be one post and we would throw a jumper down across from it and play for hours. It was like Croke Park to us. Me and the brothers and a couple of other lads from around would get games going that used to last the full day. And see in summer? The flies would ate the head of ye. They would eat you alive. You just got used to it. But you had everything a boy could want down here.

'See that wee island?' he asks, pointing to an exposed patch of ground about thirty metres from the shore. 'We all used to swim out to that in summertime and jump off and play games. There were trees to climb or you'd be heading out in the boat or across the fields. Everything you wanted as a young fella was right here. It was like you had to make a choice of what you wanted to do each morning.'

Then he takes a few steps away from the stone, his back to the water, and points through a line of trees about twenty

metres back at another desolate building, invisible unless you
knew where to look.

'There. That's home.'

The dwelling is larger than a conventional cottage, square-
shouldered and handsome, although the roof has caved in in
parts and the upstairs windows and front door are dark and
gaping. But it is the location that is striking, secluded and
somehow proud without ever giving the illusion of having been
anything other than a rustic homestead. Tommy and Annie
McGuigan raised eleven children inside those four walls. It was
basically a large living area with a loft above. There was no
electricity and no running water. The resident McGuigan
family joke was that when Daddy shouted to turn off the heat,
somebody blew out the candle. And this is not all that long ago
– it was still the McGuigan home in 1970, after the Beatles had
split up and when televisions were commonplace. In its
emptiness, the old house stands like a relic from the lost
frontier but Frank stares for a long time through the dereliction
to when fresh clothes were billowing at the gable and his
mother moved through the mellow wax light around the stove.
To when at night, he could look from his bed in the loft and
count the lights of dozens of boats spread across the black
water of the lough and wonder which one belonged to his
father. To when he would finally approach the house after
another winter walk from school when it felt like the rest of
Tyrone was indoors, the bag slung across his shoulder and his
feet and nose and knuckles raw with cold but his insides
glowing with the prospect of dinner.

'It's funny,' he says. 'You see people shelling out ten grand
for a kitchen now and then spending half their time heading up
to The Tilly Lamp for their tea. My mother used to put up hot
meals to us day in, day out, and it never occurred to us how she
did it. Miles from the shop, no running water and eleven of us
to feed. I don't know how she did it. But it never seemed to take

anything out of her. She just got on with things and never knew anything different. I often tell people where I came from but they don't believe that people used to live this far down by the lough. I suppose it is hard to imagine now.'

There is nothing that Frank cannot remember from this period of his life. The taste of his mother's food, turf smoke filling the room when the front door was opened on windy nights, the palpable exhaustion of his father returning from an overnight fishing trip. It is as if all the small details belong to yesterday and it is remarkable that Frank has such recall of his childhood when you learn what he has allowed to slide out of his consciousness. Because the memories that most men would preserve and tend to as the precious gemstones of their lives – the meaningful events – have been let fly away by Frank McGuigan. It is not so much that he has forgotten the beseeching sounds that he could evoke from the crowds across the hot and intoxicating football playgrounds of Ulster in the 1970s. It is more that he never paused to listen in the first place.

The first time he felt important was when he read his name in one of the local Tyrone newspapers. *The Observer*, he believes it was, but he can't be certain. He had played a senior game for Ardboe and the match report contained the line, 'There are signs that Frank McGuigan could be the greatest thing since Jodie O'Neill.'

O'Neill was the definitive folk hero of Tyrone football and the sixteen-year-old was flattered and amused and transfixed by this unbidden comparison that everybody else in Ardboe would also read – that his father would see. Anything that was ever said or written about him afterwards was never of any consequence. Shortly afterwards, in fact, accolades ceased to mean anything at all to him. But on the cusp of a football career that would encompass outrageously early fulfilment, he was innocent and impressionable enough to read the line over and over again. It may or may not have occurred to him that the line was so much fanciful as prescient.

For the legend factory went into production early on Frank McGuigan. He was the original teenage sensation: the boy who starred for Tyrone in the Ulster minor final of 1972 and then reappeared on the field fifteen minutes later to start in the senior final against Donegal. A summer later, he was the county's nineteen-year-old captain when Tyrone won its first Ulster championship since 1957. Ardboe won its third consecutive Tyrone championship that summer also. McGuigan was emblematic of the new and positive future of Tyrone football. He was young and masterfully skilful and was so easy-going and relaxed about his on-field performances that he seemed like a god-given antidote to the political tensions that rendered the provincial roads tense and dangerous that summer. McGuigan was little more than a boy, but he played the game with clean sophistication that made age irrelevant. Watching him was bliss shared by all generations in Tyrone. Although quiet, he was wholly at ease in the captaincy of Tyrone men many years and championship summers his senior. He just took it all in his stride: it did not seem to surprise or overawe him that Tyrone should dramatically reinvent itself as a force in football and that he should be at its epicentre. The details of that maiden Ulster championship have been erased from the recollection of the winning captain. He knows he raised the cup above his head and made a speech in Clones after that Ulster final in 1973, but only because he was told so. Frank sits on his sofa in his living room shaking his head with an expression of regret and amusement.

'Looking back on it, that was a big honour, but at the time, I never thought too much about it. Gerry O'Neill just appointed me captain and that was fine. Like, football never really worried me. It was never the be all and end all of my life. Maybe if I had my life over, it would be. I can't remember ever seeing any footage of that final. But we beat Down and to be honest I can't remember too much about it. We just went up and got the cup and my attitude was fuck it, let's get away for the celebrations. I remember taking that cup around the pubs here in Ardboe just a few weeks before we were to play Cork in an All-Ireland semi-final. But it never entered our fucking minds. We had just won Ulster and that was the summit of our ambitions. So we just kept partying.'

Or at least Frank did. His first ever drink was a bottle of Harp at an Ardboe GAA club dinner. It was the usual thing: four kids trying to be tough. McGuigan was petrified in case his father would smell the beer off him when he went home, so he left half the bottle unfinished. As it was, he needn't have bothered: word had travelled to the McGuigan house faster than Frank could walk home.

'He heard and he gave out to me. Like, Dad would have been a heavy enough drinker. So I suppose he wouldn't have wanted me to turn out an alcoholic. But, see, around this area, there was nothing only drinking after games and people were not so well ducated on the downfalls of drink. I remember seeing my mother rarin' up on Daddy after a few nights but you never considered the consequences of that. It was just something that happened and was over.'

So McGuigan went the popular way. From the beginning, he matched his more-celebrated on-field performances with equally extravagant bursts of energy in the pubs of northeast Tyrone. A typical evening might begin with a couple of pints just to quench the thirst and then the beginning of real business with a neat Powers. He was working steadily as a plasterer, and anyway, because he was Frank McGuigan, he could have toured all of Tyrone without putting his hand in his pocket. There were nights when he sat facing an endless line of amber-filled 'stacks' bought by God knows who. And if McGuigan was happy-go-lucky at the best of times, whiskey brought out the charm in him. He was a good advertisement for being drunk and because of what he could do with a football, people were happy to indulge him in the celebrations.

'Boys would see me on the Powers and more and more would land down to the table. And I loved it, don't get me wrong. I would have been the life and soul of the party. Oh, I got good and drunk though. I wouldn't say it took nothin' out of me. There would have been Monday mornings when I went back to the pub instead of work. Then, later on, I would go on these binges for a full three weeks and always exactly three weeks. What was so magical about that exact number, I never knew. But I could be drunk three times in a day then. I would go home, pass out and then head off looking for the cure and I wouldn't care what day of the week it was. And then, as quickly, after three weeks I would just stop.'

The football years of the early to mid-1970s are trapped in the fog of those intense explorations into alcohol. McGuigan is vaguely aware of the elevated position he held in his own community, but all the praise and encouragement and admiration washed off him. This is partly a consequence of the weeks spent in a boozy fugue state but also because it is his genuine theory that too much weight is placed on the game of Gaelic football. That perspective is common among those whose ability on the field separated them from the rest without any real discernible effort.

'I suppose my father was a good footballer and all of the brothers were. The game came fairly easy to me and that probably didn't help. At the same time, I lived for football. I never missed training and I put it in. I hated losing with Ardboe or Tyrone. I wanted to be a good player. People made a fuss but I wasn't bothered. Like deep down, I felt like football had no meaningful bearing on my life. To me, I was just a guy who went out plastering from Monday to Friday. I think most people thought I was fucking crazy or something because I didn't want to talk football the whole time or whatever. My family was proud of me but we were all easy-going people and that would have been left unsaid. But I only discovered all these things in the last ten years. And that's where the regrets are – like, I never knew how proud my mother was of the football.'

He was in too much of a rush to stop and think then. There is an immutable truth in all sports, but especially in Gaelic games, that tomorrow's hero is always a day away from being yesterday's man. Frank was right about that 1973 All-Ireland semi-final: Tyrone were not on the same physical or psychological wavelength as Cork and lost the match. They fled back across the borders vowing that there would always be next year and there was, but it did not trouble itself with Tyrone. After a couple of years, that Ulster championship began to look lonesome and McGuigan's affectionate turns in the bars and dancehalls of Ardboe and Cookstown were viewed with a less generous eye. Stories of his drinking inevitably got tangled up with his football life. Once, years after the event, a man reminded McGuigan of a championship game when he had captained Tyrone against Monaghan. The man had heard that when Frank went to shake Hugo Clerkin's hand before the throw-in at the halfway line, a naggin of whiskey had fallen from the waistband of his shorts. The man recounted this story as if it was an incontestable truth and Frank was so astonished that he simply nodded his head in affirmation.

'If people are going to believe that about ye, there is nothing you can do to make them think different.'

Although precise dates and score lines and opponents are frequently lost to him, McGuigan is clear that he never sullied the Tyrone jersey. He was frequently among his county's best performers in the unfulfilled years post 1973. Contrary to popular rumour, he never drank on the morning of games but there was one occasion when he admits he was unfit to play.

The night before the Ulster semi-final against Derry in 1976,

McGuigan arrived back to the house at six in the morning.
Three hours later, a taxi arrived at the door to bring him to the
game.

'The one time my Dad ever said anything to me about
football was that morning. He said, "Frank, would you ever do
the team a favour and not go today?" And Jesus, I vomited
going up the road and when we got to Clones, I didn't know
where I was. Funnily, I scored a point because the ball broke to
me and I fisted it over the bar. But I did not really know who we
were playing against or where the fuck I was. Everybody knew.
They would have smelled it off me in the dressing room, but I
suppose they were scared of saying anything to you then. Like, I
played the full game. That was the one time I wasn't fit to be on
a pitch because of drink. And why I did that was because there
was a wee fella from Ardboe training with the county and I
thought he should have been picked on that team. So me and
him went on a bender around home that night. It was fuckin'
silly. I suppose if I am truthful, I was probably half glad because
I would have been looking for a reason to get drunk anyway.'

In 1977, McGuigan went on a tour of New York as a
replacement with the All-Stars. Although he rarely travelled
further than Cookstown in the first seventeen years of his life,
once his prowess on the field established a wider audience, he
practically possessed a year-round invitation to visit the Irish-
American cities. New York appealed to McGuigan: the late
night bars, the happenstance drinking sessions with people who
shared his own enthusiasm for perseverance through bottle
after bottle, the opportunity to walk out of Gaelic Park and
turn two blocks down the street to drink in a place where
football meant nothing at all. The night that the All-Star team
was due to fly home, McGuigan was drinking in the bar at
Gaelic Park. The bus was outside to take the players back to
JFK and eventually the Tyrone man was the last of the party not
on board. Sean Doherty came up and tried to persuade him to

abandon his glass and the fun. We have to go Frank. The plane is going to leave.

'Let her fuckin' leave,' replied Frank and resumed his conversation with a few good old boys from Cookstown that he had fallen in with. And that was how he came to live in America.

'I remember waking up the next morning in an apartment that belonged to this Cookstown boy, Rocky Gallagher. He was away to work. My ticket was expired and the team was gone. So I just lay there on the floor until he came home. A couple of nights later, I got a job and that was it, I was staying. There was no reason for that decision, none at all. I just thought it was something I would try. I think there was a bit of an outcry about it at home and the brothers would have been on the phone to me a bit but I just didn't think it was a big deal. As far as I was concerned, the football in Tyrone was over. Like, I gave it all I had when I was there but I don't know, if someone had said to me, right, that's it, football is banned, I wouldn't have paid a blind bit of notice. I met my ex-wife over in New York, our first kids were born there and I was happy there. But Jesus, what did I know? Sure I was twenty-three years old.'

He was thirty when he eventually made it back home. From 1978 to 1984, Tyrone fielded championships without the most naturally gifted county man to come along in several generations. Tyrone men working the New York sites for the summer returned home with vivid reports of the majestic turns that Frank McGuigan was giving in Gaelic Park. They confirmed that he was in good form, lasting for long, long stretches without touching a drink and that he was keeping fit in a health club and – this raised eyebrows around Ardboe – enjoyed the occasional game of tennis. He played on Gaelic Park about once every three weeks so it was mainly a leisure pursuit. His wife Geraldine was born in New York, but her parents were from Tyrone and she and Frank used to court on

her summer visits home. They were reunited the very evening
that he declined to fly home with the All-Stars and that was
that. Although Geraldine knew her husband played Gaelic
football, she had little idea of the cult status he held back in
Tyrone. Then, in 1983, home came calling. Ardboe were in
trouble in the league and it was decided to fly McGuigan home
for the last two games to help the club avoid relegation. Frank
had his reservations but he could hardly refuse and, anyway, he
felt fitter than he had for years. He hadn't taken a drink in
twelve months. A group of them decided to head home, for old
times' sake.

They were about two hours out of JFK when the alarm
signals started going in the aeroplane. Frank wasn't exactly
overly enamoured with the notion of flying to begin with and
although the captain sounded calm when he announced that an
engine had caught fire, Frank could see from the expressions of
the cabin crew that this was something beyond the normal.
When the plane turned back for JFK, the other passengers were
jumpy and voluble, but two hours later, after circling to burn
off fuel, there was a steadfast silence as the angelic lights of
Manhattan materialised, with its promise of life far below.
Afterwards, McGuigan got talking to an official out in JFK and
he was assured that the problem had been grave: they had been
lucky to get out of it. All Frank knew was that his nerves were
in ribbons. He phoned Geraldine and she told him to wait, that
she would come out to collect them. In a plastic duty-free bag
beside their suitcases was a bottle of Wild Turkey that Frank
had intended presenting to a friend back home. He didn't give it
a second thought, cracking the cap and begging for the soft,
beautiful burn at the back of his throat.

Two weeks later, he was back on the drink and back on the
field in Ardboe. The prospect of flying again terrified him but
he forced himself out to the airport and although the slightest
turbulence made him break out in a sweat, his flight to Ireland

was smooth. Nothing he saw on the drive home from Dublin made him feel that the country had changed, and on the field it was the same old passion play: Ardboe won, the day was saved, McGuigan was magnificent and that night was a great night.

'Jesus, boy, ye should come home,' they said to him, tapping their glass against his own.

Now that they had seen McGuigan in the flesh again, and been assured that their recollections of his ability were founded on more than just romantic notions, a concerted plan was put in motion to bring McGuigan back. Economically, Tyrone, like the rest of the island, was shot through at that stage and many more men than Frank McGuigan were being lost to Gaelic football with every flight out of Shannon and Dublin. Men from the Ardboe club met with Art McRory, the senior manager, and officials from the county board. It was decided that they would build McGuigan a house in Ardboe: it would be something to come home to. Work would not be a problem for him. When the offer was communicated across the Atlantic, it appealed to Geraldine and Frank. Their eldest boy, also named Frank, was approaching school age and the relentless motion of city life, the early mornings and long hours were taking a toll. Ardboe offered convenience and simplicity and the promise of a happy childhood for the family. In November of 1983, they moved to Ireland and Frank resumed training with the Tyrone county panel. The following summer, at the height of the centenary celebrations and after an absence of eleven years, Tyrone won the Ulster football championship and Frank McGuigan gave one of the most masterful and enchanting individual displays of Gaelic football in the one-hundred-year history of the association.

He had stopped for chips before the accident, or so they told him. It was a custom of his after a few late ones to stop in the takeaway and knock a bit of *craic* out of whoever was serving: he broke the tedium of the late-night shift with his merriment.

It was one of those dismal November nights, a nothing week that left people in a state between agitation and gloom with the advent of Christmas. Tyrone had lost the 1984 All-Ireland semi-final to Dublin earlier that summer and football was in hibernation. It was as ordinary a weeknight as could be imagined and Frank had killed it in Forbes bar. He had had plenty but that was nothing uncommon. The fact of the matter is that Frank McGuigan drove his Hiace van through a wall just a few hundred metres from the uncompleted house that the family had yet to move into. Although the wall – the spot where Frank McGuigan's career ended – is now in a residential area, in the winter of 1984 it was outside the comfort of the streetlights and there was no one to hear the sound of metal tearing against concrete. For a long time, nobody heard the groans of the man inside. The force of the impact drove his femur through his knee bone and then caused the fibula and the hip joint to tear through the flesh, destroying the pelvis. When he regained consciousness at Altnagelvin, the sheer strain and paleness of Geraldine's face registered with him and he felt an acute pang of guilt when he saw the way his children's features were stretched with worry. And then a doctor visited and gave him the details of what had happened and told Frank that he had been foolhardy and was lucky and that his ability to walk would be permanently compromised. And when they told him his football life was over, Frank was struck by just how bereft of emotion he felt, as if they were talking about somebody else. He realised he did not mind that much. What he immediately wanted to do was walk again, just to prove the medical team wrong. That became his objective. The accident had been his fault. There was no black ice or old tyres or sharp bend to blame.

'I was drunk,' he says now. 'I was just drunk and that was it.'

With the Troubles raging and death stalking all of Ulster, it was hard to view a self-inflicted car accident as a tragedy, but a lot of people across Tyrone liked Frank and there was a constant procession to his hospital bedside. The menace and style – the perfection – that McGuigan had exhibited in that summer's Ulster final was reviewed in a more poignant light and fundraising nights were held in Ardboe and across the county. Vigorous plans to plaster and finish the house for the McGuigans were realised and the family moved in just as Frank was released from hospital.

'I was still up to my arse in plaster of Paris and I couldn't do nothing for myself. I hated that. So I worked hard to get myself up and about again. I know I was back on my feet months before they reckoned I would be.'

He resumed his drinking pattern before he had even recovered from the tremors of the accident. The complication of being Tyrone's most-revered football player had been removed for him and he concentrated on merely being Frank McGuigan the alcoholic. In a way, the accident was perfectly timed in that it set his reputation in stone and spared him the ignominy of the days when the consequences of his lifestyle would overshadow the luminosity of his skills. It spared him the dark day of not being able to get it done on the field any more. The binges became more intense and, now that he was no longer a slip of a lad in his early twenties but a family man in his thirties, completely charmless.

'See, the whole thing is not the harm you do yourself, it's the people around you. Even in a pub, you cause trouble for the barman, you slobber all over the place and you might insult someone. And I was completely oblivious to it. Maybe the first few days I would remember, but after that? Geraldine would tell me things and I would listen like I heard them for the first time. She must have thought I was joking. And then I would promise that this would be it. God knows how many times I says, "Sorry, Ger, I won't do that again, I will go for help, I will go for help.' Then a week later, I'd be off the drink and I would just think fuck it, I can beat this thing on my own.'

But there was always an excuse, a reason for one last burn-out.

After a Tyrone minor team won the Ulster championship in the 1980s, the cup was pressed to big Frank's lips and the new generation watched the old master sup deeply on their success. That night provoked another three-week spell of Frank McGuigan, clown prince of Ardboe. In the mid-1990s he went to Dublin for a league final featuring Tyrone and he was too sit-down drunk to make it into Croke Park; he spent the game slipping in and out of a dreamy euphoria while Mícheál Ó Muircheartaigh called the game on RTÉ Radio One. Sometimes Frank was one of the players starring in that intense, vibrant commentary and then he was returned to his true state: a drunk man lying in the passenger seat of a car parked among thousands of others in the north inner city, alone and far from the madding crowd.

He was drunk on and off for over a decade after the car crash. It never got to the chronic point where he was unable to function or retreated permanently from society, but gradually and remorselessly, things fell apart. Loved ones got their hearts bruised every time Frank fell and eventually they began to tire of picking him up again. There were no special reasons that caused him to embark on a spree of binge drinking. Sometimes he drank as though afflicted by an unbearable human burden when there was nothing identifiably wrong. Mundane events were as likely to spark off another trawl through the pubs and off-licences as a truly catastrophic event. In 1992 when the McGuigan family was forcibly and terribly struck with a real and horrible and scarcely believable tragedy, Frank did not need whiskey any more strongly. That time, his brother Brian, the baby and darling of the family, was drowned in New Jersey in sinister circumstances. After meeting friends in a neighbourhood bar, Brian had left to go home. The family was told that their lovely twenty-three-year-old boy, a youngster incapable of any badness, had been pushed over a pedestrian bridge into the cold, fast currents below in what was an apparently motiveless crime. Tommy McGuigan insisted on travelling across to America for his youngest son and stood on the bridge and looked on as the divers searched the brown, unfamiliar water. A lifetime on Lough Neagh and generations of learning to work and love water ended in this terrible way. The divers eventually located Brian and dragged his body in. A few days later, still in America, Tommy was travelling in the front seat of a car driven by his daughter Mary. One moment they were talking and then he was gone. It was a double funeral in Ardboe.

The American-style coffins that were flown home were so big that Frank had to have the front windows of his house removed so they could be lifted inside for the wake. Whiskey flowed during those days but there is nothing about them he will ever forget.

Frank cannot say that the numbness and shock of losing two family members in those circumstances worsened or alleviated his drinking habits. He cannot say had he not crashed his car and had he played with Tyrone in the All-Ireland final of 1986 – another loss against the last vestiges of the legendary Kerry team – that drink would have had less of a grip on him. Nor can he predict what way his life would have progressed had the family opted to stay in New York.

All he can vouch for is the fact that he drank on through the blankness, turning more and more into himself until one day he looked around and he was finally alone. After years of pleading and finally threatening, Geraldine had finally moved out with their children. For the first time, the cold voice of reason permeated the reveries of his drinking life. His immediate solution was to turn to the bottle, but when he resurfaced three weeks later, he had located his honesty and called time on what was a wilful ruination of his being.

'It was after that came the low point of my life. The family moving out hit me hard – our youngest boy was only six then and me and him were very close. I just decided that was it, enough. Why I didn't do that twenty years earlier is something I will never know. And I did it alone. I went to some meetings in Magherafelt but the talk was not about drink, it's about what you do to the people around you. They had these family days and you sit in that room in front of six or eight other couples and listen to the things you were responsible for. And you would have to be inhuman not to be affected by what you heard. I felt ashamed and that was the lowest time, hearing of the things I did. Me, like, who always thought I was a pure angel. Like, I was never, ever physically hurtful in anyway but there were other things, like lying in bed for days on end in filthy clothes and then disappearing off out the door again. Self-respect goes out the window and your wife and your children have to see that and deal with that. And the thing is, there were six other men in those meetings and they all had the same bloody story. It's a bad disease and it makes you a bore. But it is a disease. That's why I don't really blame anything or anyone or even blame myself. Alcohol is the devil. It is. Alcohol is the devil.'

Last September Frank shed tears over a football match for the first and only time.

He was on the upper tier of the Hogan stand with his brother Paddy and it was minutes after Tyrone and Armagh had concluded a stark and atmospheric and unique All-Ulster struggle of hearts and minds and bodies. Tyrone won after a dramatic and unbearably close last couple of minutes and when the whistle went, Frank trained his eyes on his son Brian, who had starred for the team at centre-half-forward but then he got swamped by the invading crowd and Frank felt overwhelmed.

'I bowed my head down because I felt like a bit of an eejit, but when I looked up again, there was boys fuckin' bawlin' their eyes out all around me. I had never seen the like of it. Normally I don't get agitated by football. There is an awful sense of pride there if Tyrone are playing well. And I suppose that game meant more to me than any game I was ever involved in because Brian was out there. It was some moment. But I still say my proudest moments were when the kids were born. Because this is still just football we are talking about.'

Frank junior and Brian both inherited the family gift for football and both made the county scene but Brian's aptitude for the game was uncommon and when you see him in the red and white of Tyrone, sleek and sloe-eyed and brightly intelligent, the similarities are uncanny. On the weekend of the final, Brian had been severely weakened by flu and conflicting news reports cast doubt on his availability until the last hour. Brian and Frank senior live together in the original family home now, and during the days before the game, Frank tried to keep his boy calm and nurse him through the illness and keep his mind off football. It is Brian's nature to fret about big occasions just as it much as it had been his father's to walk through them as if in a trance.

'Funny, Brian is twenty-four now. I was married at that age and thought I had quit the game. But I still call Brian a child. He is terrible easy-going but he lives for football. He takes it very seriously. Frank wouldn't be quite so obsessed, he would be a bit like me. And it was tough for Frank because he always had the name connection and people making comparisons and the like. That time, though, I was worried for Brian. He was devastated here before he left with the team and I didn't know if he was going to make it.'

It took his son to show Frank McGuigan why football meant so much in Tyrone and he has a clearer understanding of where he belongs – and what he once stood for – when he reviews his own football life through the new prism of sobriety. At the All-Ireland banquet, people came up to shake Frank McGuigan's hand just like they did in the old days and although he returned their grip, he made it clear that this was not about him.

'That wasn't me. That was my son out there,' he told them. 'That was his feat.'

Not so long ago, it was inconceivable that Tyrone could embark on a major football celebration without Frank McGuigan leading the charge to the bar but during the All-Ireland dinner and the homecoming, it did not even occur to him that he wished he could have a drink. He has been sober for over six years now and continues to work in the same bar in which he drank for the sake of drinking. He believes it is the best place to maintain his temperance because he sees ghosts of his former self appearing at ungodly hours on wet Monday mornings, young men blood-eyed and craven, and it reminds him of where he was. There is no sense of *Schadenfreude* in what he sees, though. It bothers him, the fact that he can foresee the pattern many months in advance and quietly he tries to talk to young lads he sees with responsibilities who drink in a certain manner or at given times or without other company. They are unaware they even have a problem. It is like a slow drowning.

'When the wife stops shouting at you for drinking, you are fucked,' he tells them, making the remark seem light but trying to convey the meaning behind it. It helps that it is Frank McGuigan talking: sometimes it gets through.

He hates to see his boys drinking. It worries him. After he started managing the Ardboe senior team, it suddenly hit him how completely the social scene revolved around the pubs. It is an automatic thing, ingrained through the generations. Sometimes Frank goes along, but the scene tires him now and leaves him cold. It is not just the inevitable detachment of the reformed addict but he believes the lifestyle is limiting. There are many days when he works in the pub and hears customers talk about the Premiership all afternoon, conversation he finds numbing and he consoles himself that he is getting old.

Frank McGuigan has never been more content. Although his marriage to Geraldine was broken beyond repair – way too much whiskey under the bridge – they became friends again and she lives just minutes away with their younger children. During the bad times, when he was constantly restless, the family used to drive into Cookstown to get the messages on a Saturday and if he was kept waiting in the car for more than twenty minutes, Frank would be like a caged animal. Now, when he brings his daughter in, he could sit outside the shops for hours at a time, perfectly serene, watching life go by.

Musing is one of his favourite preoccupations. When he returns from work and the house is quiet, sometimes he won't even turn on the television. He just sits on the couch and allows his thoughts present themselves and he gives them all the time in the world.

His re-integration to the GAA came about through persuasion. Ardboe needed a manager and Frank knew that he, above all men, owed something. The club scene in Tyrone is of a high standard and local loyalties are deep and uncompromising. When the McGuigans moved inland from Lough Neagh in 1971, it was to a modern bungalow in Moortown, part of the parish of Ardboe only by local geographic knowledge. But it meant that Frank, still living at home, switched his allegiance to his new club and lined out against several of his brothers in championship semi-finals. You played where you lived, without exception, and those stern lines of principle remain intact today. Frank is serious about management but he does not let it get under his skin.

'The games do not stress me. All that gets to me is that sometimes I see boys doing things that, well, they make it look so complicated. There is a simpler way. I still think it is a very easy game and why make it complicated?'

His relationship with the game he enlivened with colours not seen since remains complex. Make no mistake, Frank McGuigan loves the game. But he is wary of it.

After the All-Ireland final, Brian came back to the house severely weakened and listless after his efforts. He had played on energy that his body had produced on credit and it had taken its toll. Brian missed most of the homecoming tours around the county and when he noted his son's pallor, Frank questioned, not for the first time, what it was all about – this lifetime of chasing an honour that belongs to the entire county and that ultimately changes nothing.

'My attitude was that Tyrone won the All-Ireland but the players are precisely who they were the day before. Brian sat on that couch for six weeks and the weight was falling off him. He was that sick he couldn't eat. That was the reality of it. And when things calmed down again, Brian was still getting up at quarter to seven in the morning to go to the building site. People forget about that side of things.'

He knows it makes him sound like a crank. When Brian won his first All-Star award in November, McGuigan cherished it much more than he had his own back in 1984.

At an Ulster awards ceremony in honour of Brian that he and Geraldine attended, the compere inevitably began revisiting the glory days of Frank McGuigan and, as he sat in his suit, fidgeting with the cutlery, he began to feel angry despite himself. Behind the McGuigan house is a large field perfect for kicking football but because he had destroyed his leg, he was never able to kick properly with his boys when they were growing up. Had he managed his life differently, it is probable that he would still have been playing for Ardboe when they came of age. So associating his lost skills with those that his boys possess today can sound hollow. He is proud when he sees his sons playing for club or county but wants them to be judged against the present standard, not constantly paired with the man whose name and features they share and whose brightest hour is contained in a twenty-year-old video.

In the archives of BBC Ulster, about ten minutes of that 1984 Ulster final remain. It has disappeared altogether from the libraries in RTÉ and UTV. It was customary to wipe over recorded championship games even as recently as twenty years ago. Someone had the foresight to save a little from the 1984 showpiece for posterity. What the BBC has preserved begins with an edited compilation of Frank McGuigan's spellbinding contribution.

He scored eleven points from play that day. There is always something slightly ghostly about revisiting old sports events through the medium of video. It can create the same lonely feeling as an old song that once meant a lot. On that day in Clones, the sky was a washed-out monochrome and the day seemed heavy. Rain looked imminent. St Tiernach's Park was fundamentally the same, except for a glimpse of an old-fashioned two-storied farmhouse behind one of the goal ends. Among the crowd, flag-waving is the exception rather than the rule. The crowd is wearing dark, neutral colours and individual features are impossible to distinguish. Twenty years is not all that long ago, but just scanning the make-up of that crowd is as good a means as any of learning how this country has changed. There is a stoical aspect to that crowd – a heartening lack of glitter.

And Frank: his face has changed little since, but that day he was lean and pale and serious looking. The video is great because it shows his eleven scores from a distance and then goes close-up on his face. The expression never changes; he kicks his points and then trots back to his full-forward position like a man who is merely doing his job. McGuigan was physically strong then. Even allowing for the fact that all county teams then favoured shorts and jerseys that were very tight fitting, he has the strong arms and built-up shoulders of a man practised in physical work. Something in his make up and poise is reminiscent of Padraig Joyce, the present-day leading light of Galway football.

For each of his points, McGuigan is in possession of the football for no more than five seconds. As is his refrain, it is a simple game. He makes the scores look like child's play because, even when it is clear that he has total ownership of the game, the Armagh defence can do nothing to prevent him from choosing the foot he wants to kick with and then going ahead and scoring. As the BBC commentator notes in an excited, urgent east-Ulster accent, 'Tyrone voices rise in exultation' as Frank lands point after point. He scored seven of Tyrone's first eight. His tenth point is probably his finest.

A long ball is sent in – Eugene McKenna and Damien O'Hagan were the chief ball providers for most of McGuigan's scores, but the source is obscured in this instance. It must be assumed that the Armagh defensive belief was in ribbons at this stage and the centre-half-back, Colin Harvey, fumbles a ball that on any other day would be his.

Both he and Kieran McNally race to retrieve the ball, but McGuigan, loitering with his back to the goal, takes a sharp step forward and palms the ball through the pair of Armagh men and then circles around them, away from goal, to collect. In the still video frame, both defenders are caught in identical stance, crouched forwards in their orange shirts, both looking left for McGuigan who is behind them gathering possession as they desperately try to recover. McNally scrambles back towards McGuigan, who nimbly chips the ball away from the defender and picks it up. Then he takes three strides and sets himself up for a right-footed, looping kick at the posts and just when he is certain McNally has committed himself to a block, he checks inside with the classic solo-dummy. McNally's momentum carries him past McGuigan and he knows he is out of the equation now. McGuigan is already perfectly balanced and leans back to release his shot with the left, splendidly alone, with all the time in the world. The sound recorder picks up the muted sound of the crowd cheering in that muffled, far off way that you experience in swimming pools when you dive underwater. Frank doesn't even wait for the umpires to raise their white flags but resumes his position on the edge of the big square, shooting darting looks here and there, as if preoccupied by something else entirely.

'Sometimes...' Frank McGuigan says moving to get up from his couch. '... I could just sit here and ... sit.

'If I was told to sit there for twenty-four hours, that would be fine. I am just so contented. People have noticed it in me and said it to me. See, I am an awful man for sitting here and thinking, "What if?"'

People stir Frank's imagination. Because he is a fatalist, he has been able to accept life as it has fallen before him. He knows he is far from a perfect man and considers himself lucky, blessed in many ways. He has his family, his home and has managed to come through the lost years with his natural human warmth unspoiled. Sometimes the old days come back to him. In those long-gone sweltering summers in New York, he used to share an apartment with two great friends from Tyrone, Dominic Daly and Rocky Gallagher.

'Dom played minor with me for Tyrone. Like meself, he drank a fair bit but he got his life together and got married. And a few years after my accident, he hit black ice one morning [back in Tyrone] going to work and his car went into a lorry. And he died straight away. And Rocky then was coming to one of those toll booths in America and it seems he must have fallen asleep or something and he went under a lorry. All three of us lived together and we fairly threw the fuckin' mill around New York. I could well have been killed in that crash I got into and they were. They were great boys, good men. It makes you think. It makes you appreciate things.'

When he moves through the crowds at Tyrone's big games nowadays, most people still greet him by his first name. Frank: it carries echoes of a sunny, youthful time in the lives of many Tyrone people.

The theory on Frank McGuigan is that the source of Tyrone's contemporary greatness dates back to that summer's day in 1984 that would be his Ulster farewell. Tyrone football had been trapped in Ulster for the previous eleven years until McGuigan came home to liberate it. Among those in the crowd that day was Peter Canavan, the ingenious wraith of a forward from Ballygawley who would become Tyrone's symbol for hope in the 1990s and the first player from the county to lift the Sam Maguire in September of 2003. Canavan has spoken of how the experience of watching McGuigan moved him to childish dreams that afternoon.

That is not to say that McGuigan was directly responsible for the rise of Tyrone football; that distinction belongs to men like his old mentor Art McRory, his former minor team-mate Mickey Harte, to men like Eugene McKenna and Danny Ball.

But many people argue and believe that Frank McGuigan triggered something that afternoon. It is a chaos theory, just a feeling that an ephemeral hour of football that happened twenty years ago managed to influence the outcome of games played by boys of the next generation. The notion pleases Frank but it is not a claim he makes himself. Yet it ties up with the one thing he says again and again: 'Football is only a thing you do passing through life.'

It was just that he did it so beautifully that long after he believed he had let the game fall away from him and into oblivion, he learned that others had held on for him. In Ardboe and beyond, they waited until Frank McGuigan was ready to roam the local field again. They waited until he came home.

10

Wexford Forever

The Saturday morning of the first round of the Wexford junior hurling championship was full of the optimism of summer. Hot sunlight infiltrated the narrow, weather-beaten streets of Wexford Town. Its cobbled, pleasant thoroughfare smelled of fresh baking and was already beginning to crowd with shoppers and holidaymakers. Wexford is attractive in the loose and ramshackle way that Irish waterside towns can afford to be. It is an urbane 'towny' town, carelessly aware of its history and comfortable in its own skin.

A ten-minute drive delivers you from the cradle of Wexford to the home pitch of Crossabeg–Ballymurn. Once you drive past the secluded Ferrycarrig Hotel on the constantly busy Dublin Road, there is a right turn marked for Crossabeg. Although the village is only two miles off the main artery, the distance seems lengthened by the prevailing stillness, a calmness that deepens as you drive past the whitewashed grocery store at the crossroads of the village and on towards the pitch in Ballymurn.

On a fine morning in late May, it was a gorgeous drive, full of swooping dips and abrupt right turns impossible to navigate without the signposts that the club had put down. When you cross the humped bridge of the Sow river, you are in the right country. The actual pitch is located at a height so that standing near the goalposts at the river Slaney end of the field brought to mind the famous statement made by John Fitzgerald Kennedy on his visit to the ancestral homeland: 'On a clear day, you can see forever.'

'In a way we are trapped,' laughed Brian Foley, looking out on the dark green hinterland below. 'We are naturally bordered by the rivers but as well as that, the parishes of Oulart and Oylgate and Castlebridge and Shemaliers are all senior hurling clubs. We are like a small island stuck in the middle of them.'

Crossabeg and Ballymurn are two fiercely distinct and independent parishes, each with its own rich history. The communities bonded, for reasons of GAA survival, into one club in 1966. The GAA heritage of both parishes, prior to and after the amalgamation, can be traced through the bloodlines of a relatively small number of families: O'Learys, McDonalds, Murphys, Foleys, Gordons, Lamberts. For the first half of the twentieth century, organised games there peaked and ebbed. Some years, teams thrived; in fallow years they were not even fielded and players used the easy affinity with parishes to get a game with Castlebridge or Sally Beechers, a club made up from several parishes. But whatever the state of the teams, life in both Crossabeg and Ballymurn resonated with a deep love of hurling. It still does.

On the Saturday morning of the beginning of the championship, the pitch belonged to an under-fourteen skills game featuring both boys and girls. The rules differed from a normal game in that for one quarter the emphasis was on ground hurling, with solo runs disallowed, and for the next, the emphasis was on passing. It was an innovation of the county board and although the children were lukewarm about the notion of constraints, they decided to get on with it.

Leaning against the railing that borders the pitch, watching the next generation was a group of men for whom the club is kind of an obsession. Johnny Murphy is a Ballymurn legend: the first hurler of modern times from the area to represent the parish playing for Wexford. He played when the county lost consecutive All-Ireland finals to Cork in 1976 and 1977, dates that burned painfully on the retinas of all Wexford people until salvation came upon the county through the Liam Griffin-led sun-dance of 1996. Nearby stood Niall McDonald, the last Crossabeg man to play senior hurling for Wexford: he was a resolute corner-back for the first half of the 1990s, ending the season so that the county made it back to the promised land. The McDonald name echoes powerfully across all the rural parishes of Wexford Town: six of Sean McDonald's sons, including Niall, hurled for Crossabeg-Ballymurn – strong, uncomplicated, inspiring hurlers.

As John Cummins put it, 'The McDonalds weren't just hurlers, they were driven. They would lift you beyond yourself. And they were fierce bad losers.'

John has played all his life and acts as treasurer for the club as well. The Cummins name is celebrated in Wexford GAA lore. Over a single afternoon in 1905, his granduncle, Mike Cummins, won a hurling and football medal in Dublin in what was the inaugural Railway Shield. Famously, Mike walked the six miles from his house in Ballymurn at dawn that morning to take the train from Enniscorthy to the capital. He played the games and returned by evening train, the two medals in his trouser pocket as he ended his journey on foot, under moonlight.

James Kelly is a Crossabeg man and is the present-day chairman, a post that is tougher to quit than it is to attain. Only four men have been honoured with it since the club was formed in 1966. 'Thankfully, we brought in a five year rule at the last annual meeting so I can bow out next year,' he said.

They were all family men, reared in the parishes in the 1960s and 1970s when it was still wedded to the traditions and manners of the preceding centuries. All agreed that the locality had changed greatly in the last twenty years, not so much in physical appearance as in mindset and attitude. They attributed the differences to the usual faultlines: affluence, lack of time and the steady dissolution of neighbourliness. Crossabeg-Ballymurn GAA Club remains the most potent symbol of identity for both parishes and that, as well as a love of hurling, is as good a reason as any to work to ensure its survival. That and perhaps also that the continuing association with Crossabeg-Ballymurn keeps them in touch with their youth as the middle years encroach; by pushing the club towards its tomorrows, they are fanning the flames of its past.

Crossabeg–Ballymurn's recent history reads like a moral tale. Ten years ago, at the height of its first and only incarnation as a senior club, the team came within five minutes of qualifying for a county final. They lost through a series of late goals against Oulart the Ballagh, then also on a hot and bold flush of senior ambition. Oulart went on to claim that year's county championship and established itself as a perennially respectable senior club.

'And the funny thing was, they had been coming for a while then,' said Johnny Murphy. 'And I think if we had beaten them that year, it would have been the end of them.'

Instead, Crossabeg–Ballymurn slid. In 1999, they preserved their senior status in a relegation game, but the following autumn, they were relegated with a team that featured many men pushing for a place in the senior final just six years earlier.

Johnny Murphy rates losing that game, a humdrum end-of-season encounter in the larger scheme of things, as the worst day of his hurling life, leaving him with a knot in his throat that was worse than the All-Ireland final losses in the 1970s.

'Because with this, you were among your own.'

It is said that they locked the dressing room after that match and for an hour let nobody in and there was no talking.

'I never want to be in another room like it,' said John Cummins. 'It was terrible. Grown men cried hard. It was just an awful feeling because we knew we had lost something that was going to be very hard to recover.'

And so it went. Two seasons later, they plummeted through the intermediate grade to junior level, the fallen angels of Wexford hurling. The speed of that decline, a decade in which they went from really contending with the best in the county to the more fundamental concerns about the future of the club, is the backdrop against which they work. This is not the ropiest phase of the club's history but it has its own uncertainties: those heavily involved in running the club are constantly beset by the feeling that its momentum is constantly in danger of stalling.

That is why Johnny Murphy, the manager of the team, was on a high at the arrival of the championship date. By neat coincidence, a decade after their most glittering epoch, they were drawn to face Oulart the Ballagh again – at junior level this time.

'This is the day we have been training for since Christmas,' said Johnny. 'Like, we have been trying to do things properly anyhow and we reckon it is time we stopped sliding. We reckon we can move back up a grade this year. That's the intention anyhow. I'll spend the day just driving around visiting all the boys, making sure they are all right and talking about the game. I can't help meself. It's just something I like to do.'

On the Friday evening, in Liam Griffin's Ferrycarrig Hotel, I met with Brian Foley and Annis Kehoe and Niall McDonald to talk about what running a contemporary GAA club in this country entails. They were all busy people. Brian had just returned from athletics with his daughter. Niall's wife Jetta had given birth to a little girl just seven weeks earlier. Annis had been out canvassing in local elections and was due to attend a twenty-first birthday party. In addition, she had promised herself she was going to make a pot of home-made jam that evening and would arise at dawn to run her customary five miles before heading on a week-long working trip around the west coast of Ireland as a tour guide. The are all friends but not so much in a social way, more through these hectic, hastily convened meetings to discuss the state of Crossabeg–Ballymurn.

Brian has an accountant's head for dates and figures and a historian's soul when it comes to the club. The son of publicans, he grew up immersed in conversation of local hurling and has a keen knowledge of the genealogy of friends of his youth and of the children playing the game today. He stopped hurling in his early twenties when he went away to study, but after returning to live in the locality, he immediately became involved in the club again at juvenile level.

'The worst statistic from our point of view is that from the fifth and sixth classes in Crossabeg Primary School: there is just one boy playing hurling. When we began going into schools three or four years ago, we found we had trouble recruiting. Kids just weren't that interested. So we sent out circulars at under-eight level and we have about eighty kids now. But in the Crossabeg side, there are so many other things going on – soccer and gymnastics and athletics – that they don't just have the intensity or feeling for hurling that we all had growing up. In fairness, that is not the case in Ballymurn. The habit of hurling every single day still exists there and it shows. Like, our main team now only has two players from Crossabeg.'

Annis Kehoe played camogie growing up in Crannford but has been involved in Crossabeg since her children were small, acting now as the PRO for the club and turning up to drive children to games and to support the teams. Because it is closer to the main road than Ballymurn, new housing developments are beginning to spring up around the village, ostensibly bringing more potential club members to the community.

'In comparison to other clubs, though, we aren't as good at getting new people to come in and get involved,' she said. 'Some people offer to help out because they feel they should but others just don't want to get involved. People feel that they don't have the time and that they are under enough pressure. And they probably are. But it is amazing what you can fit into a day if you force yourself.'

About ten years ago, precisely when the senior team were pushing for county glory, a really fine Crossabeg–Ballymurn minor bunch came along. It was just one of those coincidences of birth and talent that brought together a group of boys for whom the game came more effortlessly than the rest. They swept all before them as they progressed through the juvenile grades and as expected they advanced to the county minor final in 1994. Ten years later, no more than three of that team are still playing the game. They just vanished.

'It is an incredible thing,' said Brian Foley. 'Many of them are still about. They will be sitting around the stand at the championship game when they should be out there playing. I mean, these guys had real ability but they just walked away from it.'

When they were emerging though, in tandem with the senior squad, Crossabeg–Ballymurn was identified as a model club in Wexford, an example of how a rural team with modest resources could challenge with the best of them. Niall McDonald kept a close-enough eye on that generation. He noticed that they were treated almost deferentially in the parish and that they were breezily indifferent about the games they won.

'Perhaps it came too easily for them in the beginning. You can't win too often as far as I am concerned but you have to be wary of what comes with that habit. Those guys probably expected things to fall into their laps because that was their early experience and when things began to get rough, they found they didn't want to know. Like, we have a group of under-fourteen players now coming through and I worry they are going to go the same way. They won a competition there recently and the club brought them down to the Oak Tavern for a meal. Now, maybe I'm hard but I think that is unnecessary at that age. I worry if they get accustomed to that when they are fourteen, what will they be expecting in five or six years' time?'

The ease with which that 1994 minor team just melted shocked the more senior guys in the club. The reasons were not strictly confined to hurling either. Teenagers had more money in their pockets; many of them were driving cars that either belonged to their parents or that they had bought themselves. The distance from Wexford Town – a troublesome hour of hitching in the 1970s and 1980s – became negligible and its Friday night attractions, with a new Omniplex and a healthy night-club scene – held a stronger allure than hurling in the parish.

'It was like,' says Brian Foley, 'they wanted to hurl but only when it suited. There was a reluctance to be tied down by the game. There was always a get-out clause to the commitment that was given – yeah, I'll come if it suits me. It was very hard to take because if you had seen these boys as a team when they were young, you would have said that Crossabeg–Ballymurn was set up for the next generation.'

The following morning, I asked Johnny Murphy about that minor team. His own son Johnny – one of the few to persevere with the game into adulthood – played on that side.

'He'd still be friends too with a lot of them. But I don't know what happened to them. I can't explain it. It was a terrible thing. The only thing I can put it down to was they got a ferocious beating from Rathnure at minor level, it must have been by seventeen or eighteen points. Like, Rathnure were very strong at that time too and were expected to win that game but maybe not by so much. After that, I felt something died in them. It knocked the spirit out of them a bit. And as well, life was different. It didn't have to matter so much. There is a fair bit out there now to turn a fella's head. Changed times. It wasn't like when the McDonald boys were growing up.'

Niall McDonald grew up on a dairy farm with five brothers. Their father Sean hurled as a Sunday pastime and encouraged his boys to play the game but never excessively. They discovered their fascination with the sport themselves. They had an uncle, Fr Fintan McDonald, whose touch and skill with a hurl had been a source of stories in the house since they were young children. When Fr Fintan was home from the missions in Kenya for a couple of weeks every summer, Sean and his brother and the boys would tap around well after dusk in a field behind the house.

'Never competitive games, just stuff like first-time hitting and keeping the ball in the air for as long as we could. But it got as serious as any game.'

The priest, though, had a lovely touch, languid and effortless despite having left hurling far behind him, and their father was a strong, clean, uncompromising hurler and at least some of those qualities seeped into the boys. Diarmuid, John and Niall all played for Wexford. But it was with the club that the McDonald name was primarily associated. There was one season when McDonald boys formed the spine of the Crossabeg–Ballymurn team, from full-back through to full-forward, all physically imposing, fair and holding no great respect for illustrious reputations. Niall McDonald made his first senior steps for Crossabeg–Ballymurn just when Johnny Murphy's career was winding down.

'The admiration we had for Johnny was incredible. Like, to go from a small club like ours to play in an All-Ireland final for Wexford was some feat. And he was a beautiful hurler, fast and neat. I was put midfield with him for my debut game for the club and I think I got four points just by running off his shoulder and waiting for him to play me a pass. He made it seem simple.'

The club was rich in people then. As with all GAA clubs, the development of Crossabeg–Ballymurn was illuminated by certain names that will always be remembered for whatever reason. Cauley Gordon, a fearsome hurler from the Sixties, cropped up in innumerable conversations as the perennial driver of a red Hiace van, always coming to or from some under-age match or other, its suspension creaking and ruined by delivering generations of kids to pitches around Wexford. He is widely regarded as having been the broker in the original alliance between the two parishes. Brian Foley remembers hearing pub talk to the effect that Crossabeg weren't too pushed on the notion of joining up with Ballymurn. But Gordon was one of those ferociously positive sorts who hurled well past his prime. At one league game where he turned up as a driver, it happened that Crossabeg were short a couple of players. Gordon borrowed boots and lined out at corner-forward. It was said he was sixty years of age then but that was probably a conservative estimate.

It was travelling around and listening to men like Gordon that gave Niall McDonald and his brothers an understanding of the club. He cannot say precisely when its importance in their lives became pre-eminent but it was early.

The dates when Crossabeg–Ballymurn won titles are spare. A 1972 junior final, lost after a replay, is still remembered bitterly by those who played. In 1974, they finally won that grade. In 1975, an under-twenty-one team from the parishes won county honours.

Brian Foley played on the under-twenty-one team that won the county championship in 1982 along with Diarmuid

McDonald. But the breakthrough for the club was winning the intermediate title in 1988.

'My brother John was exceptionally strong,' remembered Niall. 'He used to go on these solo runs and he was so powerful that nobody could stop him, especially at under-age level. But even after we all started playing for the senior team, he was the constant worry for other teams. My mother rarely went to see games because she was worried for us and it was just as well because John used to come off after some of those games hardly able to walk with the way hurls were broken off him. His legs were in bits.'

There was one game, when Crossabeg were four points down against Buffers Alley, when John McDonald burst through on a solo run and took a hurl around the nose. He carried on and a hurl was smashed off his thigh and he still kept going. By the time that sequence of play ended, three McDonald men lay on the ground. In the end, they lost the game by twenty-two points.

'But we were learning all the time that the senior clubs weren't infallible and we were gradually getting closer to their standard.'

By the beginning of the 1990s, Crossabeg-Ballymurn had bottled a mood, a sense that they had tapped into a higher level of the game, and it made them ambitious. Team training, once a loose arrangement, acquired a near-religious dimension and became deeply enjoyable. Numbers were consistently up at thirty or thirty-five members and there was a glow about the squad. Ideas that a few years earlier – and later – had seemed daft felt like the most natural thing in the world at the time. They took to meeting up on a nearby beach at dawn to run together. One morning, Johnny Murphy arranged it so all the cars in which they had driven were relocated a mile or so up the road, just to lengthen the session and add a bit of mischief to the day. It was a blissful period, with no excuses or grumbling and marked by the possibility of actually setting the standard in Wexford hurling. That was what they were chasing.

Niall McDonald's presence on the Wexford senior team helped spread a sense of worth and belonging among his club team. He still insists that John and Diarmuid were more versatile hurlers than he was but the Wexford selectors became happy and secure in his performance at corner-back and he just locked that position down. Over the years, he sparred with some of the most highly lauded forwards of the modern game: Nicky English, John Troy, DJ Carey.

Between 1992 and 1994, Wexford lost three consecutive Leinster finals. Of those defeats, the unforgettable moment, the play that will stay crystallised, is Carey's last-minute goal in the 1991 Leinster semi-final. McDonald had been shadowing him so well that the Kilkenny player, the nation just becoming aware of the full range of his gifts, was moved to full forward. A high ball came in and McDonald followed his man out to meet it. 'If I had stayed, it would have dropped right down on top of me but I had to cover the player.'

DJ was alive to the half chance and broke away cleanly from the pack, the most feared black-and-amber player bearing down on goal, as if it had been prophesied. He buried the chance, the grace note of a taut classic that ended 2-09 to 0-13. The outcome seemed obedient to the laws of the Leinster game: Wexford's summer was over, while Kilkenny marched on to the All-Ireland final.

Niall McDonald would insist his career represented the antithesis of whatever 'stardom' is supposed to entail. And yet to survive as one of the best backs in the sport during an era when hurling was coming back into bloom is a sporting feat of huge significance, a level of achievement that only a tiny percentage of hurlers ever manage to attain. The worst score he ever gave was 2-3.

'And that, funnily, was against Laois. I actually didn't play too badly in that game either, it was just the way the ball broke. Against the more noted players, they were probably better hurlers than me but I managed to find ways of closing them down – most of the time.'

He suffered for his art, the victim of a terrible incident in a league game against Tipperary that left him with severe facial damage. In retrospect, the entire period is tinged in a wistful light: it was nearly perfect. In that legendary game against Oulart, the Crossabeg back line weathered severe pressure in the last ten minutes. Near his own goal line McDonald rose to take a dropping ball and created enough space to effect a clearance. But the trajectory of the ball was low and it rapped off another Crossabeg player and bounced back into the net. It was an absolute freak goal, a once-in-a-lifetime occurrence. With the Crossabeg-Ballymurn players still numb, a young Oulart player called John Moydon got control of the ball from the puc-out and in one of those movements that appeared to unfold in slow motion, found a gap and fired another goal. The fate of Crossabeg-Ballymurn changed that suddenly: it was almost a violent close to their most hopeful and promising season and there was a sense of inevitability when Oulart went on to win the county final.

Niall McDonald hurled the 1995 season with Wexford but the combined disappointments of the previous three seasons had created a lukewarm team and they lost the Leinster semi-final to reigning All-Ireland champions Offaly by 1-10 to 2-14. When the panel met up in the autumn of that season to listen to the evangelical and urgent Liam Griffin, McDonald was among those not invited back to the panel after a preliminary training weekend in Waterford. He was taken aback by the decision but reasoned, after conversations with the management, that the situation wasn't terminal.

'We decided I would go back to the club and keep playing and training away and that we would take another look at things a bit later on. And I was playing fairly well with the club that season.'

But the call never came. A truth that dawned on him during the seasons when he was practically immovable from the Wexford defence hit him from a different perspective.

Once the door closes on a county man, it is hard to rediscover the combination. The dynamism shifts and even though you keep playing the game you always believed you played, it is as if everyone has stopped watching. Niall McDonald never complained or grew resentful when it became apparent that Liam Griffin was planning without him: he had too much pride, too much class. He inherited his father's stoicism as well as his strong wrists. When the summer of 1996 rolled around, it was clear that Wexford had inhaled some of the rebellious toxins generated by Clare the summer before. Kilkenny and Offaly were toppled on the way to a Leinster championship. McDonald consoled himself that he could at last sit back and watch the glory of a classic championship from a good seat. There was a sense of predestination about the semi-final win over Galway and suddenly, that August, something life-affirming was happening in the county as Wexford prepared for its first All-Ireland hurling final since 1977.

'We made a weekend of it for my mother and father,' Niall said. 'We sent them up to Clontarf Castle and got them tickets for a show and for the game. Dad died the following year and I know that he said privately later that he found the 1996 final hard to enjoy, that he wished one of us had have been out there.'

Another Crossabeg man, Johnny Murphy, sat up in the new Cusack stand, now glistening and elegant in comparison to its sullen companion across the field, and tried not to think about those lost moments in the 1970s. Small things flashed before his mind: Tony Doran being dragged down in the last minutes of 1976 but no call, Seánie O'Leary of Cork seemingly dropping his hurl – a ploy outlawed that season – to palm a goal for the winners. He tried to banish them and surrender himself to the heavenly possibility of witnessing a first Wexford All-Ireland victory since he was a young boy.

'And I was delighted for them, I was. I celebrated as hard as anyone. But I won't pretend there wasn't a small bit of me choked up when I saw the way the crowd reacted on the field afterwards. It kind of hit home to me what we had missed out on.'

Niall McDonald was contemplative about what he missed out on. He still is. Eight years later, he is still in regular contact with Liam Griffin in relation to club and under-age matters in Wexford and has a good relationship with him. And Griffin speaks with genuine admiration for McDonald. But neither man ever broached the subject of McDonald's absence from the 1996 panel. It came down to a number of intangibles: timing, a judgement call, pure luck. If Wexford had suffered injuries early in that league, he might have been drafted right back in. If: it all came down to that and although Griffin is a wordsmith, there are moments between sports people when the unspoken is the best acknowledgement of something that has come to pass.

Niall McDonald hurled on resolutely and honourably with Crossabeg-Ballymurn as the bad times settled down for a spell on the club. The harmony and sense of well-being that was summoned so easily in 1994 just evaporated: numbers at training dipped, some players were more committed than others. A few guys retired. Others, tired by what they saw as declining standards, transferred to neighbouring clubs. Collie Kehoe was one of those guys and he actually played against Crossabeg-Ballymurn on the day they were relegated.

'Collie was frustrated, that was why he left. Nobody blamed him but I suppose it made it all the harder for us afterwards.'

Listening to Niall McDonald talk openly and dispassionately

about the highs and lows of his hurling life brought to mind the oft-used phrase, 'a true servant of the game'. Perhaps that is what he was without ever being servile to it. He played on his own terms and abided to his own sense of fairness and how the game should be played. He had a judicial appreciation of what he did well and of what other players did well and like all those who make it to the highest level, he learned how to thrive in the grey areas between those absolutes. He hurled on through the seasons, surprised to register that his mid-thirties had arrived without much ado and that he had reached, without feeling it, the stage where he could rightfully claim the grand-old-man status of the team.

In 1987, in his teens, he spent a summer in America. At college in Waterford, he played alongside guys like Michael Duignan of Offaly and Colm Bonnar of Tipperary. Between the college's competitions and club and then county involvement, he forgot what holidays were. Early this year, he came to a decision that it was time he and Jetta took a break. And he decided it was time to retire.

Even a fleeting visit to Wexford is enough to confirm the subtle sense of separateness of the county, an independence of soul and temperament that forms the basis of its society. Growing up in Donegal, Wexford was a distant rumour of strawberries and eternal sunshine. It might as well have existed on the continent but for the flash of purple-and-yellow jerseys that appeared on *The Sunday Game* every now and then and for the history lessons on 1798 that featured in all Irish classrooms.

Maybe it is an act of the imagination but because 1798 remains such a glimmering and potent date, there is a unique feel about the countryside in Wexford, a restless nature that transferred itself to the Gaelic movement.

The GAA was organised soon after the inception of the association in Thurles. A number of Crossabeg men – including a John McDonald and a James Murphy met with a number of men from other fledgling clubs at No 2, Rowe Street in Wexford in October of 1885, at the request of the Wexford National League.

The team played its first game against Parnellstown in March of 1886. After a return game a week later, the Parnellstown players issued a complaint at the county-board meeting that one of their players had been knocked out by a Crossabeg man making injudicious use of his knee. The board formally proposed to ban the use of the knee for future games.

The early days of Crossabeg GAA events are all detailed in a book researched by Annis Kehoe and other locals to coincide with the Wexford bicentennial celebrations in 1998. The group spent months selecting from the excellent archives in *The Wexford People* office to unearth all the contemporary reports of community life in Crossabeg: the parish and its people. Gaelic games featured prominently.

As a report written by the editor of *The Wexford People* on the occasion of an inter-county match against Avondale in 1886 suggests, the novel sight of organised sport was greeted with enthusiasm.

'Truly we have entered a new era in history of Irish Athletics on the completion of this first ever inter-county match since this dear land of ours was cursed by the so called Act of Legislative Union. Not one of the thousands of spectators whose good fortune it was to have passed their Hallowe'en Eve of the year 1886 on the picturesque slopes of Avondale will ever forget a sight which, in all probability, will be unique in their memories of the past and many of them in the autumn of their lives will feel proud in relating the event to their children as our own grandfathers did of the deeds of Vinegar Hill and the stormy fights which aroused the echoes of the Glens of Old Wicklow in the memorable year of '98.'

Crossabeg parish made a name for itself almost immediately.

Although the GAA was struggling on a national level in 1892, the hurlers of Crossabeg and nearby Castlebridge had qualified to represent Wexford in the All-Ireland hurling final. The previous year's competition had been delayed because of the sudden death of Charles Stewart Parnell in October, so the 1891 final, against Ballyduff of Kerry, was fixed for 21 Feburary 1892 at Clonturk, but it was delayed for a week because of a heavy snowfall. Each team lined out with twenty-one players. Although the ground was still frozen hard and the day viciously cold, the Kerry men played in their bare feet. The score was level at 1-2 apiece at full-time and at the break before additional time, the Kerry team left the field and took shelter while the Crossabeg players stayed on the field. Half an hour passed, during which time they became shivery and blue with cold. Kerry prevailed – their first and only All-Ireland hurling title – on a scoreline of 2-4 to 1-5.

PJ Devlin of *The Celt* newspaper wrote: 'It was such a contest as has never been seen before in a native arena. It may be youthful fancy or senile myopia, but I think there was more of the sport of the ancient Fianna that day than was ever before.' Around Crossabeg, though, the game became known as 'the barefoot robbery'.

In the early days of the association, playing fields were 'kindly donated' by local farmers. One of the chief benefactors of Crossabeg was James Shortle. In her notes for the parish book – the first of three planned volumes – Annis Kehoe kept a great account of a policeman's time in Crossabeg, taken from *The Wexford People* in 1888.

During the period, threatening notices had begun to appear, protesting against Gladstone's Protection of Person and Properties Act, with many posted on the church grounds and on the gravestones at Sion. The Constable of Crossabeg decided the only way to catch the miscreants was to post a member of his force in the graveyard overnight.

'None of us cared to accept this duty,' the unnamed officer wrote. 'There was a rumour long ago that a number of rebels were shot by the military and yeomanry in '98 near the chapel and that their corpses were buried in the churchyard – whose ghosts would have small respect for a policeman.'

There were countless village tales of ethereal pike men roaming the churchyard at the dead of night. As a consequence, just one policeman, young and new to the area, volunteered for the posting. At about eleven o'clock, positioned behind a headstone, he was awakened from a slumber by the sound of two men climbing the wall of the churchyard and then proceeding to a nearby tree, onto which they began hammering a written notice.

'Endeavouring to vault the railings, my overcoat caught on the spikes, my sword striking against the railings, all this making a racket in the still silent night. As soon as I could extricate myself and gain my feet I could hear my two neighbours invoking every saint in the calendar to aid them, and I the supposed ghost.'

One of the intruders fled. The other fainted. The constable carried him to a nearby stream and tried to revive him but the man remained out cold until he was restored in the local station with a glass of brandy. It turned out that the notice the two men had been posting, far from being politically motivated simply read: 'Potatoes for sale 5/- per barrell, apply to James Shortle, St Edmunds.'

Whether this was the same Mr Shortle as provided a pitch for Crossabeg is unknown.

But it was on the strength of such tales, apocryphal and true, that Gaelic games prospered. The further Annis Kehoe and the other researchers delved into the written archives and spoke to families around the parish, the deeper their appreciation of living history became. The house of John Rossiter, who led the Crossabeg contingent at Oulart Hill in 1798, is still a private residence today. The stone-washed house of John Hay, who was hanged on Wexford bridge during the rebellion, is also perfectly preserved.

He is buried in Kilmallock cemetery, just a couple of miles from the pitch in Ballymurn. It has been marked by one of the sepia-coloured signposts that are used to distinguish places and buildings of historical note.

The graveyard gate stays locked but visitors can climb over a low stone stile. The oldest graves are to the left of the ground, shaded by trees. The inscriptions are still legible even though many of the plain, curved slabs predate 1798. John Hay, who apparently joined the local rebel forces after giving way to forceful persuasion, and fought at Vinegar Hill: when the rebellion dwindled, he returned to his home in Newcastle to find his wife gone and the interior ransacked. He hid out in the woods for some time but was caught and condemned to hang on Wexford bridge, of which he had been a shareholder. His body was thrown into the water but was reclaimed by a relative and he is now buried in the family vault in Kilmallock. Today, it is a disquieting sight: a steel grate covering the stone steps that lead down to the chamber and a flagpole high above the commemorative stones that glint like a day lantern in the warm sunlight.

Elsewhere in the cemetery is the grave of Mike Cummins, the Crossabeg dual Railway medallist in 1905 who also played on Wexford's first All-Ireland winning team in 1910. When Mike died in 1948, hurling people from across the county and beyond gathered among the solemn stones and their chiselled inscriptions. It is the bare dates that catch the eye, terse acknowledgements of people who lived in times of wild grandeur and extremity, people whose deeds and spirit are now remembered through summer pageantry and in song. On most days, Kilmallock cemetery has few visitors and even when it is warm and blue-skied, the place is cool in atmosphere and guarded in its secrets. And many of the names decorating the slabs settled in the ground for centuries were the same as those of the young men who would line out in Crossabeg's first hurling match of the 2004 summer season.

By six o'clock, the sun was still high over Wexford and with the boutiques closing down and the pubs and restaurants in the lull period, the town fell somnolent and dreamy. Wexford Park is located at a height, above the town, and slowly the cars began to gather, exhaust fumes shimmering, windows down. A championship football game between Roscommon and Sligo was being broadcast live on the radio from Markievicz Park and every so often, the hazy quietude of the summer evening was broken by Brian Carthy's rhapsodic commentary drifting from a passing car. It sounded tense and remote, the way that a half-caught passage of live radio sport does when you are blanked out on a beach.

The players came in twos and threes, parking their cars as though in a hurry. All players have their habits. Some arrive at double speed and snatch their bag from the boot like a doctor on an emergency house call. Others dawdle. One young player lit a cigarette before ambling into the ground, a huge sports bag slung over his shoulder.

Johnny Murphy had instructed his boys to be at the ground an hour before the throw-in. There were two junior games scheduled for that evening and somebody had written with a marker on a plain white sheet of paper the names of all the competing teams, and had placed it on the dressing-room doors.

When Johnny made his way down the stone corridor, most of his team had already arrived. Ginger-coloured and fresh-faced, Johnny looks much younger than a man who hurled in an All-Ireland final almost thirty years ago and he has retained the tidy cut of a low-centred athlete. He clapped his hands as he walked down the corridor, like a hungry man on his way to a wedding banquet. After looking in on the boys, he went over to talk with Fr James Finn, who had travelled from a pilgrimage in Knock to be back for the game. Brian Foley had said that Fr Finn was the biggest hurling fan to assume the parish house for quite a few decades. He had promised Johnny that he would dedicate a few prayers at the Mayo shrine.

In a way, Wexford Park was too grand a ground to house a junior game, with its new stand easily absorbing the crowd that had begun to trickle in through the two turnstiles. It would have been wonderful to watch a game of this importance in Ballymurn, where the field is tightly embroidered by a fence that people park right up against, so they watch games from the car on rainy days.

This was an evening for ice cream and short sleeves, though. We sat in the Crossabeg section of the crowd, which was split among families and teenagers and former players. John Cummins was already there when we arrived. He had met an Oulart man earlier in the day, in Wexford Town who had promised him that this was the strongest junior team the Ballagh had fielded in many years. It was not encouraging news as Oulart were favourites to begin with.

John, after faithfully promising their safe return to his aunt, had brought along his granduncle's Railway and All-Ireland medals for me to see. Rather than produce them in the stands, we went down underneath to the St Martin's dressing room which was still vacant. None of the medals was any larger than the old ten-pence coin with the salmon decoration. All were perfectly preserved, with tiny shamrocks adorning one and the date and name of the competitions etched onto the back.

All three fitted perfectly in the palm of John's hand as we made a botched attempt to take a photograph. Polished and treated with great care, the gold medals looked disconcertingly shiny and new, as if too recently forged to date back to the afternoon at the beginning of the last century when Mike Cummins received them.

'My aunt guards them,' John laughed. 'She is the only one who knows where they are stored.'

While we were studying the medals, the boys from the Martin's team came blustering down the corridor and into the room.

'Out ta fuck,' growled one in a good-natured way.

Seeing us crouched over the medals, a small crowd gathered around John expectantly. They were mostly teenagers, their faces flushed from the day's sun and in anticipation of their game, the second of the evening. John allowed them to pass the medals around through hands with nails bitten to the quick, scraped from summer work. A low whistle echoed through the dressing room when he explained the origins of the medals.

'Jesus. You sellin' them?'

The others laughed at this but they were impressed and were stilled for a few moments as they leaned over each other's shoulders to catch a clear look at the medals and to see for themselves the impossibly ancient dates. 1905. 1910. Mike Cummins would not have been too much older the evening he delivered them to Enniscorthy, tapping his pocket to make sure his newly minted prizes were still there, the carriages creaking as the train moved remorselessly towards the south. The boys handed the medals back to John with slow, deliberate respect and broke away from the circle, becoming animated and loud again.

When we returned, the teams were on the field, going through the motions of warm-up drills, nonchalant in the heat. Johnny Murphy stood at the end of the field opposite the stand, alone and contemplative. Margaret Kenny, the team trainer from Enniscorthy, took the team through a series of short sprints and stretches. Then the teams departed the field and both managers bolted the dressing-room doors and, at either end of the corridor, their voices carried, imparting their separate message. When the managers finished, the players responded with a communal exhortation and amid oaths and clattering boots they moved towards the field again, wound up and ready.

Niall and Jetta McDonald arrived with their girls just before the anthem. As his brother Diarmuid was on holiday in Portugal, this was the first Crossabeg-Ballymurn team to line out without a McDonald for as long as most people could remember.

It was also Niall's first championship game since his late boyhood as a spectator and he grinned in acknowledgement of that as he moved through some people he knew, carrying his baby girl Alana and a bag with bottles and snacks for Shaunín, their two-year-old.

'Now, love, come around until you see what it is all about,' he said to Alana, turning her around on his lap.

He scanned the Oulart team for players he knew. Sean Dunne, whose brother Liam was one of the great Wexford players of modern times, was out there.

'A class player. Just winding down now,' Niall said. It was mainly a young team though, filled with Oulart minor kids on the up.

We stood for the national anthem, the scattering of people in the stand tilting towards the flag that fluttered across the park. This must have been the strangest sensation for Niall McDonald, for whom gripping a hurl and clearing his mind during the traditional rendition had become second nature. He admitted that he had been apprehensive about how he would feel but sitting there and hearing his neighbours cheer as the last bars sounded felt surprisingly natural.

He began pointing out some of the Crossabeg lads. John Cummins' brother Mike, wearing number eleven, was captain. Johnny Murphy, a tricky wraith of a player whose talents mirrored those of his father, was in at full forward. There were several Doyles and O'Learys.

The great thing about watching hurling among a small crowd of people is that the acoustics are amplified. Ash resounds on ash and the sound of the ball being driven clear is lonely, like that of a hunter's gun going off in the woods. You can hear the shouts and curses of the individual players. When the play comes near the sideline, you could hear the velocity of the *sliotar* as it flew through the air. That was the music of the evening, broken by the shouts of encouragement all around us, plaintive and urgent.

Crossabeg started brightly, taking possession at the throw-in and really clattering into Oulart, Johnny Murphy's words still ringing in their heads. They strung together a series of early moves that yielded no scores. Then Oulart swept up the field and knocked over a point with ominously little fuss.

'Simple scores,' murmured Niall. 'That could be the difference.'

He was right. The game settled into a rhythm in which Crossabeg seemed to hurl more but Oulart managed scores with simplicity. They went ahead 1-04 to 0-03 after twenty minutes; 1-08 to 0-7 after half an hour.

Niall studied the game without much emotion although it represented a deeply personal moment for him: his first seventy minutes as an ex-hurler. The hardest thing for all serious sportsmen is saying goodbye and hurlers seem more attached than most. John Keane, the great Waterford player from the 1950s, spent his last days travelling the deep south hooking up with his former foes from his playing days, hurlers from Limerick, Tipperary, and Cork. He died on the road, still saying his goodbyes. For Niall McDonald, you sense it will be an easier departure.

'It's funny, I can watch games without ever having to shout

or say much,' he said. 'I don't know why that is. My father was the exact same way.'

Shauníní occupied herself by climbing to the uppermost row of seats in the stand and skipping across, blissfully unconcerned about matters on the field. Niall kept glancing over his shoulder, checking on her. The first half passed quickly. The highlight was a beautiful point from a sideline cut by Brian O'Leary. The Crossabeg section of the crowd applauded hard, their shouts echoing around the ground. In the shade of the stand it was becoming a bit chilly but the light of the field was still a rich ochre and it was warm. At half-time it was 1-09 to 0-10 in favour of Oulart, an encouraging score for Crossabeg.

During the break, the conversation turned to Wexford's chances in the All-Ireland championship. Although Niall made the transition to spectator again after his inter-county life finished, he said that in recent years, he had not gone to see his county play for three seasons or more. That was partly because he had grown tired of the hassle of trying to deal with the constant demands for tickets and partly because he had just grown out of the habit. He had grown fond of spending Sundays with his family.

The resumption of any fast-scoring game after half-time can be dangerous. There is always the likelihood of one team being caught in a mental lull. We were just settling in for the second half when the Oulart team created a lovely goal straight from the throw-in. It was a score that suggested the outcome of the game was now inevitable. John Cummins turned to shake his head and told Niall what he had heard about the quality of the Oulart team. He said that Diarmuid McDonald would be doing his nut stranded out in Portugal. They knew he would be ringing shortly to find out the result. The minutes passed and Oulart comfortably held onto a six- or seven-point lead, tapping over a free or managing a point whenever Crossabeg looked like making a rally. For the Crossabeg supporters, it was infuriating because for the most part there was little in quality between the teams. It was as if the outcome was fated or predestined.

With a few minutes left, I decided to leave Niall to watch the closing of the game in peace. Crossabeg, trailing by a couple of goals and facing a comfortable Oulart defence, looked destined for another courageous loss. They would have another opportunity in the championship but it suggested nothing auspicious for the season ahead. There was nothing shameful or wrong with that: the vast majority of hurling and Gaelic football clubs exist in precisely the same state of struggle and hope, pushing on towards the unwritten seasons ahead. On the sideline, Johnny Murphy was crouched forward and lost in the final minutes of the game, a million miles away from anything other than the next score. Walking underneath the tunnel, you could see the teams for the next game caged in the dressing rooms, making their solemn vows.

Two boys sat on the front wall of their house across the road from Wexford Park, squinting and bold-faced in the evening sun, listening to the noise coming from the pitch and wishing for something out of the ordinary to happen.

Late that evening, Niall McDonald left a message on the phone. The reception was poor but the mood was vivid. In the two minutes of the game, something improbable had happened. It was as if Crossabeg had forgotten or ignored history. They had scored a couple of goals and finished the game exultantly.

'It was funny, they were all over Oulart in the end,' Niall said, speaking calmly but you could hear the delight in his voice. He sounded thrilled, as if, after everything, the game was still new and mysterious to him, as if he was relieved to know it would always claim a piece of his heart.